Shakespeare's Political Realism

Shakespeare's Political Realism

The English History Plays

Tim Spiekerman

State University of New York Press

Published by
State University of New York Press, Albany

Printed in the United States of America

For information, address State University of New York Press, 90 State Street, Suite 700, Albany, NY 12207

Production by Marilyn P. Semerad
Marketing by Michael Campochiaro

Library of Congress Cataloging-in-Publication Data

Spiekerman, Tim, 1963–
Shakespeare's political realism : the English history plays / Tim Spiekerman.
p. cm.
Includes bibliographical references and index.
ISBN 0–7914–4867–3 (alk. paper) — ISBN 0–7914–4868–1 (pbk. : alk. paper)
1. Shakespeare, William, 1564–1616—Histories. 2. Shakespeare, William, 1564–1616—Political and social views. 3. Machiavelli, Niccolá, 1469–1527—Influence. 4. Politics and literature—Great Britain—History. 5. Political plays, English—History and criticism. 6. Historical drama, English—History and criticism. 7. Kings and rulers in literature. 8. Politics in literature. 9. Realism in literature. 10. Great Britain—History—1606–1687—Historiography. I. Title.

PR2982.S63 2001
822.3'3—dc21 00–038765

10 9 8 7 6 5 4 3 2 1

To my parents

Contents

Acknowledgments

This book has been a long time in the making. Along the way, numerous people have offered helpful criticism and advice, and I would like to thank them. Allan Bloom inspired me to write about Shakespeare; my debt to him is everywhere evident in this book. Nathan Tarcov, Saul Bellow, Ralph Lerner, Pam Jensen, Fred Baumann, Michael Zuckert, Steve Kautz, Paul Ulrich, Chris Nadon, and Lorna Knott all read various versions of all or part of what became this book. Their assistance, support, and suggestions were invaluable.

I would like to give special thanks to the anonymous reviewers for SUNY Press, who read my manuscript with unusual care and offered thoughtful and constructive criticism, as well as encouragement.

An earlier and shorter version of chapter four was published as "The Education of Hal" in *Shakespeare's Political Pageant: Essays in Politics and Literature*, ed. Joseph Alulis and Vickie Sullivan (Lanham, MD: Rowman and Littlefield, 1996). I worked closely with Joe Alulis, a talented editor and a Shakespeare pro. Vickie Sullivan helped me fine-tune and articulate my argument. A version of chapter two was published as "A Legitimate Crisis: Shakespeare's *King John*," in a symposium on politics and literature guest-edited by Michael and Catherine Zuckert for *Legal Studies Forum* (volume 22, number 4, 1998). I would like to thank James Elkins for his speedy and precise editorial advice.

Finally, I must acknowledge my parents, whose support, optimism, and gentle prodding ("Is it done yet?") kept me on track over the years. Thank you.

Chapter One

Introduction: Shakespeare's Politics

Dramatizing Politics

While skepticism about the existence of timeless truths and enduring human characteristics is now common and respectable, Shakespeare, who is usually thought to have written about such things, remains enormously popular. The poet who wrote four centuries ago about Human Experience is still an undisputed hit in the classroom, at the theater, and, perhaps most spectacularly, in the local cinema. Generation X flocked to the movies to watch *Romeo and Juliet*, apparently still *the* play about first love. Movie-goers have also turned to Shakespeare in recent years to experience the dysfunctional family (*Hamlet*), racism (*Othello*), military courage (*Henry V*), betrayal in friendship (*My Own Private Idaho*, featuring Hal and Falstaff), and tyrannical political ambition (*Richard III*). Unlike so many other "classic" authors, Shakespeare still resonates.[1]

But while Shakespeare has always been acknowledged as the poet of love and, more generally, one of the keenest observers of human psychology, his reputation as a political thinker, or even as an author much concerned with politics, is less secure. As one critic points out, the word "politics" does not even occur in Shakespeare. And the word "politic," which does, connotes a base concern with appearances for the sake of political gain.[2] In fact, the "orthodox view" until early in this century was that Shakespeare had little of interest to say about political matters.[3] The historian A. F. Pollard concluded that "no period of English literature has less to do with politics than that during which English letters reached their zenith, and no English writer's attitudes toward the questions with which alone political history are concerned is more obscure or less important than Shakespeare's."[4]

But twentieth century critics like L. C. Knights reject the view that Shakespeare is essentially apolitical: "we may properly speak of Shakespeare's political philosophy," because "he showed throughout his career a lively concern with men not only in their private and personal, but also in their public and formal, relations. And this concern included questions of power and subordination, of mutual relations within a constituted society, of the ends and methods of public action. . . . "[5] Alvin Kernan is perhaps even more impressed with the political nature of Shakespeare's plays:

> Of all the major writers in the Western literary tradition, there is none who deals so consistently and so profoundly with political matters as Shakespeare. He wrote almost exclusively of courts and aristocratic life, and matters of state, of law, of kingship, and of dynastic succession are always prominent parts of his dramatic matter. This is true even in comedies like *As You Like It* or *The Tempest* where the personal experiences which form the body of the play are set within frameworks of a political situation involving usurpation and the restoration of a dukedom to its rightful owner. But it is even more obviously true in Shakespeare's history plays and in his tragedies where the political issues are the very substance of the plays and where crucial matters of state are explored with remarkable precision and in great depth.[6]

Allan Bloom thinks that Shakespeare is an "eminently political author" and that his history plays in particular are "political with a vengeance."[7]

But with the notable exception of *Macbeth*, Shakespeare's most famous plays don't so obviously seem to be about politics. If one were asked briefly to describe the theme of *Hamlet*, or *Lear*, or *Romeo and Juliet*, the word politics probably wouldn't make it into the first paragraph, let alone the first sentence. And yet Hamlet, much to his dismay and rather reluctantly, is a political actor responding to a political act. The family squabbles over inheritance in *King Lear* are decidedly political, for the inheritance in question is a kingdom. Even *Romeo and Juliet* cannot be fully appreciated without some knowledge of the political situation in Italy, where powerful families fill the vacuum left by impotent political entities. Romeo and Juliet are forbidden to love one another because their politically rivalrous families hate one another: love is the casualty of politics. In plays like *The Tempest* and *As You Like It*, the action revolves around the theft and abuse of political power, which is eventually restored to those who can exercise it properly.

All ten of Shakespeare's English history plays are named after politicians. And they're all about the same thing: who gets to rule. Of course they're specifically about who gets to rule in thirteenth- to sixteenth-century England, but the plots are political plots (literally) and the action—assassination, treason, civil war, foreign conquest—doesn't seem peculiarly English or distinctly medieval. While one must pay attention to the historical setting of Shakespeare's plays, it would be silly to maintain that every coup d'etat is unique.

Given the titles of recent influential books about Shakespeare—*Shakespeare Left and Right; Political Shakespeare: New Essays in Cultural Materialism; Shakespeare Reproduced: The Text in History and Ideology*—it may be unnecessary to argue that Shakespeare's plays are *about* politics. The political treatment of Shakespearean texts is now routine in the most prominent critical circles. In fact, the political treatment of all literary authors, whether it be Jane Austen or Allen Ginsberg, is now common. But the claim that all literature is political may dilute the claim that Shakespeare in particular is political and it seems, furthermore, to be perfectly compatible with the notion that Shakespeare, like any other author, is merely timely, his plays the witting or unwitting reflection of his era. For historicist critics, Shakespeare is both political and politically irrelevant. While one can scrutinize his plays for evidence of misogyny or proto-feminism, racism or enlightened cosmopolitanism, reactionary monarchism or nascent liberalism, one will not learn from Shakespeare what politics is or what one's political opinions ought to be. Shakespeare, for example, either is or is not a colonialist, but it is taken for granted that colonialism is evil. Thus recent political studies of Shakespeare often seem more like the search for an ally or a whipping boy than for a teacher.

Such a course makes sense if Shakespeare has nothing to teach us about politics, and given his stature and popularity, one might expect to bolster one's own political agenda by appealing to his authority. Conversely, one might be doing others a service by pointing out the unpalatable political and social positions embedded in otherwise entertaining dramas. But I would like in this book to entertain the possibility that Shakespeare is an author from whom we can learn something significant about politics. Perhaps reading the English history plays in order to fill out what E. M. W. Tillyard called "the Elizabethan World Picture," or to grade Shakespeare according to our own political convictions, is unnecessarily limiting.

Of course, critics have always tried to discern Shakespeare's positions on the political issues of his time. Was he a Tudor apologist? Did he believe in the doctrine of the divine right of kings? Was he a big England or a little England man? What did he think of the papacy? Answers to questions like these are of more than merely historical interest, for properly rephrased, such questions may bear on contemporary issues like the separation of Church and State or the ethics of offensive foreign war. More provocatively, if a man of Shakespeare's intelligence did in fact think that rulers owe their authority to God, then some readers, at least, might be prompted to rethink their liberal views about the proper source of political authority.

While Shakespeare may have been interested in at least some of the political issues that also interest us, I would like to investigate the broader claim that he can teach us something about the nature of "the political" as such. Does politics have an essence? Are there, in other words, universal aspects of political practice and does Shakespeare tell us something about them? If the political sphere is limited or finite, if politics always has been and always will be practiced within familiar and well-traveled boundaries, then Shakespeare's distance in time from us and our concerns is ultimately unimportant. The question is whether he saw what is essential about politics and whether we can recover such a vision by studying his plays.

President Lincoln confessed to having "gone over perhaps as frequently as any unprofessional reader" several of Shakespeare's plays, all of which have distinctly political themes (*King Lear, Hamlet, Macbeth, Richard III*, and *Henry VIII*). His favorite details the clash of ambition and conscience: "I think nothing equals Macbeth. It is wonderful."[8] Now, Lincoln may only have been making an aesthetic judgment, but one might suppose that he was also impressed by the content of *Macbeth*, and found that the political world dramatized in that play bore some resemblance to the one he inhabited. While Lincoln climbed to power by more acceptable means than Macbeth did, he was clearly an ambitious man. Responding to Senator Douglas's hints that his positions were motivated by a desire for high office, ultimately the presidency, Lincoln admitted to being "desperately selfish," although no "more selfish than Judge Douglas" himself.[9] Perhaps Lincoln's attraction to *Macbeth* should be seen as an acknowledgment by the nineteenth-century president that Shakespeare understood what he faced.

If ambition seems to be a universal aspect of political life, so too does the concept of "legitimacy," which is the most salient theme of the English history plays. At stake in these plays is the question not only of who will rule, but of who is *supposed* to rule, a distinction which arises, as Machiavelli points out, because "the passion for ruling is . . . so great that it not only enters the breasts of those who have a claim to the kingdom but also into the breasts of those who have not."[10] Legitimacy, that is, the proper acquisition and use of political power, will remain a problem so long as the desire for power arises in those who shouldn't have it. In the plays I will be treating, such a desire arises seventy-five percent of the time—John, Henry IV, and Henry V are illegitimate rulers—which suggests that ambition is doled out in larger doses than is respect for legitimacy. History suggests that the gentlemen listed above are unexceptional: those who choose politics as a vocation often lack a degree.

Lest I prematurely prejudice readers against several Shakespearean kings, it should be pointed out that "desperately selfish" men can and do pursue justice, and that "legitimate" power can be abused. The proper use of political power, Shakespeare's overarching theme in the history plays, need not preclude ambition, and may not include a legal claim. Who should have power, what means are acceptable to acquire it, and how it is best exercised are all questions that Shakespeare treats with subtlety and depth in the plays I will examine. They are basic questions, as pertinent now as then.

Politics and History

If, as I have suggested, Shakespeare is a political author, the political landscape he surveys in the history plays may seem somewhat unfamiliar to a modern audience. Shakespeare treats monarchy,[11] and we are liberal democrats. Christianity dominated politics in Shakespeare's time; it doesn't now. Most generally, what politics was understood to encompass seems in some ways narrower in the history plays than it does now. As Michael Walzer explains,

> A politics of conflict and competition for power, of faction, intrigue, and open war is probably universal in human history. Not so a politics of party organization and methodical activity, opposition and reform, radical ideology and revolution. The history of reform and revolution is relatively short compared, for example, with that of the political order itself or of the power struggle. The detached appraisal of a going system, the programmatic expression of discontent and aspiration, the organization of zealous men for sustained political activity: it is surely fair to say that these three together are aspects only of the modern, that is, the postmedieval political world.[12]

One would be hard pressed to identify King John's "ideology," Richard II's "program," or Henry V's "vision of the common good"—such language is entirely foreign to the political world Shakespeare describes. Even the wars and rebellions that suffuse the history plays seem part of another world: "[f]eudal wars were largely the chaotic struggles of aggressive noble families, 'over-mighty subjects' of weak kings. Rebellions were most often the desperate, furious risings of nonpolitical peasants or proletarians, unorganized, helpless, with only the crudest of programs."[13]

I do not mean to suggest here that power politics unaccompanied by large ideological claims is unknown in the modern world, only that for Shakespeare and his audience, such a politics was normal and unspectacular, tolerated in a way that it rarely would be now, and even respectable. "Ambition" and "conquest" were not yet dirty words. But if the politics Shakespeare describes in the history plays is not "programmatic" or "ideological" in the modern sense Walzer has in mind, it was nonetheless informed by general principles. A reader of the history plays could be excused if he saw only naked struggles for power, but such struggles took place in the context of established political preconceptions, and here some historical background is useful.

The problem of legitimacy came to sight in the sixteenth century in the most practical way, as a question of obedience and disobedience. As Irving Ribner remarks, "the dominant political question which produced the history plays . . . was thus the terms of political obedience. Under what conditions, if ever, was rebellion against a lawful monarch justified?"[14] The prevalent answer, popularly expressed in the 1571 homily, *Against Disobedience and Wilful Rebellion,* was never.[15] According to the homily, obedience is "the principle virtue of all virtues" because God's first command to Adam was to obey. Satan was the original rebel, disobedience the original sin. In the Bible, the homily notes, both good and evil kings rule by God's will. Evil rulers are just as legitimate as good ones, and can be understood as God's punishment for the people's sins. There will always be some who dislike a particular king, and if they have the right to rebel, rebellion would be commonplace. Rebels, the homily concludes, are vicious, and vicious men shouldn't judge their king:

> What an unworthy matter were it then to make the naughtiest subjects, and most inclined to rebellion and all evil, judges over their princes, over their government, and over their counsellors, to determine which of them be good or tolerable, and which be evil and so intolerable that they must needs be removed by rebels. . . . [A] rebel is worse than the worst prince, and rebellion worse than the worst government of the worst prince. . . .[16]

If the homily offered practical guidance on when subjects should obey their ruler (always) and when they should disobey him (never), behind it stood an ambitious and scrupulously detailed account of the nature of men's relations to one another. The universe, the absolutists argued, is hierarchical, and this hierarchy is evident among men:

> . . . men were known to be unequal and their inequality was most often described in direct analogy to the cosmic hierarchy. Within the great chain there were discovered a whole series of lesser chains. . . . The idea could hardly be avoided that such a lesser chain, corresponding to the order of animals and angels, existed also among men. . . . [T]he feudal hierarchy of status and degree seemed to imitate perfectly the great chain. . . . [T]he degrees of the great chain were quite simply repeated among men, establishing in human society precisely the same order and harmony which prevailed in the universe.[17]

Political relations, or the terms of obedience owed by inferiors to superiors, were simply a reflection of the structure of the world. Political order, mimicking the order of the universe as a whole, thus depended on a proper appreciation of each man's place and the degrees that naturally separated ruler from ruled. This is the meaning, simply put, of the oft-repeated phrase, "order and degree":

> . . . order among men had to be hierarchical because *there was no other kind*. "If things or persons be ordered, this doth imply that they are distinguished by degrees. For order is a gradual disposition." The lives of men were determined by status and degree: only within the forms of this determination might they live together and relate to one another with certainty and peace.[18]

There were, however, dissenters from the absolutist political creed and its hierarchical metaphysics. Ribner suggests that while absolutism "was the dominant and most loudly proclaimed political doctrine in Tudor England, . . . we must not believe that it was universally accepted. The very vehemence with which it was proclaimed over and over again would suggest that the English people needed urgently to be convinced of it."[19] In his *Short Treatise of Politicke Power* (1571), the political theorist John Ponet attacked the notion of "passive obedience." Ponet argued that natural law, which is the law of God, is determinable by reason; but because men are too corrupt to rule themselves by reason alone, God gave them government and laws. The purpose of government, according to Ponet, was to replace man's corrupt reason and so allow him to live in harmony with God's laws. God, however, is neutral on the question of what *form* political authority ought to take. This—and here is the decisive point—is up to the people, for whose benefit government is instituted:

> God, therefore, conferred political authority upon the community to distribute and to control as it saw fit. It is the community, and not God, which establishes democracy or monarchy, and where there is monarchy, the king is responsible to the community and the community is responsible to God. . . . If the ruler is unworthy, the people may revoke the authority they have placed in him. It is a rule of nature that evil princes must be deposed and tyrants punished by death.[20]

At the same time Ponet and others questioned political absolutism, the idea of "order and degree" came under suspicion. As Walzer notes,

> Sixteenth-century Englishmen were extraordinarily preoccupied with the historical fact of social mutability . . . [which] . . . called the whole harmonious and hierarchical world view into question. Rebel, usurper, conqueror, tyrant—all were objects of sixteenth-century speculation and dramatic representation. The great chain could hardly account for them;

> they were unnatural and monstrous, yet all human history taught their reality. The son might kill his father and subjects assassinate their king. . . . Puritan writers, employing many of the old images but enlarging upon the idea of sin, produced descriptions of chaos which sounded very much like Hobbes' view of nature. And if chaos were natural, there was no great chain.[21]

The sixteenth century, then, understood the problem of legitimacy primarily in terms of obedience. The question "Who should rule?" became "When should men obey?" Absolutists and resistance theorists disagreed about the answer to the latter question, but there was little disagreement about the first question: monarchy was the only realistic alternative. Whether to obey this king here and now was the pressing question, not whether there should be a king at all, or, at a further remove, whether the universe was ordered or chaotic. Philosophical speculations about the order of the universe did, however, intrude upon practical politics in the following way: if the world, and especially the social and political world, were not hierarchically ordered, then the questions of who ought to rule and whether rebellion could ever be justified, were open questions. It is in this manner that Shakespeare takes up the question of legitimacy in the history plays. In the struggle for political power that is the central concern of each play, Shakespeare's rulers and would-be rulers make various claims about why they, and not some other, ought to rule. Even the most self-interested of Shakespeare's actors seek more than mere power: they seek legitimate power, if only because it is more secure. Just what constitutes legitimate political authority and how one can acquire it is thus of pressing concern to Shakespeare's characters: the question of legitimacy arises naturally from the dramatic action. We are confronted with specific choices between actual men—John or Arthur, Richard II or Bolingbroke, Henry IV or Hotspur—who desire to rule in an actual polity.

How to Read Shakespeare

I argued previously that reading Shakespeare as a political author is both plausible and commonplace, and that despite differences in historical context, Shakespeare still might be able to teach *us* something about politics. Most contemporary political critics (I am thinking particularly, although not exclusively, of the new historicists) would accept the first half of this statement, but reject the second: Shakespeare may be "political," but he has nothing to teach us; and he has nothing to teach us because he lived in different, and politically infantile, times. We may be able to locate Shakespeare's political views on the historical map, but we cannot learn from him.

One of the most powerful and influential schools of contemporary Shakespeare criticism, the new historicist school, attempts to place Shakespeare in historical context and identify his political views. Since the purpose of this book is to uncover Shakespeare's political teaching, and since part of that project involves dealing with Shakespeare's use of history, I want to distinguish my own approach from other political approaches to Shakespeare that look to history to help explain his plays. While new historicism is a complicated and diverse movement, one might begin by noting its apparently Marxist genealogy. Like Marxists, new historicists are preoccupied with history, give a deterministic account of human production (in this case, literary production), and have egalitarian political commitments. The relation between their historicism and their political commitments is not, to me anyway, altogether clear, but one almost always finds both orientations present in a new historicist reading of a Shakespearean play.

According to a friendly critic, "the fundamental move of new-historicist critics" is "trying to see the text as essentially generated from, and directed toward the politics of a historically remote period."[22] For new historicists, literary texts are intimately related to a specific historical context—they arise out of and validate that context—and the relation is a subordinate and deterministic one: "their whole endeavor is to situate the literary text in social history and thus to see it in a determined and secondary position."[23] In treating literary texts as *determined* by their environment, these critics take a decisive step beyond the common practice of referring to extra-textual influences (biography and history) to shed light on the meaning of a literary work. For the new historicists, a literary text is a historical document, a reliable reflection of the social and political views that dominated at the time. It must, in fact, be a reliable reflection of its environment, for that is all that historicism allows for: human beings are products of their environment; autonomy and creativity are illusions. This means that Shakespeare wrote for and about only his own time, for he could not do otherwise.

To the obvious objection that few if any historical contexts are simply one-dimensional, and that it is therefore difficult to identify the single context an author supposedly reflects, new historicists have an interesting answer: all literary productions serve the interests of the *dominant* ideology.[24] Apparently heterodox or subversive activity is just that—apparently, but not really, subversive. As Cantor explains, "any move against a system is reconstructed as a move within that system, and hence acts of outright rebellion become the surest evidence of orthodoxy."[25] This Foucauldian principle (Greenblatt calls it "subversion and containment") may be a necessary consequence of the historicist critique of human autonomy, but as Cantor's humorous restatement below implies, it cannot possibly persuade those who do not already accept the historicist critique:

> According to Freudianism, if you say you hate your father, you hate your father; if you say you love your father, you also hate your father. According to the New Historicism, if you say you support orthodoxy, you support orthodoxy; if you say you attack orthodoxy, you also support orthodoxy.[26]

On this view, one can be certain not only that Shakespeare is a mouthpiece for Tudor political orthodoxy, but that anything he says which seems to oppose this view in fact serves to validate it.

If new historicists approach Shakespeare's plays as historical documents that reflect the reigning political ideas and commitments of his time, they do so not in a detached, scientific manner, but as vigorous partisans of their own political convictions. What is new about the new historicism is political commitment:

> Traditional Shakespeare critics seemed to have a simple scholarly interest in how the ideas of Shakespeare and his contemporaries differed from those of our own day. . . . The Elizabethans believed that monarchy was the best form of government; we believe democracy is. For the old historicists that is just the way things are—different ages think in different ways. Traditional Shakespeare scholars did not appear to be pushing any kind of agenda and, in particular, they did not seem obsessed with asserting their superiority as people of the twentieth century over Shakespeare, the Elizabethan. . . . In short, the old historicism tried to uncover the distinctively Elizabethan ideas in Shakespeare, but it did not subject them to an inquisition. . . . The New Historicists inject a new passion into discussions of the historical limitations of Shakespeare's thought by examining them in

> the context of today's political issues. They are interested in the ways that Shakespeare's plays reflect the race, class, and gender prejudices of his day.[27]

By exposing Shakespeare as a supporter of aristocratic privilege, or colonialism, or slavery, the new historicists seek not merely to situate his work in its historical context, but to take him to task for holding oppressive political views.[28] The unstated premise is that while we can learn nothing from Shakespeare, he could certainly learn much from us.

Pechter objects to the identification of new historicism with political partisanship: "[d]espite the political advocacy of many new-historicist critics, it would be wrong, I think, to regard the new historicism itself as necessarily or essentially associated with political action, if for no other reason than that such a view would exclude the most powerful of its practitioners, Stephen Greenblatt."[29] But consider the following comments by Greenblatt about the insomnia of Shakespeare's Henry IV:

> Who knows? perhaps it is even true; perhaps in a society in which the overwhelming majority of men and women had next to nothing, the few who were rich and powerful did lie awake at night. . . . We are invited to take measure of his suffering, to understand . . . the costs of power. And we are invited to understand these costs in order to ratify the power, to accept the grotesque and cruelly unequal distribution of possessions: everything for the few, nothing to the many. The rulers earn, or at least pay for, their exalted positions through suffering, and this suffering ennobles, if it does not exactly cleanse, the lies and betrayals upon which this position depends.[30]

This passage is useful because it makes clear Greenblatt's partisanship as well as his view that Shakespeare is complicit in what can only be seen as a political crime—perpetuating "the grotesque and cruelly unequal distribution of possessions." More often than not, the new historicist project of placing Shakespeare in historical context means exposing and condemning his unfortunate inegalitarianism.

In contrast, Annabel Patterson argues that Shakespeare was a democrat.[31] While her work shares the new historicist preoccupation with historical context,[32] her Shakespeare is an autonomous thinker capable of "as much perspicaciousness . . . as is now assumed by his most sophisticated readers."[33] Shakespeare had an intention,[34] and that intention was to (carefully) align himself with an emerging populist political movement. But like the new historicists, Patterson's own political commitments are featured prominently in her criticism. She wants to demonstrate not only that Shakespeare was committed to "ordinary working people,"[35] but that she is too. She describes her book thus:

> Deliberately written in the most accessible style I can muster; lightly annotated so as not to suggest one must come to such arguments through a long negotiation with the academic authorities on the subject; and priced, by negotiation with the publisher, within the reach of almost anyone who buys paperback books, it aspires, simply, to the largest and most popular audience that can be reached.[36]

Like Greenblatt, Patterson is an overtly political critic; unlike Greenblatt, she finds in Shakespeare a comrade. Both, however, share in common the conviction that what is important about Shakespeare's political views is whether he agrees or disagrees with a settled (egalitarian) political agenda. In trying to demonstrate that Shakespeare was either a friend or an enemy of the people, contemporary political critics presuppose that he cannot teach us anything about politics.

The alternative I am proposing, and will in the course of this book argue for, is that Shakespeare can indeed teach us something about politics. This presupposes an openness to the proposition that politics in Shakespeare's time was not insuperably different from politics now, that Lincoln was not simply deluded in identifying with *Macbeth*. Like Patterson, I too rely upon "certain categories of thought that some have declared obsolete," namely authorship, self-determination, and intention.[37] That Shakespeare was incapable of rising above and reflecting upon his own time seems to me unproven and probably unprovable. I am not ready to abandon the old-fashioned but still prominent view that "we turn to Shakespeare" not because he is simply typical of his time, but "because he seems to tower over his contemporaries."[38]

This study also presupposes a more expansive view of politics than one is likely to find among most contemporary political critics. I am interested not only in whether Shakespeare was an elitist or a democrat, but whether his observations about political practice in medieval England reveal something fundamental about politics as such. In fact, I do not find much evidence to support the view that

Shakespeare was a political partisan in the usual sense of that term. He strikes me more as an observer than an advocate, and the range of his observations about politics far exceeds the current interest in race, class, and gender issues. The kinds of questions that I am interested in pursuing arise from the plays themselves. Who legitimately deserves to rule? Does ambition pose a permanent threat to political stability and justice? Is reverence for political tradition a relic of the past, or a perennial possibility? Is war, whether foreign or civil, always more likely than peace? Is prudence or morality a superior standard for political action? Shakespeare provides us in his history plays with an exhilarating and cogent account of how politics is practiced. It would be a shame, in my view, to forego a detailed examination of Shakespeare's political actors and the contexts *they* face in order to pursue a narrow and contemporary view of what counts as politics.

One can assume that Shakespeare had a political intention, but any attempt to recover his teaching bumps up against an immediate and massive difficulty: Shakespeare *himself* doesn't say anything in these plays. How can one say anything about what Shakespeare thought if one cannot point to a single instance of what Shakespeare, as opposed to one of his characters, said? It can be difficult enough to recover the teaching of those thinkers who speak in their own name, forthrightly offering theses and arguments to back them up. Shakespeare is not one of them. But then neither is Milton, and everyone would agree, I think, that *Paradise Lost* tells us something about Milton's view of Christianity.[39]

How, then, as a practical matter, does one go about unearthing Shakespeare's views? Most importantly, we have Shakespeare's characters. They may seem admirable or loathsome, talented or incompetent, sneaky or honest, amusing or dull, but all of them share one thing in common: Shakespeare made them. And it seems to me plausible that one should see signs of the maker in what he's made. If a given character appears admirable or amusing, it is not farfetched to infer that Shakespeare himself admires or is amused by him. He, after all, made him that way. But how do we know that our take on a character gibes with Shakespeare's? How do we know whether he finds the same things admirable that we do? I, and I think most readers and critics, begin with the assumption that Shakespeare is moral in the most ordinary sense of the term: he is for those characters who appear to be good and against those who appear to be bad. This, however, is only the beginning point. One must then proceed to look for evidence that supports or undermines this initial assumption. Take, for example, Hotspur. Our first impressions are undoubtedly good ones: he is a man of unquestionable honor and courage, fiercely loyal to his relations, playfully loving with his wife, and if he has a temper, he also has a sense of humor and a generous spirit. But we soon learn that Hotspur is an unwitting tool of others much smarter than himself, that he naively expects others to be as loyal as he is, that his courage is not tempered by prudence. We learn why Hotspur fails in politics, and, more generally, we learn something about the ineffectiveness of honor in political life. But the most difficult judgment remains: Does Shakespeare still admire this political failure, or does he intend for us to see that what seemed admirable in Hotspur really isn't? This goes to the root of the whole problem of Shakespeare's views on the relation of morality and politics. It seems to me that one cannot answer this question about Hotspur until one examines all of the characters in the history plays who succeed, and all who fail, to see if any patterns emerge.

I also begin from the assumption that Shakespeare is politically orthodox for his time, that he is a supporter of hereditary monarchy, a believer in the divine right of kings, and comfortable with a large role for religion in politics. As above, I then look for evidence to support or undermine this initial assumption. Since three of the four Shakespearean kings I treat are usurpers, and since the king most closely identified with divine right is toppled and murdered, political orthodoxy is always under attack in the history plays. But how does one decide which side Shakespeare is on? One must, I think, look to the characters who represent political orthodoxy and those who attack it and try to determine what Shakespeare thinks of them. If, for example, Richard II comes off looking very bad and his opponent Bolingbroke very good, one can begin to wonder just how supportive Shakespeare could really be of hereditary monarchy and divine right.

Almost all of the characters in the history plays are historical figures (Falstaff is the most interesting exception), which means that Shakespeare's creativity is limited by facts. He cannot make his characters say or do just anything. But while Shakespeare is generally quite faithful to the historical record,[40] he does take liberties, which usually involve compressing time. He also, like any historian, emphasizes some things and marginalizes, or even leaves out, others, and it is here, I think, that one gets a glimpse into what Shakespeare thinks important. The most famous example of the outright omission of a seemingly significant historical event is Shakespeare's failure to mention the Magna Carta in *King John*. One has to wonder why Shakespeare chose not to treat an important part of King John's reign, whether this tells us something about his views of constitutionalism, and why he thought John's struggle with the pope a more worthy subject to dramatize. In other cases Shakespeare almost seems to be using history selectively to make a given character look good or bad. Historians may know that King Richard II probably had to kill Gloucester to preserve his own life and throne, but readers of Shakespeare's play do not. The play opens after the murder, tells us nothing about Richard's long struggle with Gloucester, and offers favorable testimonials to Gloucester's character. Shakespeare seems to be intentionally slanting things against Richard, and one must ask why. In *Henry V*, Shakespeare omits a small but significant historical detail about the battle at Agincourt, which makes Henry look better than he would otherwise. In fact, Henry was cornered by the French while attempting to retreat to Calais, and only fought at Agincourt after the French refused his offer to give up Harfleur, a town he had won earlier in the war. Shakespeare barely alludes to the retreat, says nothing about the offer of Harfleur, and has Henry proudly rejecting all French demands and almost taunting them to engage his tired and ragged troops. Why does Shakespeare make Henry look more heroic than the historical facts warrant? The way Shakespeare presents history would seem to tell us something about his own views.

These brief comments on method are intended only to show how it might be possible to discern Shakespeare's political views. But any interpretive strategy must be put to a practical test: does it provide plausible readings of the plays? I offer below interpretations of five plays where I spend a good deal of time speculating on Shakespeare's political views. But readers should be forewarned: Shakespeare does not have a politics in the usual sense of that term. He does not offer policy suggestions or solutions, he does not reveal himself as a man of the Left or the Right, and it would be difficult to say whether he's a monarchist or a republican—which is not to say that Shakespeare is not a profound political thinker. He does explore general political themes like ambition, the nature of legitimacy, the power of political tradition, the limitations of constitutionalism, the difference between tyranny and kingship, and the role of religion and morality in politics. He is a keen observer of political practice with an eye for the permanent political problems.

The Problem of Legitimacy

In the broadest sense, legitimacy is usually understood to mean the allocation of political power on some basis other than brute force. John Locke puts it quite clearly in the introduction to his *Second Treatise:*

> . . . he that will not give just occasion, to think that all Government in the World is the product only of Force and Violence, and that Men live together by no other Rules but that of Beasts, where the strongest carries it, and so lay a Foundation for perpetual Disorder and Mischief, Tumult, Sedition and Rebellion, . . . must of necessity find out another rise of Government, another Original of Political Power, and another way of designing and knowing the Persons that have it. . . .[41]

But the general agreement that political legitimacy involves something other than force quickly dissipates on the question of what that "something other" should be. Concrete accounts of what constitutes legitimate political authority vary from age to age, and from country to country. Locke gives one answer, his divine right opponent Filmer another, Marx and Lenin a third. The answer to the question "Who should rule?" will always depend on whom one asks.

The term legitimacy is often taken more narrowly to refer to questions of succession. In this narrow sense, legitimacy is almost a procedural matter: a legitimate ruler is the one upon whom political power is rightly conferred in accordance with certain prescribed rules. The answer to the question of who should rule becomes narrowly technical: the first son of the king; the choice of the aristocracy; the individual elected by the people or the senate or the party. But by reducing legitimacy to a matter of rules or procedures, more fundamental questions are obscured. Why these rules? Why this individual rather than some other? Political legitimacy will always involve an answer to the question of who should rule, but the short, procedural answer points inevitably beyond itself.

The distinction between the narrow and the broad sense of legitimacy ought, nevertheless, to be maintained. For if one is concerned above all else with political order, then the peaceful transmission of power is ultimately more important than its proper exercise. Hobbes, for example, takes his political bearings by the *summum malum*, arguing that most any kind of order is preferable to the evil of anarchy and civil war. And since civil war is caused by confusion over who deserves to rule, procedural clarity is the most crucial aspect of politics.

Of course, procedures for transmitting rule, no matter how well established and respected, cannot guarantee good rulers. In a discussion of hereditary kingship, Aristotle notes that if the descendants of kings ". . . turn out to be ordinary persons, the result will be mischievous."[42] The talent to rule is not necessarily passed from father to son. This is not a problem limited to hereditary political systems. As Howard White points out, "there is no evidence that either heredity or election guarantees wise and just rule or leadership, though there are myths in both monarchy and democracy that they do."[43] Such myths may break down when men are confronted with an incompetent or unduly harsh ruler, or when a charismatic rebel convinces enough people that there are better ways than the ones they are accustomed to.

Legitimate politics is often equated with what is customary or traditional, with what has been handed down. This view of political propriety was typical, according to Michael Walzer, in the feudal Middle Ages:

> For the rational consideration of political methods, . . . [the feudal system] . . . substituted a blind adherence to customary ways. Men came to inherit not merely their land and possessions, but also their social place and their moral and personal commitments. Reverence for tradition paralleled the reverence for fathers and lords and similarly precluded impersonal devotion to ideas, parties, or states.[44]

In his chapter on custom in *The Machiavellian Moment,* J. G. A. Pocock turns to Sir John Fortesque—" . . . an English lawyer and the kind of amateur of philosophy who helps us understand the ideas of an age by coarsening them slightly . . . "[45]—to illustrate the idea of a customary or traditional politics. Arguing for the superiority of English laws[46] to all others, Fortesque found it necessary to distinguish between natural laws and those based on custom. Natural laws are the same everywhere and always: a good or just law in Venice is a good or just law in England. Customary laws, on the other hand, derive their authority from their suitability to a particular people in a particular place. Laws suitable to Venetians may not be suitable to Englishmen. But how, then, can one claim the English laws are superior to all others? They are better, Fortesque argues, because they are older: they have met the test of time. While England has been ruled by Britons, Romans, Saxons, Danes, and Normans,

> . . . the realm has been continuously ruled by the same customs as it is now, customs which, if they had not been the best, some of those kings would have changed for the sake of justice or by the impulse of caprice, and totally abolished them. . . . Indeed, neither the civil laws of the Romans, so deeply rooted by the uses of so many ages, nor the laws of the Venetians, which are renowned above all others for their antiquity . . . nor the laws of any Christian kingdom, are so rooted in antiquity. Hence there is no gainsaying nor legitimate doubt but that the customs of the English are not only good but the best.[47]

The superiority of one custom over another cannot be rationally determined—one could not reconstruct what a good custom would be—because "suitability" depends on experience, and experience takes time. As Pocock says,

> Each man must use his own judgement of the particulars he happens to know, and the only way of extending its sphere beyond the merely private is by combining it with other men's judgements of their particular knowledge. Since there is no organized critique of particular judgement—since it is like (though not identical with) an art rather than a science—one of the few criteria by which one judgement can claim *a priori* superiority over another is that of the number of men whose experience has gone to its making. The judgement of three hundred men is by that figure more likely to be the best than that of one man; the judgement of many generations than that of the men now living; the oldest custom than the custom slightly less old.[48]

There is, however, a higher or more sophisticated argument for equating the legitimate with what is customary. Quoting Aristotle, Fortesque argues that "use becomes another nature." Experience transforms our original nature in such a way that we develop a "second nature": we develop a love for what we're used to.[49] Or, as Pocock nicely puts it, " . . . my customs have become so much a part of myself that they must be right for me."[50] Similar arguments for a politics based on custom were made famous centuries later by Edmund Burke, "a direct heir," according to Pocock, "of this way of thinking."[51] "Veneration of antiquity," Burke said, "is congenial to the human mind"; tradition "is a vestment which accommodates itself to the body." It is natural for men to accept a particular political order because it seems to have existed "time out of mind."[52]

But whether one justifies political tradition on the basis of quantitative experience or on its (secondary) naturalness, one must acknowledge, as Pocock points out, that such arguments are "self-validating":

> In custom, experience judged what had proved good and satisfactory; it judged also what had proved adapted to the particular nature, or "genius," of the people, and this judgement was likely to be self-fulfilling, since use and custom created this "second nature" as well as evaluating it—the past was perfect indeed.[53]

"[T]he people," Pocock adds, "could not tell you why the customs they observe are good or those they abandon bad, not merely because the people are not philosophers, but because the philosopher himself could not tell you."[54] The philosopher could not tell you because the argument that a particular political arrangement is best because it is old and because it is ours is not a rational argument. It has, nevertheless, always captivated men and continues to do so. Even in the United States, which was founded on rational political principles—"self-evident truths"—respect for our political arrangement is commonly expressed as "reverence" for a constitution which is good (and which ought not to be tampered with) because it is old and because it is ours.[55]

In practice, the identification of legitimacy with tradition does not always result in the slavish acceptance of custom. In the "medieval mind," according to Pocock, the distinction between custom and what (was new, but) was expected to become customary was "habitually slurred over"; and creative legal minds "knew well enough how to make new statute law by reinterpreting old,"[56] a practice which continues today. Shrewd politicians have always been adept at making the new seem old, the innovative seem customary. Even Machiavelli, renowned for his novelty and no friend of custom, sometimes advises new princes to present their rule as a seamless continuation of the past.[57]

Of course, departures from political tradition are not always disguised. It may well be argued openly that the customary way is the wrong way, that what seems politically suitable should not. Men can get used to all kinds of questionable practices; habituation needn't always entail justice. Arguments for political innovation thus almost inevitably turn on the question of justice.[58] If "the ordinary importance of legitimacy" has something to do with the orderly transfer of political power, "its extraordinary importance," according to White, "rests on its identification with justice. If the legitimate way of succession is the only just way, then legitimacy is indeed one of the most important questions, perhaps the most important question, of political philosophy."[59] The equation of political legitimacy with justice is the obvious alternative to its equation with custom or tradition. Political tradition, as we saw above, is self-validating: its very existence is taken as proof of its suitability and goodness. In order to deny the legitimacy of tradition, one must appeal to a standard other than experience; one must, that is, appeal to nature or reason. "Justice," as White says, "is more extensive or more comprehensive than legitimacy. Justice, in other words, may be natural while legitimacy rests on constitutional law."[60]

But what exactly does it mean to appeal to nature in justifying a particular political arrangement? Every polity makes some kind of claim to justice, no matter how disingenuous, and justice is always thought to be somehow natural. Defenders of political tradition argue that inherited customs are just because experience teaches us that they suit us, and insofar as they suit us, these customs are somehow natural. But this does not mean that all appeals to nature are equal and that one cannot make distinctions amongst them. Political traditionalists and political innovators may alike appeal to justice and to nature, but they do so in different ways. The "second nature" argument, which appeals to experience, is obviously different than the "first nature" argument, which appeals to a rational, non-historical standard. These arguments lay bare fundamental philosophical differences. Are we really only, as a radical traditionalist (or historicist) might have it, what we inherit? Or is there an ineradicable human tendency to recognize some things as just and others as unjust, everywhere and always? If the latter is true, then there may well be circumstances in which, as White says, "it is possible to distinguish the just regime from the legitimate regime."[61] Put otherwise, it may be possible to distinguish what is legitimate according to tradition or custom, and what is legitimate according to nature or reason. To take a clear-cut case, a hereditary monarch who rules despotically may be legitimate in one sense and illegitimate in another.

Such confusion arises in part from the fact that "legitimacy" refers to two separate, although related, political phenomena. It refers both to the quality of political rule and the way in which power is transferred from one ruler to the next. Who should rightly come to power and how that power should be properly exercised are both questions to which the term "legitimacy" tries to provide an answer. The problem is that the answers might be different: authority that is legitimately come by might not be legitimately exercised, and authority that is illegitimately come by might be exercised legitimately. The hereditary monarch, to repeat the example used above, may be a despot; the man who then seizes his throne without the benefit of a hereditary claim may be an exemplary ruler. Those who recur to nature or reason when arguing about the meaning of legitimacy are typically more concerned with the quality of rule than with procedures for succession: "if there are, as Jefferson put it, a 'natural *aristoi*' who should rule because they have the virtue and talents to rule, the real problem is to find the rulers, to identify the natural *aristoi*, not to transmit power in a constitutional way." But, White continues,

> . . . neither Jefferson nor anyone else . . . found a way for the natural *aristoi* to inherit rule from the natural *aristoi* or to be assured of election. The brutal problem of power intruded on the gentle style of rule. . . . There might be a natural way to rule, but the natural way to transmit rule was problematic.[62]

So long as the procedures for transmitting political authority do not guarantee just or desirable rulers, legitimacy will remain a problem.

If the identification of political legitimacy with custom or with justice is common and respectable, its identification with force is neither. Discussions of legitimacy usually take for granted the distinction between mere possession of power and its proper acquisition and use. Those passionately ambitious men who owe their authority to brute force—who rule because they can—are rarely deemed legitimate, and would rarely claim to be legitimate, by virtue of force alone. And yet there are precedents for such political candor. After killing Richard

III and ascending the throne of England, King Henry VII made *possession* of the throne a legal right, no matter the credentials of the pretender. Machiavelli certainly recognizes the distinction between legitimate and illegitimate political authority, but he does not respect it: he teaches men with no claim to a kingdom how to become kings. The identification of legitimacy with force is really tantamount to denying the distinction between legitimacy and illegitimacy altogether. It is perhaps only a slight exaggeration to say that for Machiavelli, legitimate authority is not a special kind of authority, but authority pure and simple, however gotten and however used. The legitimate ruler, on this view, is the one in power, as well as the one who is strong enough or clever enough to topple him.[63]

Legitimacy is ordinarily identified with the law: legitimate political authority is *legal* authority. But when one asks how the laws themselves are justified, about the basis of what is legal, one is sure to encounter one of the three arguments (or some combination thereof) discussed above. The law derives its authority, that is, from either custom, (natural) justice, or force. "[A]ll English law," as Pocock notes, "was common law, common law was custom, custom rested on the presumption of immemoriality; property, social structure, and government existed as defined by the law and were therefore presumed to be immemorial."[64] The argument that positive law is just because it accords with nature was a common refrain among proponents of the U.S. Constitution. Arguing for the adoption of the proposed Constitution, James Madison appealed "to the transcendent law of nature and of nature's God, which declares that the safety and happiness of society are the objects at which all political institutions aim, and to which all institutions must be sacrificed."[65] The argument that laws are justified by simple force, that "might equals right," was made famous by Thrasymachus in Plato's *Republic:*

> . . . each ruling group sets down laws for its own advantage; a democracy sets down democratic laws; a tyranny, tyrannic laws; and others do the same. And they declare that what they have set down—their own advantage—is just for the ruled, and the man who departs from it they punish as a breaker of the law and a doer of unjust deeds. . . . [I]n every city the same thing is just, the advantage of the established ruling body. . . . [E]verywhere justice is the same thing, the advantage of the stronger.[66]

Finally, while the identification of legitimate political authority with the consent of the governed may seem more precise than its identification with what is legal, "consent" is a notoriously pliable term, especially when one allows for the distinction between tacit and explicit consent. Explicit consent (i.e., election) will certainly limit the range of governments held to be legitimate. But tacit consent (i.e., recognition of authority through obedience) can be presumed by any ruler who manages to hold on to power. Definitions of legitimacy may then begin with discussions of what is legal and what is consented to, but they ought not to end there.

Shakespeare and Machiavelli

Like most of the new historicists today, E. M. W. Tillyard argued more than fifty years ago that Shakespeare is an orthodox Elizabethan conservative, a defender of order and degree who assumes that legitimate political authority is ultimately supported by heaven.[67] Tillyard's Shakespeare, according to one dissenting critic, is an "all-weathers champion of the Establishment."[68] But Tillyard acknowledges the possibility that Shakespeare ignored the "thought-idiom of his age . . . by following the doctrines of Machiavelli."[69] "The Machiavellian figure," as Tracy Strong says, "radically questions the world of order and degree. These are men with no background, or none that matters, who through force of will and cunning of intellect climb to positions of dominance and authority."[70]

Elizabethans, according to M. M. Reese, had a "strange love-hate relationship with Machiavelli. . . . " They were "appalled because he defied all their cherished dogmas about order and degree, and yet fascinated because everyday experience taught them that in many respects he might very well be right."[71] Machiavelli is not known for his sensitivity to questions of political legitimacy; his view of legitimate rule is commonly summed up in the phrase, "might equals right." Shakespeare's Richard II underlines this Machiavellian teaching when he says to his deposer and eventual murderer, "Well you deserve. They well deserve to have / That know the strong'st and surest way to get" (*RII* III.iii.200–01).[72] But is this Shakespeare's view as well? Do the history plays, as Stephen Greenblatt argues, "confirm the Machiavellian hypothesis of the origin of princely power in force and fraud"?[73] What, in general, does Shakespeare think of Machiavelli?

That Shakespeare knew of Machiavelli is certain: there are three references to him in his plays, two in the Histories.[74] It is not certain, however, that Shakespeare knew Machiavelli's writings firsthand. The most critics and historians can establish is that he *could* have read him, that copies of *The Prince*, both in Latin and in English, were available and read by educated sixteenth-century Englishmen.[75] The most compelling evidence that Shakespeare knew Machiavelli's writings is also the most impressionistic: one needs only a casual acquaintance with *The Prince* and *The Discourses* to hear persistent echoes in Shakespeare's plays. The plot of *Measure for Measure*, for example, bears an uncanny resemblance to the Remirro de Orca/Cesare Borgia story recounted by Machiavelli in chapter 8 of *The Prince*.[76] It seems that one could illustrate almost any Machiavellian principle with an example from one of Shakespeare's plays. This may prove only that both men knew a lot about politics; but it also proves that Shakespeare knew what Machiavelli knew, whether or not he'd read him.

The list of Shakespearean characters who have been called, by one critic or another, "Machiavellian," is extensive: Aaron, Iago, Edmund, Octavius, Cassius, Macbeth, Claudio, Faulconbridge, Henry IV, Henry V, Richard III. Whether a particular "Machiavellian" character is true to type or a mere caricature, and whether Shakespeare admires or disdains him, is debatable in each case. But the fact that so many of Shakespeare's characters strike a whole range of readers as "Machiavellian" argues at least that Shakespeare was preoccupied with a recognizable political type. Of course, politicians who do the kinds of things Machiavelli brazenly recommends have always existed, and their appearance in highly political plays like Shakespeare's could be expected. But I think a case can be made for a deeper connection between Shakespeare and Machiavelli, for their writings share remarkably similar concerns. Both men address the question of how political power is acquired and maintained; both scrutinize the relation between morality, particularly Christian morality, and political practice; and both criticize the Roman Catholic Church in its capacity as a political actor. Shakespeare and Machiavelli confront the same issues.

The Prince is often described as a manual or handbook that explains how to successfully acquire and maintain political power. Numerous rulers are known to have consulted it regularly (Richelieu, Frederick of Prussia, Bismarck, Hitler, Stalin, Lenin); Mussolini even wrote about it.[77] The history plays, whose plots almost always involve a contest for power, often seem like dramatizations of Machiavellian principles. If *The Prince* is a terse manual, the Histories are more like rich case studies. As a general rule, what works and doesn't work for Shakespeare's characters corresponds to Machiavelli's rules and maxims. Let me give two brief examples. In chapter 17 of *The Prince*, Machiavelli says that "above all, [a prince] must abstain from the property of others, because men forget the death of a father more quickly than the loss of a patrimony."[78] This shocking and incredible statement is borne out in Shakespeare's *Richard II*. When Richard murdered Bolingbroke's popular uncle, he was able to weather all opposition. But when, upon Gaunt's death, Richard seized Bolingbroke's inheritance, Bolingbroke returned from exile to recover his patrimony and soon after installed himself as king. Machiavelli continually cautions new princes to beware of those "friends" who helped them to power, for "you cannot keep as friends those who have put you there because you cannot satisfy them in the mode they had presumed. . . . "[79] On the flip-side, those who help a prince to power are themselves in danger, for "whoever is the cause of someone's becoming powerful is ruined: for that power has been caused by him either with industry or with force, and both the one and the other of these two are suspect to whoever has become powerful."[80] Machiavelli's counsel here is almost a summary of Bolingbroke's career. Helped to power by the Percys (*Richard II*), he spends the remainder of his career (*1,2 Henry IV*) at war with them. Had Bolingbroke followed Machiavelli's advice and eliminated the Percys instead of first trying to satisfy them, he might have enjoyed a more peaceful reign.

Machiavelli's most general advice about how to acquire and maintain political power is deceptively simple: a prince should ignore morality. Those who think of the afterlife are not likely to flourish politically in this life. Machiavelli says that the desire to be good is "very laudable" but politically naive, " . . . for a man who wants to make a profession of good in all regards must come to ruin among so many who are not good."[81] Because good guys finish last, a prince or potential prince must "learn to be able not to be good, and to use this and not use it according to necessity."[82] Machiavelli's advice is deceptively simple because the ability to ignore morality is not. It must be "learned," and one may not get many chances to experiment—a single mistake can be fatal. At least as a practical matter, Shakespeare agrees with Machiavelli's analysis. As Paul Cantor notes, "the recurrent political tragedy portrayed in Shakespeare's plays (including the histories) is that somehow the evil characters push their way to the top of the political order, while the morally good and humane characters either fail to achieve rule, or, if they do, cannot maintain it properly."[83] It is worth pointing out here that three of the four Shakespearean kings I will be treating are murderers and that this, of itself, does not wholly discredit them in Shakespeare's eyes. Shakespeare is perfectly aware of the ambiguous relation between morality and political success and he knows that what is politically necessary may often be indistinguishable from evil.

If Machiavelli's teaching were limited to the rather pedestrian assertion that because good guys finish last they ought, at times, to act like bad guys, then one could comfortably label Shakespeare a Machiavellian. But Machiavelli's teaching is more radical. He questions the goodness of what is ordinarily held to be good and the badness of what is ordinarily held to be bad: " . . . for if one considers everything well, one will find something appears to be virtue, which if pursued would be one's ruin, and something else appears to be vice, which if pursued results in one's security and well-being."[84] Thus it is not the case, as Machiavelli earlier led us to believe, that what is commonly held to be good *is* good, but that "human conditions do not permit it."[85] "Virtues" are not necessarily virtuous and "vices" are not necessarily vicious. Machiavelli demonstrates, for example, that what appears to be merciful can in fact be extremely cruel, and that what appears to be cruel can in fact be merciful.[86] Machiavelli's intention is not, however, simply to point out common misunderstandings of what is genuinely moral. He intends instead to redefine morality according to a new and distinctly political standard, as what promotes a prince's "security and well-being."

This radical critique of morality has two practical consequences. First, ordinary moral concerns ought to take a back seat to a prince's primary goal, the pursuit of security. Contrary to what is often said of

Machiavelli, this does not mean that a prince should practice only treachery, deceit, and ruthless villainy. Rather, he should do what is necessary under the circumstances, which sometimes demand virtue, other times vice. Second, and more disturbingly, a prince ought to pretend to be good—even though he's not—in order to cultivate a reputation for possessing all of those qualities that are held to be virtuous:

> A prince . . . should appear all mercy, all faith, all humanity, all religion . . . [I]t is not necessary for a prince to have all the above-mentioned qualities in fact, but it is indeed necessary to appear to have them. Nay, I dare say this, that by having them and always observing them, they are harmful; and by appearing to have them, they are useful. . . . [87]

The following lines, spoken by Shakespeare's Richard III, are a perfect expression of the moral hypocrisy Machiavelli recommends: "And thus I clothe my naked villainy / With odd old ends stol'n forth of Holy Writ, / And seem a saint, when most I play the devil" (*RIII* I.iii.336–38).

Does Shakespeare go this far with Machiavelli? Does he reject the common understanding of morality and, in addition, advise princes to practice moral hypocrisy? There is some evidence that he does. Henry VI is a gentle Christian who is Shakespeare's only genuinely decent and pious king. But he is weak and politically ineffective, and this seems to be a direct consequence of his moral character. Henry VI is too good for politics, which is to say he's a bad king. As Reese remarks, "politics is not an occupation for the over-scrupulous or the chicken-hearted, and when the alternative to strong government is the probable disintegration of society, there is no place on the throne . . . for a monk *manque* like Henry VI."[88] Shakespeare's Henry V, on the other hand, is far more concerned with reputation than with true virtue. But his "pseudo-morality"[89] serves England well; he is a more capable and effective king than his son. There is, of course, the question of where Shakespeare's sympathies lie. When Wyndham Lewis asks whether or not Shakespeare was a Machiavellian, he declares that "the answer would have to be complex" but " . . . one thing however can be decided at once where Othello, at least, is concerned . . . [H]e was not on the side of Othello's small destroyer."[90] Shakespeare may have recognized, as John Danby argues, that "the machiavel . . . was bound to succeed" while finding that prospect deeply troubling.[91] The observation that political success depends on the extent to which one follows Machiavelli's advice may, as Howard White says, have turned Shakespeare into a political pessimist: "the immense interest in politics and the broad understanding of its devious ways are accompanied, often enough, by a mistrust bordering on revulsion and a coldness not free of contempt. . . . Apparently Shakespeare did not think too highly of political life."[92]

Whatever Shakespeare's final opinion about political life may be, like Machiavelli, he sees that modern politics cannot be adequately understood apart from the Christianity which always somehow informs it. Machiavelli views the crippling effects of morality on politics as a peculiarly modern, that is, Christian, phenomenon. Christianity, he observes,

> . . . appears to have made the world weak, and to have handed it over as prey to the wicked, who run it successfully and securely since they are well aware that the generality of men, with paradise for their goal, consider how best to bear, rather than how best to avenge, their injuries.[93]

Shakespeare, according to John Alvis, was well aware of this problem: "portrayals of the acquiescence of Christian realms to usurpers, tyrants, or corrupt rulers in the English history plays, *Macbeth,* and *Hamlet,* suggest that Shakespeare sought to focus on the same malady Machiavelli had detected."[94] Because men, as Machiavelli says, "are less bold than they used to be,"[95] the political liberty characteristic of republican government is rarer than it used to be. While Shakespeare is not concerned in the history plays with republics, he is concerned with liberty insofar as he opposes the passive acceptance of corrupt and tyrannical monarchs.[96] Of the plays I will be treating, this is most apparent in *Richard II.* When Richard murders a popular political opponent, the weak-willed response of the murdered man's brother is representative of public opinion and typifies the submissive Christian reaction to the abuse of power:

> God's is the quarrel—for God's substitute,
> His deputy anointed in His sight,
> Hath caus'd his death; the which if wrongfully,
> Let heaven revenge, for I may never lift
> An angry arm against His minister. (*RII* I.ii.37–41)

Bolingbroke, the lone nobleman who dares to oppose Richard, appears to have Shakespeare's support.

Christian moral teaching, according to Machiavelli, infects rulers as well as ruled. This is made clearest in *The Prince,* which, unlike *The Discourses,* is addressed to princes and, although Machiavelli never uses the word in that work, to tyrants. *The Prince* is filled with historical examples used to illustrate particular political points. It is nearly always the case that ancient rulers are held up as models, while modern (i.e., Christian) rulers are faulted, characteristically for being too moral. Even the clever and brutal Cesare Borgia, the nominal hero of *The Prince,* fails in the end because he is too trusting. Shakespeare's kings are Christian kings and as a general rule, the bad Christians are better politicians than the good Christians. More precisely, one's effectiveness as a ruler in the political world Shakespeare dramatizes seems to depend on one's willingness to depart from Christian moral teaching.

Henry V provides a complicating case: he is the most successful of Shakespeare's kings and he is a Christian. There is, however, some evidence that Henry V is Christian by design rather than by conviction. If this is true, he would be a perfect exemplar of Machiavelli's teaching. For despite his criticism of Christian morality, Machiavelli thinks religion can be politically useful. Of all the virtues, none, according to Machiavelli, is more important for a prince to appear to have than religion.[97] Religion serves as an umbrella for the rest of the virtues and because it is based on a private belief, it is easy to fake and difficult for others to question. Machiavelli concludes his chapter on "faith" by praising "a certain prince of present times" who "never preaches anything but peace and faith, and is very hostile to both. If he had observed both, he would have had either his reputation or his state taken away from him many times."[98] On one of those rare occasions when Machiavelli praises a modern, he chooses a figure who, despite his pose, is "hostile" to Christian teaching. Shakespeare's opinion of his Machiavellian characters—if it can be discerned—will necessarily reveal something about his opinion of Christianity.

Shakespeare does seem to share Machiavelli's hostility toward the Church as a political actor. The Church, according to Machiavelli, possesses a unique combination of political strengths and weaknesses:

> . . . though the Church has its headquarters in Italy and has temporal power, neither its power nor its virtue has been sufficiently great for it to be

> able to usurp power in Italy and become its leader; nor yet, on the other hand, has it been so weak that it could not, when afraid of losing its dominion over things temporal, call upon one of the powers to defend it against an Italian state that had become too powerful.[99]

If the Church's strength lies in its powerful moral grip over men, its weakness springs from the same source: Christ's teaching is incompatible with military prowess, or, to put it more bluntly, priests cannot fight. Thus the Church must rely on others to do its fighting for it. It is capable of great mischief and intrigue, but it cannot conquer on its own and it cannot always control those armies it enlists to promote its temporal aims. One could learn all of this by reading *King John.* In *John,* an ambitious Roman Catholic pope plots to remove the English king, using his moral authority to turn the English people against John and recruiting the French to topple him. But, true to Machiavelli's analysis, the Church loses control of the French army, which, once set in motion, pursues its own aims rather than Rome's.

Shakespeare's Church officials, for the most part, fit Machiavelli's description—"there is less religion among them than elsewhere."[100] In *Henry V,* the Archbishop of Canterbury declares that "miracles are ceas'd" (*HV* I.i.67), and in *King John,* the papal legate pokes fun at the masses for ascribing divine intentions to impersonal nature (*John* III.iii.153–59). Shakespeare's divines are politic plotters and schemers, hypocritical users of religion whose eyes are fixed firmly on this world rather than the next. They are, in a word, Machiavellians. Machiavelli advises princes to treat the Church like any other political actor because that is how it will act toward you as prince. John (for a while, at least) and Henry V take Machiavelli's advice and their policy toward the Church seems to meet with Shakespeare's approval.

I hope to have shown above that Shakespeare and Machiavelli are preoccupied with the same moral, religious, and political issues. But it is one thing to say that Shakespeare portrays Machiavellian characters and explores Machiavellian themes; it is quite another to say that Shakespeare agrees with Machiavelli. Is Shakespeare, then, a Machiavellian?

Arguing for the political nature of the history plays, L. C. Knights notes confidently that "Shakespeare's political realism is not of course Machiavellian realism. . . . "[101] He does not say why this is so, but his opinion of Shakespeare's relation to Machiavelli is a common one. "Literary critics," as Alvis points out, "tend to regard Shakespeare as an adversary of Machiavelli. . . . "[102] This is clearly Tillyard's position (Shakespeare "used Machiavelli to make a challenge"[103]), and Reese suggests that Shakespeare's seemingly orthodox defense of Tudor conventions was motivated more by a desire to resist Machiavellianism than by any genuine belief in "order and degree."[104]

Many critics, however, are quick to distinguish the real Machiavelli from "the pseudo-Machiavellian villain of the public stage"[105] who had become a stock figure in Elizabethan drama. "The popular idea of Machiavelli," according to Prior, "was in many respects a misconstruction, often approaching parody and not based on knowledge of the original work itself."[106] Machiavellianism became synonymous in the public mind with evil:

> . . . the word [Machiavel] was a label attached to a fairly large package into which . . . [Elizabethans] . . . stored almost everything of which they disapproved, much of it not specifically Machiavellian. At other times and in other places Popery, Presbytery, Jacobin, atheist, Fascist, imperialist, Communist have served a similarly convenient purpose.[107]

There seems to be a general consensus among scholars that Shakespeare was an intelligent critic of the real Machiavelli, who was not as evil as his popularizers made him out to be. Machiavelli is famous for his formulation that the ends justify the means:

> It is a sound maxim that reprehensible actions may be justified by their effects, and that when the effect is good . . . it always justifies the action.[108]

But while the popularizers of Machiavelli concentrated on his advocacy of "reprehensible" means, they neglected his advocacy of noble ends. Machiavelli, Reese argues, was an Italian patriot and this "powerful strain of patriotism—even, in a strange way, idealism—. . . dignified and justified his work."[109] The problem, of course, is that Machiavelli's political advice is available to everyone, regardless of their motives. According to Prior, this is precisely Shakespeare's point in *Richard III*:

> The desire to do good implies a social impulse, a care for others which is at odds with the total contempt which Richard feels for the rest of mankind and which, Shakespeare implies, is inherent in the assumptions underlying the Machiavellian idea of power.[110]

This view of Machiavelli, as a well-intentioned bumbler who was too shortsighted to see the pernicious effects his teaching might have when practiced by evil men, is common among Shakespeare critics. Shakespeare is then credited with pointing out the obvious—that Machiavelli's teaching could be abused—and characterized as a kind of friendly critic, impressed by Machiavelli's knowledge of political reality but fearful lest it fall into the wrong hands. Both Ribner's and Reese's Shakespeare turns out to be what might be called a "cautious Machiavellian":

> Within the limits of the law, power has its own special morality. This is not a permission for Machiavellian deceits and ruthlessness, *although the distinction is obviously fine-drawn*: which is why it is so important that virtuous men should have power, and that those who have power should be virtuous. But it does acknowledge the simple truth that kings and subjects are required by their function to have different values.[111]

> For Shakespeare the good king must first be a good man, *but nevertheless*, insofar as the immediate problems of government were concerned, Shakespeare may have come to envision the successful ruler as having public qualities not dissimilar from those espoused by Machiavelli.[112]

Shakespeare, on this view, learned a lot from Machiavelli, but took only as much as would allow him to remain respectably moral. The question is whether this is possible. The selective practice of virtue is surely incompatible with a simple respect for virtue. Just how does one determine on which side of the finely drawn moral line a politician stands? And if it is political circumstances which finally dictate a ruler's moral behavior, would not morality be subservient to politics?[113]

In attempting to defend Machiavelli against his popularizing opponents, these critics may be guilty of sanitizing him beyond recognition. The man who, according to popular opinion, taught wicked ways to wicked men is defended on the one hand for being a dispassionate scientist, and on the other for being a passionate patriot. They do not explain why patriotism, whether Italian or English, ought to justify the political treachery Machiavelli advocates. Neither do they consider just how patriotic a man whose advice is available to everyone could possibly be. (In chapter three of *The Prince,* Machiavelli even offers explicit advice to the French on how they could be more effective conquerors of Italy.) Machiavelli's patriotism clearly is not of the ordinary variety. And his "science" is not only shocking to ordinary sensibilities, but intentionally so. Machiavelli surely knew his teaching would be attractive to ambitious, unscrupulous men; these, after all, are the kinds of men he often champions. To cite one particularly provocative example, Machiavelli praises Hannibal for his "inhuman cruelty" and "other virtues."[114] It is little wonder, then, as Tillyard notes, that "the plain man smelt out something fundamentally wrong" in Machiavelli.[115] Perhaps the intuition of the "plain man" and the "grotesque image of the original"[116] portrayed on the stage bear a closer resemblance to the real Machiavelli than these critics would admit.

The question, then, is how Shakespeare compares to this untamed Machiavelli. I do not intend to answer the question here, only to point out the kinds of considerations that ought to guide any inquiry into Shakespeare's relation to Machiavelli.

Is there for Shakespeare a fundamental difference between a tyrant and a king? Aristotle makes the classic distinction on the basis of motives: a king pursues the common good, a tyrant his own good. Machiavelli has very little to say about justice[117] and identifies the common good with the selfish interest of the popular class. He also intentionally blurs the distinction between tyrant and king, praising rulers in *The Prince* whom he calls tyrants in *The Discourses.*[118] Does Shakespeare blur this distinction as well? If not, according to what criteria does he make the distinction? The usual answer is patriotism. But what exactly does love of country warrant a king to do? Can it, for example, justify murder and offensive foreign invasions?

Shakespeare's view of legitimate political authority will ultimately depend on his view of what men are like and thus what they are capable of. Machiavelli begins from the proposition that "all men are wicked."[119] This leads him to expect less of politics than other thinkers have, to downgrade justice and elevate stability and security. Shakespeare, according to Reese, has a more positive view of man's nature than does Machiavelli:

> He feels that on the whole men do not behave like that; or when they do, they are not whole men. It is surely significant that he provides almost every one of his Machiavellians with some sort of pathological excuse for their behaviour. . . . Machiavellianism, in Shakespeare's view, is the creed of men who have been morally perverted by misfortune.[120]

Shakespeare's view of legitimacy will depend, similarly, on his view of what the world is like—does it support justice? Machiavelli's pessimism on this point is most strikingly stated in chapter 15 of *The Prince*: "many have imagined republics and principalities that have never been seen or known to exist in truth; for it is so far from how one lives to how one should live that he who lets go of what is done for what should be done learns his ruin rather than his preservation." Reese, whose opinion on this matter is fairly typical, argues that Shakespeare was more optimistic about the possibility of just government, and that his optimism had a religious foundation:

> Shakespeare believed in a universe created and made intelligible by God. . . . Government was made necessary by the fall, and to that extent was marred by human error. But God's design assured its eternal righteousness, and this was a vital corrective of the Machiavellian view of the state as a man-made contrivance, existing only because human life was brutish and solitary, and incapable in itself of being a school of virtue.[121]

Divine support for legitimacy is treated explicitly by Shakespeare in *Richard II*, but it is not at all clear that this play provides decisive evidence for Reese's thesis.

Any consideration of Shakespeare's relation to Machiavelli must also take into account the very different manner in which they present their teaching. Machiavelli is bold and shocking. Shakespeare, by comparison, seems subdued, partly because he never speaks in his own name: if one of Shakespeare's characters says bold and shocking things, one need not associate them with Shakespeare himself. The diversity of views attributed to Shakespeare shows that he can be taken many ways. As we saw above, he has been characterized as politically orthodox, typical of his time. I do not share this view and go out of my way to emphasize those unorthodox things that may not seem obvious on the surface (notably, what's good about John and Henry IV, who are both usurpers, and what's bad about Richard II, whose claim to the throne is impeccable). But it is not hard to see why Shakespeare is usually taken to be morally respectable, a champion of political decency. Unlike Machiavelli, Shakespeare seems to take great care not to offend conventional views. He never, for example, openly advocates political murder. He may in some instances support it, but one has to piece together the evidence from clues and may have to remain satisfied with plausible conjecture. Nowhere in Shakespeare can one find the direct advice Machiavelli offers usurping princes—eliminate the bloodline! But even if Shakespeare could be shown in the end to be sympathetic to a good deal of Machiavelli's teaching, his reticence in announcing as much would itself point to a significant difference. One of Machiavelli's novelties is the brazenly open way in which he challenges the reigning moral and religious dogmas. Shakespeare's cautious manner of presentation may conceal similarly unconventional views, but such caution shows a certain respect for convention and may ultimately be in the service of moral decency. If Shakespeare agrees with part of Machiavelli's teaching, he doesn't agree with him that it ought to be trumpeted to the world.

Shakespeare seems to go beyond Machiavelli in his examination of the souls of those politicians who practice what Machiavelli preaches:

> . . . it may be that Shakespeare's original contribution to our understanding of political power is the insight he provides into how men respond to the moral conflicts inherent in the exercise of power. In support of this view is Meinecke's opinion: 'The ability to think [of *raison d'etat*] in terms of inner conflicts, violations and tragic problems, presupposes a more modern and sophisticated mentality which perhaps only began in Shakespeare.'[122]

Shakespeare, according to Prior, is a better psychologist than Machiavelli. I think such a conclusion is hasty, for Machiavelli offers an impressive account of human motivations; he may be blunt, but he is not unsophisticated. "The moral conflicts inherent in the exercise of power," especially the conflict between Christian moral teaching and political necessity, are at the very center of Machiavelli's thought. One might say, however, that Machiavelli's concern with moral conflict is more practical than Shakespeare's, that he is preoccupied with morality only insofar as it relates to political success or failure. Shakespeare gives us a deeper picture of the phenomenon itself, allowing us to share the self-doubt, even agony, of men caught between the warring claims of ambition and conscience. Does Shakespeare's greater attention to the problem of conscience signal a greater respect for its claim upon men? Machiavelli thinks conscience is a fraud and seems to have little sympathy for its victims, a view shared by Shakespeare's Richard III: "Conscience is but a word that cowards use, / Devis'd at first to keep the strong in awe. / Our strong arms be our conscience, swords our law" (*Richard III* V.iii.310–12).

Does Shakespeare agree with Richard here? Whatever Shakespeare's final view about the status of conscience may be, he does seem to have some sympathy for those of his characters caught in its grip.[123] On the other hand, Shakespeare is clearly fond of Falstaff, a man whose vigorous pursuit of the non-political pleasures is unencumbered by moral doubt.

For Machiavelli, politics—or, to use contemporary parlance, relations of power—are all. While Reese notes that "the distinguishing quality of the English histories is that here, and here alone, political virtue is the only standard of reference," he also says that "Shakespeare never supposed that politics made up the whole of life, or that the dedicated statesman was in that respect alone a complete man."[124] To say that Shakespeare is a Machiavellian in the deepest sense, one would have to show that of all the human types he portrays (prince, priest, poet, lover, philosopher), the politician is the most clear-sighted and the others somehow deluded. This would require an examination and comparison of all of his plays, which is clearly beyond the scope of this inquiry. But one could point to several plays which seem to cast doubt on the notion that politics is for Shakespeare the best and highest pursuit. In *Antony and Cleopatra*, for example, Antony chooses Cleopatra over empire—"the whole world, really the whole world, for a woman"[125]—and is a more compelling and sympathetic character than Octavius, whose single-minded dedication to politics earns him the title of Caesar. In the history plays there is Falstaff, a connoisseur of witty conversation and sensual pleasure, whose life offers a counterpoint to the ambitious politicians who surround him. Shakespeare's view of Falstaff, who is arguably the most interesting and surely the most controversial character in the history plays, ought to provide some insight into his view of politics in general and its rank amongst the human pursuits.

Chapter Two

King John

As is typical of his English history plays, the plot of Shakespeare's *King John* is driven by a violent struggle for political power.[1] It features conspiracy, treason, assassination, moral corruption, poisoning, civil war, and foreign conquest. In short, Shakespeare's subject matter in this play is political crisis, a crisis brought on by confusion—to put it politely—over who should be king of England.

This confusion over who should rule is in some ways decidedly artificial, for all of the characters in *King John* agree that Arthur is the legitimate or legal king of England. But Arthur lives powerless on the continent, and England is ruled by the illegitimate King John, who has no intention of abandoning the throne. Legitimacy doesn't seem to matter much. Or, perhaps more accurately, legitimacy is both acknowledged and ignored—hence the political crisis.

Because Shakespeare is often thought to be an orthodox Elizabethan conservative,[2] sometimes even a propagandist for hereditary monarchy,[3] one might expect him to offer in *King John* a vigorous defense of political custom, that is, a defense of Arthur's legitimate hereditary claim to the throne against the usurping King John. While I suppose it would be possible to read the play this way, to my knowledge no one does. And this is due to the fact that Arthur's claim is anything but straightforward: he is both undeniably legitimate and, because he is sponsored by England's greatest enemies, undeniably dangerous to English sovereignty. Perhaps, Shakespeare seems to ask in *King John*, there are situations in which it is prudent, even imperative, to ignore political custom. But if this is one of those situations, then Shakespeare will have written a play defending the illegitimate claim of a selfish murderer to rule England. Could he possibly have intended that?

The Question of Legitimacy

King John's legitimacy is questioned at the very beginning of the play. An ambassador from France demands that John abdicate his throne, on threat of war, to Arthur, whom he calls the "right royal sovereign" (I.i.15).[4] Elsewhere Arthur is referred to as the "lawful king," "this oppressed boy," "England's king" (II.i.95, 177, 311). At one point even King John's most loyal ally, the Bastard (Philip Faulconbridge), acknowledges Arthur's legitimacy, calling him "the life, the right and truth of all this realm" (IV.iii.144). John alone believes in his title to rule, but his mother corrects him only forty lines into the play:

> *King John:* Our strong possession and our right for us.
>
> *Eleanor:* Your strong possession much more than your right,
> Or else it must go wrong with you and me:
> So much my conscience whispers in your ear,
> Which none but heaven, and you, and I, shall hear.
> (I.i.39–43)

In fact, most Tudor historians seem to have accepted John's legitimacy. Holinshed reports that a dying Richard I named John his heir, and John was supported by England's leading nobles, mostly because he was an adult and present in England. Arthur, who had some claim to throne, was a twelve-year-old boy born in Brittany who had never set foot in England.[5] But Shakespeare's King John is clearly a usurper.

If John is illegitimate, however, Arthur's claim is also problematic. He is young and unformed and seems to have little interest in either pursuing the throne or ruling:

> Good my mother, peace!
> I would that I were low laid in my grave:

> I am not worth this coil that's made for me. [weeps] (II.i.163–65)
>
> . . . .
>
> By my christendom,
> So I were out of prison and kept sheep,
> I would be as merry as the day is long . . . (IV.i.16–18)

Arthur has no domestic support in England and is, on his own admission, "powerless" (II.i.15), that is, utterly dependent on foreign sponsors. In short, Arthur is a pawn—of his mother, who wants to be queen, of the French and their Austrian allies, who want to topple John and control (or dismantle) the Angevin Empire, and of the pope, who also has designs on England.

Thus Shakespeare makes two things clear at the outset of *King John*: Arthur is both the legitimate king of England and a grave threat to its autonomy. The case for John, which is also the case for English sovereignty, seems overwhelming. But King John is not a particularly attractive or admirable figure. He is not a clear-sighted defender of English sovereignty in a difficult situation; his breach of political custom is neither reluctant nor nuanced. From beginning to end, John is nothing more than a selfish politician who has power and will do anything—including invading France and assassinating Arthur—to keep it.

Because of Arthur's friends and John's character, a play which frames itself in terms of a legitimacy dispute becomes a blow by blow account of the struggle for power between talented, ambitious, and unscrupulous politicians, ultimately between a murderer king and an atheist cardinal. The conflict between political tradition and national sovereignty with which the play opens gives way almost immediately to the theme of force and fraud.

Statesmanship and Realism

John responds to King Philip's demand that he abdicate the throne to Arthur by invading France. Meeting outside the walled town of Angiers,[6] the king of England and the king of France exchange high-minded and passionate rhetoric, Philip arguing for the justice of Arthur's claim, John defending England's sovereignty:

King Philip: England we love; and for that England's sake
With burden of our armour here we sweat.
This toil of ours should be a work of thine;
But thou from loving England art so far,
That thou hast underwrought his lawful king,
Cut off the sequence of posterity,
Outfaced infant state, and done a rape
Upon the maiden virtue of the crown.
. . . .
How comes it then that thou art call'd a king,
When living blood doth in these temples beat,
Which owe the crown that thou o'ermasterest?

King John: From whom hast thou this great commission,
France, To draw my answer from thy articles?

K. Philip: From that supernal judge that stirs good thoughts
In any beast[7] of strong authority
To look into the blots and stains of right.
That judge hath made me guardian to this boy:
Under whose warrant I impeach thy wrong
And by whose help I mean to chastise it.

K. John: Alack, thou dost usurp authority. (II.i.91–98, 107–18)

After an inconclusive battle and the refusal of the fearful town to commit to either John or Philip (and Arthur), the Bastard suggests that the two armies temporarily join forces to conquer Angiers; afterwards, they can renew the battle to determine who will rule it.[8] Thus threatened, the citizens of Angiers suggest a peaceful solution, proposing a royal wedding between John's cousin Blanche and Philip's son Lewis. After it is agreed upon, the two monarchs draw up a peace agreement whereby John is recognized as the undisputed ruler of England and Philip is given a large portion of England's continental provinces. With the legitimacy dispute settled and with a good deal of Philip's geographical ambitions sated, the play appears to be over.

Commenting on the peace, the Bastard gets it just about right:

Mad World! mad kings! mad composition!
John, to stop Arthur's title in the whole,

> Hath willingly departed with a part:
> And France, whose armour conscience buckled on,
> Whom zeal and charity brought to the field
> As God's own soldier, rounded [whispered] in the ear
> With that same purpose-changer, that sly divel,
> . . . .
> That smooth-fac'd gentleman, tickling commodity,
> Commodity [self-interest], the bias of the world
> (II.i.561-67, 573-4)

The high rhetoric of both kings only masked low self-interest: John wanted to keep his throne, Philip wanted land. In having his John give away so much more than the historical King John did,[9] Shakespeare probably intended to emphasize the lengths to which John would go to preserve his personal power (as opposed to England's national integrity). Philip forthrightly admits to abandoning Constance and Arthur's cause for his own: "In her right we came; / Which we, God knows, have turn'd another way, / To our own vantage" (II.i.548–50). Arthur is forgotten in all this, then remembered as an afterthought and given Angiers, mostly to console his mother.

Before turning to the entrance of Cardinal Pandulf, before, that is, turning to his incendiary mixture of moralism and cunning that will fuel the extraordinary violence of the remainder of the play, a word should be said in favor of these unprincipled, deal-making politicians. King John is motivated solely by a desire to remain in power, but his self-interest coincides with England's interest. Arthur is a twelve-year-old boy with a foreign sponsor and no visible domestic support. In resisting Arthur's lawful claim, albeit for selfish reasons, John resists the threat of an aggressive foreign power and so defends English sovereignty. King Philip may at first understand himself as the champion of justice, but he happily settles for land instead, and probably had no more in mind from the beginning. John loses part of England, but gains security and peace. Philip loses the respect of Arthur's mother and perhaps some self-respect, but he gains territory and peace. These are sober kings, not, as the Bastard half-jokingly described them, "mad kings": John's willingness to depart with a part and Philip's willingness to unbuckle his conscience serves both countries reasonably well.[10] In light of the treachery, violence, and massive bloodshed that will follow as soon as Pandulf arrives on the scene, the peaceful compromise these unprincipled deal-makers have brought about looks like sound politics.

This is not to say that Shakespeare flatly endorses a view of politics that only has room for self-interested realists, or that he rejects the Bastard's plea for a more principled approach. In fact, the same character who here criticizes John and Philip will later save England and, perhaps more importantly, may save us, from the depressing view that politics is little more than a race to the moral bottom. But there are worse alternatives than the "moderate realism" these two kings represent. John and Philip are selfish, but not without some moral sense. Philip seems embarrassed by his betrayal of Constance and will later feel responsible for her grief over Arthur's imprisonment. John, as we shall see, is capable of great crimes, but also of remorse. Both men are more moral than they appear to be. Pandulf, the papal legate who dominates the remainder of the play, is less moral than he seems to be, and far more dangerous—to peace and to anything resembling justice.

Moralism and Cunning: Enter Cardinal Pandulf

The peace that secures John's kingship and Philip's territorial gains is short-lived. On orders from the Pope, Pandulf demands that King John install Rome's choice as Archbishop of England, something John has in the past declined to do. John refuses, as Pandulf certainly expected he would, and once again assumes his role as the defender of English sovereignty:

> Thou canst not, cardinal, devise a name
> So slight, unworthy and ridiculous,
> To charge me to an answer, as the pope.
> . . . .
> Where we do reign, we will alone uphold
> Without th' assistance of a mortal hand:
> So tell the pope, all reverence set apart
> To him and his usurp'd authority. (III.i.75–77, 83–86)

King Philip accuses John of blasphemy, but it would be a mistake to conclude that John lacks respect for the pope and his emissary. It just isn't religious respect. John is acutely aware of the moral, and as a consequence, political power Rome exercises over men, and he correctly predicts King Philip's inability to resist it: "you and all the kings of Christendom / Are led so grossly by this meddling priest, / Dreading the curse that money may buy out; / . . . I alone, alone do me oppose / Against the pope" (III.i.88–90, 95–6). Pandulf promptly excommunicates John and promises canonization and sainthood to his murderer. John's ability to resist the religious blackmail of Rome offers no protection against those who cannot. John has met his match and knows it.

Turning to King Philip, Pandulf demands that France abandon the peace and meet the enemies of Christendom on the battlefield. Philip is torn. He's satisfied with the recent agreement, but fearful of the pope. Rather than admitting forthrightly that he prefers land, peace, and marriage to a holy war, King Philip tries to persuade Pandulf that it would be immoral for him to break his agreement with John, a shallow argument considering the ease with which he broke his agreement with Arthur and Constance. For Philip's son Lewis, the choice is an easy one, "the light loss of England for a friend" being far preferable to the "purchase of a heavy curse from Rome" (III.i.131–32). Lewis's spiritual fear overpowers any thoughts of enjoying his new marriage in peace. After repeated threats of excommunication, Philip comes to the same conclusion, submitting to Rome and agreeing to renew the war. Unlike John, this deal-maker has religion. Philip's political self-interest loses out to an interest in the fate of his soul, and as a consequence, the world quickly becomes a more dangerous place.

England wins the ensuing battle decisively, killing the Duke of Austria, capturing Arthur, fortifying their continental possessions, and thoroughly dispiriting the French. But as John and Pandulf know, nothing is over, and both prepare for more war. The race to the moral bottom now begins in earnest.

All of John's options are risky, including those he settles on, which are probably the best but certainly the most repugnant. John first orders the Bastard to ransack the Church, which is sure to be a center of domestic opposition. If he cannot count on the clergy's support against Rome, he can at least try to neutralize them with a reign of terror, and he can certainly use their wealth to finance his war. John's biggest decision concerns Arthur. If he releases him, perhaps to live in exile in France, John is back where he began, subject to a lifelong threat to his throne from Arthur himself and from those who would use him, as the French did, to advance their own interests. If he keeps him in prison, he renders Arthur an object of pity as well as a symbolic center of legitimate opposition—again, for life. If he kills him, Arthur can never be king, but his murder could be expected to ignite domestic outrage, which could be exploited by enemies at home and abroad. On the other hand, if John could weather the initial outrage over Arthur's murder, he might plausibly hope that it would fade over time. Thus all of John's options involve certain risk, whether in the short term or the long term.

The matter is further complicated by the fact that John expects Pandulf to convince the French to invade England.[11] And it is this pressing consideration, I think, that finally pushes John to opt for murder. One might have expected just the opposite, domestic outrage being the thing John can least afford during an invasion. But it is possible that John thinks Arthur would do more to aid the anticipated French invasion alive than dead. By eliminating Arthur, John deprives the French of the ability to characterize themselves as liberators who come only to rescue and install the rightful English king. Without Arthur, the French cannot connect their invasion to England's higher good. John may also hope that his crime would not look quite so serious to a country preoccupied with a foreign invasion. Sensitive to the domestic threat, John tries to arrange some good will in advance of the news of Arthur's death by publicly re-crowning himself and privately bribing his nobles (IV.ii.43–46).

John's decision to kill Arthur may be morally repugnant, but it does make political sense, both as a means to preserve his kingship and as a means to save England from a successful conquest. Short of giving up the throne or allowing Rome and France the opportunity to rule England in Arthur's name, John has little choice. This, in any event, is Pandulf's thinking. He expects John to kill Arthur—for at least some of the reasons attributed to John here—and plans his whole strategy around it.

Once John has made his decision to kill Arthur, whatever his exact reasons, he slowly falls apart. In one of his creepier performances in this play, John tries to console his recently captured and soon to be murdered nephew: "Cousin, look not sad: / Thy grandam loves thee; and thy uncle will / As dear be to thee as thy father was" (III.ii.12–14). John's kindness to Arthur here makes his recruitment of Arthur's assassin, just a few lines later, seem more monstrous than it would have otherwise. Perhaps Shakespeare had something else in mind: John doesn't really think of himself as a killer. When it comes to recruiting Hubert to kill Arthur, John is incapable of directness. He dances around the subject for thirty-six lines:

> . . . I had a thing to say,
> But I will fit it with some better tune.
> . . . .
> I had a thing to say, but let it go
> . . . .
> . . . if that thou couldst see me without eyes,
> Hear me without thine ears, and make reply
> Without a tongue, using conceit alone,
> Without eyes, ears, and harmful sound of words;
> Then, in despite of brooded watchful day,
> I would into thy bosom pour my thoughts:
> But, ah, I will not. (III.ii.35–36, 43, 58–64)

He cannot say it. And when he gains the courage to hint at his meaning, he cannot say Arthur's name:

> Good Hubert, Hubert, Hubert, throw thine eye
> On yon young boy; I'll tell thee what, my friend,
> He is a very serpent in my way;
> And wheresoe'r this foot of mine doth tread,
> He lies before me: dost thou understand me? (III.ii.69–73)

Because Hubert cannot, or will not, understand him, John is finally forced into chilling, monosyllabic directness:

> *John:* Death.
>
> *Hubert:* My lord?
>
> *John:* A grave.
>
> *Hubert:* He shall not live.
>
> *John:* Enough.[12]

John is a reluctant murderer. The moral doubt that will, in the end, cripple him, is evident even here.

Pandulf is unencumbered by moral doubt. His strategy, like John's, revolves around Arthur. He too wants Arthur dead, but unlike John, he finds the prospect "wonderful" (III.iii.178). Pandulf plans to capitalize on English outrage over Arthur's death: John will divide, and the French will conquer. But first, he must get the dispirited French to find the idea of benefiting from the murder of a teenage boy as delightful as he does. And to do this, he must corrupt King Philip's son.

In selling his strategy for conquering England to Lewis, Pandulf sheds his religious garb and reveals himself as a naked Machiavellian. He makes no further attempt at religious blackmail, already having played the excommunication card to lure the French back onto the battlefield, where they performed miserably. Pandulf may think that in crying wolf again he would not be listened to and, furthermore, that the dejected French are more in need of inspiration than of spiritual terror. So Pandulf abandons his religious stick for a carrot: Lewis can be king of England. But before tempting Lewis with the prize of power, Pandulf must make him comfortable with the idea of Arthur's murder. He first gently tests the waters by asking Lewis if he is sad about Arthur's imprisonment. Lewis is indeed sad, and Pandulf now knows that he is dealing with a decent man who hasn't thought the situation through: "[y]our mind is all as youthful as your blood" (III.iii.125). Political grown-ups, he implies and soon demonstrates, see opportunities where others see cause for grief. Playing reality instructor to naive youth, Pandulf lays out the necessity of Arthur's murder:

> John has seiz'd Arthur; and it cannot be
> That, whiles warm life plays in that infant's veins,
> The misplac'd John should entertain an hour,
> One minute, nay, one quiet breath of rest.
> A sceptre snatch'd with an unruly hand
> Must be as boisterously maintain'd as gain'd;
>
> . . . .
>
> That John may stand, then, Arthur needs must fall.
> (III.iii.131–36, 139)

Pandulf is clearly trying to shock Lewis with a picture of how politics is actually practiced, but he is also trying to comfort him. Because Arthur's death is inevitable, as certain as sunrise, Lewis needn't trouble himself about it. It's as good as done, so the question is what course to follow. And as Pandulf surely hoped, this is just what Lewis asks: "But what shall I gain by young Arthur's fall?" (III.iii.141). You will gain the throne of England, Pandulf explains, claiming it through your new wife Blanche.[13]

Now that Lewis is acclimated to the idea of Arthur's murder and has been given a motive to invade England, Pandulf reveals the details of his divide and conquer strategy: Arthur's death will "cool the hearts" and "freeze up" the "zeal" of John's supporters (III.iii.149–50), who will rise up in dissent and welcome Lewis's assistance in deposing John. In order to ensure that dissent, Pandulf will play on English superstition, spreading the word that God himself desires John's fall:

> No natural exhalation in the sky,
> No natural scope of nature, no distemper'd day,
> No common wind, no customed event,
> But they will pluck away his natural cause
> And call them meteors, prodigies and signs,
> Abortives, presages, and tongues of heaven,
> Plainly denouncing vengeance upon John. (III.iii.153–59)

It is worth noting that the man who speaks condescendingly of those who would mistake a natural event for a sign from heaven is a cardinal.

Now that he has seen the logic of Pandulf's plan and can taste the English crown, Lewis poses a problem: what if John merely imprisons Arthur, but doesn't kill him? "[W]hen he shall hear of your approach," Pandulf answers, "[i]f that young Arthur be not gone already, / Even at that news he dies" (III.iii.162–64). Lewis does not object. The man who earlier admitted to grief over Arthur's imprisonment is now prepared to cause his death in order to serve his own ambitions. Cardinal Pandulf has thoroughly corrupted Lewis. He has created a power-hungry killer.

News of Arthur's death has exactly the effect in England that Pandulf predicted and helped to ensure. John's nobles suspect him and, once their suspicions are confirmed, turn against him. The

English people become "strangely fantasied; / Possess'd with rumours, full of idle dreams, / Not knowing what they fear, but full of fear" (IV.ii.144-46). When five moons are reported seen, they are interpreted as heavenly signs implicating John in Arthur's death (IV.ii.184–87). Peter of Pomphret (said by one historian to have been in the pay of Rome[14]) prophesies among the people of John's imminent fall. Meanwhile, the French land in England.

Pope Innocent III, the man who stands behind Pandulf, once wrote that "[t]he Lord left to St. Peter the governance not of the church only but of the whole world."[15] Whether we are to understand Pandulf as the embodiment of the pope or as a reflection of the pope's wisdom in choosing lieutenants, Pandulf is an extraordinary politician.[16] Without a single soldier to back him, Pandulf forces the French to abandon an advantageous peace, and after being routed on the battlefield in their own backyard, he persuades them to turn around and invade England. With the help of his spiritual soldiers, he convinces the English populace that God himself desires John's fall. He makes King Philip fear damnation and transforms Lewis from a God-fearing youth into an unscrupulous killing machine. Pandulf knows which buttons to push to mold men to his will. In his single-minded and farseeing devotion to the pope's political agenda, he appears himself to be wholly unaffected by moral or religious claims, something which cannot be said of any other character in the play besides Lewis, whom he personally corrupts.[17] Simply put, King John's talented foe is a textbook Machiavellian.

John is most worried that his angry nobles will join with the French in opposing him, and confides to the Bastard that he has "a way to win their loves again" (IV.ii.167). While John never reveals his plan, we can assume he intends to try to blame Arthur's death on Hubert.[18] But when he confronts Hubert, John's political motive for shifting responsibility gets tangled up with a moral motive for shifting responsibility: he cannot stand to think of himself as a murderer. And so John begins, as if he were barely acquainted with the whole matter, by asking Hubert why he murdered Arthur. When an astonished Hubert objects that he was simply doing John's will, John accuses him of misinterpreting his "humours for a warrant / To break within the bloody house of life" (IV.ii.209–10). Hubert then produces the warrant, and John is unable any longer to sustain his fantasy: "O, when the last accompt 'twixt heaven and earth / Is to be made, then shall this hand and seal / Witness against us to damnation!" (IV.ii.216–18). All the kings of Christendom may not fear the pope, but all apparently fear for the fate of their souls. King John is a Christian. His moral terror leads him next to blame Hubert for planting the thought of murder, which he wouldn't have had by himself, and finally for not trying to stop him—"hadst thou but shook thy head or made a pause . . . " (IV.ii.231). These are the desperate maneuvers of a confessed sinner, not the sober calculations of a politician. The difference between John and Pandulf could not be greater.

But Arthur is not dead: Hubert got cold feet. John is delighted by Hubert's admission and the politician in him rises from the dead as he commands Hubert to inform his nobles of the good news. But one wonders just how completely the politician in John has taken over, for he apologizes to Hubert for thinking *him* a murderer, which may well be a renewed effort to grapple with his own guilt. Unbeknownst to Hubert or John, Arthur is in fact dead, having suffered a fatal accident while trying to escape from prison. But when we next see John, who is still oblivious of Arthur's fate, we find him cowering at Pandulf's feet, delivering over his crown and receiving it back beholden to the pope. In exchange for his submission to Rome, Pandulf has agreed to call off Lewis's troops. But why does John, who believes Arthur alive, submit to Pandulf rather than waiting to hear from his nobles, or toughing it out without them? John's precipitous and thoughtless decision makes no political sense, but this may be Shakespeare's point: it is not a political decision at all. By prostrating himself before the Church, John is seeking a kind of absolution for his sin. At the end of this scene, which begins with a submission to the pope, John quits politics altogether, putting the Bastard, his last loyal ally, in charge of his crumbling kingdom.[19]

As the Bastard predicted to John, Pandulf cannot call off the war. Lewis, reminding us of the once vigorous King John, will not obey the cardinal, refusing to be an "instrument . . . [t]o any sovereign state throughout the world," refusing to be "Rome's slave" (V.ii.81–82, 97). And in his proud defiance, a defiance that Pandulf made possible by corrupting him, Lewis points to the fatal flaw in Pandulf's policy: "What penny hath Rome borne, / What men provided, what munitions sent, / To underprop this action?" (V.ii.96–98). None, of course, because priests can't fight. Rome can wage moral war, but it must rely on others on the battlefield, and it cannot always control those armies it recruits to carry out its temporal aims.[20] Trying to distinguish Rome's policy of spiritual obedience from mere worldly gain, Pandulf tells Lewis that "[y]ou look but on the outside of this work" (V.ii.109). Understandably, Lewis finds the distinction irrelevant:

> Outside or inside, I will not return
> Till my attempt so much be glorified
> As to my ample hope was promised
> Before I drew this gallant head of war . . . (V.ii.110–13)

Pandulf can't control Lewis, because Lewis, thanks to Pandulf, is immune to religious blackmail. Again reminding us of the robust early John, Lewis is more concerned with political power than he is with the fate of his soul.

The differences in the ways John and Pandulf recruit their killers reveal fundamental differences in their characters. The fact that John has so much trouble saying what he wants of Hubert indicates his underlying moral misgivings, which surface soon after. Pandulf, by contrast, is brutally direct. The recruits themselves also seem to reflect the character of their recruiters. John's executioner finds himself unable to harm Arthur. Pandulf's creation is a perfect imitation of his teacher, so perfect that he turns against Pandulf himself.

The Bastard

Lewis does not prevail in his contest with John's remaining loyalists, who are commanded by the Bastard, a man who is both prudent and moral, who has all the right sentiments and makes all the right moves. All of the Machiavellians—John, Pandulf, and Lewis—lose out in the end, and England is saved by a decent man, who hands the throne over to John's son and heir—like Arthur, just a boy. But does the apparent lesson of this play—that *realpolitik* is doomed to failure—really stand up? To investigate this question, I turn to the Bastard and to the reasons for his victory over Lewis.

The Bastard is both politically savvy and morally sound. When John informs him of his pact with Rome, the Bastard apprises the situation quickly and recommends the only prudent course:

Let us, my leige, to arms!
Perchance the cardinal cannot make your peace;
Or if he do, let it at least be said
They saw we had a purpose of defence. (V.i.73–76)

Charged with prosecuting the war, the Bastard lies to Lewis that John never fully trusted Pandulf, using him more "for sport than need," and so is fully prepared "[t]o feast upon whole thousands of French" (V.ii.175, 178). And his bold words are matched by action, earning him backhanded praise from one of John's revolting nobles: "I did not think the king so stor'd with friends. / . . . That misbegotten divel, Faulconbridge, / . . . alone upholds the day" (V.iv.1, 4–5). In short, the Bastard does what John would have done prior to his moral collapse.

He does, however, differ with John over Arthur. While standing over Arthur's dead body earlier in the play, the Bastard is caught short: "I am amaz'd, methinks, and lose my way / Among the thorns and dangers of this world" (IV.iii.140–41). But his moral crisis does not lead him to publicly oppose John, as it did John's nobles, who found themselves forced into a traitorous alliance with the French in order to save themselves.[21] And with John dead and the war won, the Bastard makes no attempt to seize power for himself, as he surely could have, instead supporting John's son and heir, the boy-king Henry III.[22] He appears to be without political ambition, and he has surely learned from his association with John the devastating consequences of such ambition.

But the Bastard's decency may come at the cost of clear-sightedness. Does he ever understand the threat that Arthur, whom he eulogizes as "the life, the right and truth of all this realm" (IV.iii.144), poses to English sovereignty? As Pandulf succinctly put it, "[t]hat John may stand, then, Arthur needs must fall" (III.iii.139). And John *must* stand if England is to resist foreign control. The Bastard seems to lack the brutal clarity of John and Pandulf, a clarity fueled in both cases by ambition. While the Bastard's selfless decency serves England well in this instance, it appears to be incompatible in his case with a recognition of the threat that Arthur poses to England, and incompatible as well with an ability to deal with him harshly.[23] One need not be ambitious in order to recognize and deal with one's enemies, but it certainly helps.

Let us turn, finally, to the war itself, and ask ourselves if it can be understood as the victory of decency over Machiavellianism. Lewis surrenders after confronting two facts: the re-defection of the English nobles, who return to John, and the loss of his military reinforcements in a storm at sea. The latter setback is due to fortune, and so can't be understood as a commentary on Lewis's political methods. Shakespeare may even have intended to emphasize the accidental nature of Lewis's loss, for most of the available source material reports that English ships, not a storm, were responsible for sinking Lewis's reinforcements.[24] The re-defection of the English nobles, however, can be understood as a commentary on Lewis's political methods, for it is the result of the betrayal of a dying French lord who cannot abide Lewis's treachery, and who therefore warns the nobles that Lewis intends to kill them as soon as he wins the war and seizes the throne. But if the loss of the English nobles is a direct result of a moral intention to subvert Lewis, Lord Melun's conscience only pricks him as he nears death, and thus his betrayal depends first on the fact that he is wounded and second on the fact that he lives long enough to deliver his warning. Had he survived the battle unharmed, Melun may never have warned the nobles of their fate. Had he died instantly, one of Lewis's reasons for quitting the war would have disappeared with him. There is a possibility that Lewis might have prevailed without the English nobles, so long as he didn't lose his reinforcements at sea. Even then, he still might have prevailed, for he surrenders without knowing that the Bastard has lost more than half of his own troops in a flood.[25] The Bastard's victory is surely a victory for decency over Machiavellianism, but the causal links are slight and perhaps even non-existent.

Why do the Machiavellians fail? Is it because they are Machiavellians, or because they are not Machiavellian enough? First, it's not so certain that Lewis's failure can be attributed to his political methods. He may simply be a victim of fate, and fate is blind. John fails because he is too moral. He really just gives up, crippled by his conscience. Ultimately, he appears to care more about the fate of his soul than he does about political success. Pandulf fails because he has no army, and because he decides that in order to get one, he must relinquish moral control over Lewis. But Pandulf really is a remarkable politician, a cardinal who believes that the only sin is ignorance, and who benefits from the fact that most men are incapable of such a belief. We see, I think, in Shakespeare's treatment of Pandulf, some of the same admiration that Machiavelli has for Pope Alexander. Of course, Shakespeare, like Machiavelli, shows us the horrors that Christian moralism can unleash upon the political world—King John, incidently, was poisoned by a monk (V.vi.23–31)—and he understands the necessary limitations of ecclesiastical politics. But are we to conclude that Machiavellian politics is ultimately ineffective, or that Pandulf with an army would be invincible? Pandulf with an army means only a more effective combination of force and fraud, and Shakespeare will investigate another combination in his next history play, *Richard II,* which explores the doctrine of the divine right of kings. Someone in England was apparently paying attention to Pandulf and his boss.

Justice

Arguably, Shakespeare intends for us to learn from *King John* that things are better in Europe before God enters politics in act 3, that John and Philip's moderate realism is preferable to Pandulf's Christian moralism, which is but a mask for immoderate realism. John and Philip's political vision is selfish and hypocritical, although both men are likely to have had some awareness of each other's true aims. Politics thus becomes a kind of competition or game whose end is securing power, but it is a game in which limits are respected and compromise is possible. Insofar as this political universe is guided by calculated self-interest, it is predictable, if predictably uninspiring. When one compares Europe before and after act 3, one must conclude that the world is a better place prior to the pope's meddling and that John and Philip's political vision is, if nothing else, more amenable to peace and security than is Pandulf's.

When God enters politics, the stakes are raised and extremism is the natural result, for God doesn't compromise. Shakespeare makes this clearest by repeating the (historically spurious) tale that King John was poisoned by a monk. Fear for one's soul also leads to extremism, shown best when King Philip takes leave of his political common sense in response to Pandulf's threats of damnation. With God's apparent blessing, monarchs are subject to assassination and armies are hijacked by priests. The men who are directing all this action with threats of divine retribution—Pandulf and the pope—are themselves without religion. As Machiavelli teaches, the ability to manipulate the conscience of others while remaining conscienceless oneself is a politically formidable combination.

The Bastard, who is plucked from obscurity and thrown into the very center of European politics, matures rapidly over the course of the play. His boyish delight in the trappings of power and his happy-go-lucky tolerance of John and Philip's low politics[26] gives way to a weightier demeanor when he becomes the de facto king of England. The Bastard offers us a political alternative to John and Philip on the one hand and Pandulf on the other. A moral realist, that is, a man with some experience of how ambitious politicians actually behave, he nevertheless remains uncynical, finally guided by a sense of decency and justice. But are moralism and realism compatible in practice? In the Bastard's case, they appear not to be, for his feelings for Arthur come into conflict with his concern for England, leaving him decent but incoherent. As Colmo points out,

> From a strictly political point of view, the least rational speech Richard makes is the one in which, having found the boy dead, he calls Arthur 'The life, the right, and truth of all this realm'. . . . Richard's speech about Arthur is confused. Is Arthur at any time anything other than a pawn of the French? Is it not for Arthur that so many French and English soldiers fall before Angiers?

Colmo continues that "[w]hile the unscrupulous Pandulf might have seen Arthur merely in such a light, we know that Shakespeare did not. Shakespeare does not allow us to see Arthur only from a political point of view."[27] In contrast, I think we must see Arthur in such a light and that Shakespeare makes it so difficult precisely in order to highlight the danger that sentimentality poses to sober politics, a sentimentality from which no decent man is immune,[28] but which must be overcome lest the hardhearted and amoral always emerge victorious.

So we are left in *King John* with a mixed message. Shakespeare seems to encourage our indentification with the Bastard, but warns that his decency comes at the cost of clear-sightedness. If possible at all, genuine moral realism will be rare. The next best alternative is also shown to be problematic: John and Philip's moderate realism may be preferable to Pandulf's opportunistic Christian moralism, but it is no match for it. Neither monarch proves capable of pursuing a consistent policy of enlightened self-interest. Both ultimately submit to moral claims (Philip submits to the pope, John to his conscience) which undermine their own and their country's well-being. Even if John and Philip were capable of resisting the Pope, it is not clear that their subjects would continue to support them. With covert prodding from Rome, the English people are led to believe that God disapproves of their king; they appear to crave moral authority even at the cost of sovereignty and peace.

If something like justice does prevail in *King John*, its victory is heavily dependent on chance. The happy ending in *King John* covers over but does not wholly obscure the precariousness and fragility of justice.

Chapter Three

King Richard II

In *King John,* Shakespeare dramatized a political crisis brought on by a legitimacy dispute, which pitted the sitting king against the legitimate pretender and his French allies. The crisis was exacerbated by the worldly ambitions of the pope, who had his own designs on England. One hundred sixty-one years later, the man who possesses the English throne, King Richard II, is undeniably legitimate.[1] And like the pope who plagued King John, Richard derives his authority directly from God. But Richard's double right to rule—both hereditary and divine—does not eliminate competition for the throne: he is challenged at the beginning of the play and murdered by the end.

Calling himself "an anointed king," "the deputy elected by the Lord" (III.ii.55, 57), King Richard is Shakespeare's only portrait of a divine right king. John Figgis, author of the definitive study of divine right, traces the genesis of this political doctrine to the ambitious Roman popes:

> It is in the gradual rise of Papal claims to universal supremacy, that are first put forth those notions which form the basis of all theories of Divine Right; the conception of sovereignty, of the absolute freedom from positive laws of some power in an organized human society; the claim that this sovereignty is vested in a single person by God, and that resistance to the sovereign is the worst of sins.[2]

King John's early stand against the pope is a step along the way in the development of the divine right of kings, which arises "as a contradiction and a counter-theory to that of Papal supremacy."[3] In Shakespeare's King Richard, we meet the embodiment of that "counter-theory," a king who claims to have been anointed by God to rule and who is responsible to no one else.

But Richard, unlike those cynical and unbelieving Roman Catholic officials in *King John* who use religion as a political weapon, truly believes he is divinely authorized to rule. He inherits the pope's divine authority without any of his political savvy. Richard is a genuinely naive ruler: believing that God protects him, he fails to protect himself, and so becomes the tragic victim of a doctrine designed to fortify his rule. *Richard II* is a tragedy.[4] The question is whether this beautifully sad play dramatizes a merely personal tragedy—"the lamentable tale of me," as Richard puts it (V.i.44)—or a political tragedy as well.

Bolingbroke's Motives

Richard II opens with an accusation of treason, which may or may not be directed at the king. Henry Bolingbroke charges Thomas Mowbray with plotting against King Richard as well as with murdering Gloucester, a popular and once powerful nobleman who died under mysterious circumstances while awaiting trial for treason. Bolingbroke's motive in accusing Mowbray is as mysterious as Gloucester's death. He may be trying simply to secure Richard's kingship by exposing a traitor and to secure justice for Gloucester by exposing his killer. On the other hand, this may be a thinly veiled attempt to embarrass and undermine King Richard, the opening salvo in Bolingbroke's ultimately successful campaign for the crown.

Richard suspects the latter. Linked by rumor to Gloucester's death, Richard believes that he is Bolingbroke's real target, his kingship Bolingbroke's real aim: "how high a pitch his resolution soars!" (I.i.109). The historical King Richard was presumed to have been responsible for Gloucester's death and Shakespeare's audience would have taken this for granted.[5] While the identity of Gloucester's killer is never definitively settled in the play, no one doubts that Richard ordered his death. In the quarrel between Gloucester's brother and his widow, for example, the question is not whether Richard is responsible for the murder, but what should be done about it. Arguing that one's primary allegiance ought to be to one's blood relations, Gloucester's wife pleads with Gaunt to avenge his brother's death:

> Finds brotherhood in thee no sharper spur?
> Hath love in thy old blood no living fire?
> . . . .
> Ah, Gaunt, his blood was thine! (I.ii.9–10, 22)

Of course, Richard too is a blood relation; he is also a divine right king. Failing to move Gaunt, the duchess changes tactics and appeals to the less noble, though perhaps more pressing, desire for self-preservation:

> In suff'ring thus thy brother to be slaught'red,
> Thou showest the naked pathway to thy life,
> Teaching stern murder how to butcher thee.
> . . . .
> . . . to safeguard thine own life,
> The best way is to venge my Gloucester's death. (I.ii.30–32, 35–36)

But Gaunt will not act. While he claims to feel outrage, he cannot bring himself to challenge Richard, God's representative, for God must have his reasons:

> God's is the quarrel—for God's substitute,
> His deputy anointed in His sight,
> Hath caus'd his death; the which if wrongfully,
> Let heaven revenge, for I may never lift
> An angry arm against His minister. (I.ii.37–41)

The duchess thus gives up, pinning her hopes for justice on Bolingbroke.

Whatever his exact intentions, Bolingbroke's accusation unsettles Richard's awkward but sustainable position of being presumed both guilty and untouchable. Because the last thing the king needs is a rigorous public inquiry into Gloucester's death, he attempts to quash the whole matter at the outset: "wrath-kindled gentlemen, by rul'd by me, / Let's purge this choler without letting blood— . . . Forget, forgive, conclude and be agreed" (I.i.152–53, 156). But Bolingbroke resists

Richard's attempt to impose a peaceful settlement and Richard, still trying to avoid a public hearing, orders a trial by combat, a legal duel that was supposed to result in divine justice—the man who dies is guilty. But this solution is problematic: if Richard's ally Mowbray should prevail, the king might be blamed for two murders rather than one; if Bolingbroke should prevail, Mowbray and, by implication, Richard himself might be deemed guilty in the eyes of God. Calling off the trial by combat, Richard decides finally to make his problems literally go away, banishing Mowbray for life and Bolingbroke for six years. Mowbray's harsher sentence implies guilt, but the king offers no verdict, and Mowbray quietly accepts his fate. The relatively light sentence Bolingbroke receives seems designed to appease his powerful father while suggesting, at the same time, that Bolingbroke's concern for England is dangerous and probably self-interested. In fact, Richard implies when spelling out the terms of their banishment that both men may have been conspiring against him:

> You shall never, so help you truth and God,
> Embrace each other's love in banishment,
>
> . . . .
>
> Nor never by advised purpose meet
> To plot, contrive, or complot any ill
> 'Gainst us, our state, our subjects, or our land. (I.iii.183–84, 188–90)

Delicately turning attention from a past murder toward the future stability of England, Richard succeeds (for now) in burying the Gloucester affair by banishing an awkward friend and a potentially dangerous enemy.

Immediately after securing his kingship in England, Richard is faced with a rebellion in Ireland. In order to finance his Irish expedition, Richard seizes the assets of Gaunt, who has just died. Gaunt's title and estate should rightly devolve to his son and it is to claim what has been taken from him that Bolingbroke purportedly returns early from his banishment.[6] But as with the Gloucester affair, Bolingbroke's motives are not clear. Is he really only interested in claiming his stolen inheritance, or is this the second and decisive stage in a long planned strategy to unseat King Richard? Earlier in the play, Gaunt tried to comfort his banished son with Stoic platitudes, telling him to imagine his exile as "a travel that thou tak'st for pleasure," or, better yet, "think not the king did banish thee, / But thou the king" (I.iii.262, 279–80). While Gaunt's words were perfectly innocent, Bolingbroke may have been thinking as much all along.[7]

Still, in their dealings with one another, Bolingbroke comes off looking much better than Richard does. Whether Bolingbroke is innocently pursuing justice or deviously pursuing the throne, Richard is still a murderer and a thief. And if Shakespeare allows and perhaps even encourages us to think well of Bolingbroke, he makes no attempt to justify Richard's behavior. This is not to say that it cannot be justified.

In Richard's defense, Gloucester had to be killed. While Gaunt refers to his brother as a "plain, well-meaning soul" (II.i.128), the historical Gloucester was nothing of the kind.[8] Holinshed describes him as "fierce of nature, hasty, wilful . . . and in this greatly to be discomended, that he was ever repining against the king in all things."[9] Gloucester more or less ran the country during Richard's minority. He was extremely popular and Hume describes him as "a prince of ambition and genius."[10] But when Richard was grown, Gloucester didn't want to relinquish his power, and during a period when his faction gained the upper hand against Richard's, he killed most of the king's partisans. For this, Hume labels him "the inexorable tyrant."[11] According to Froissart, Gloucester tried to get Richard's heir, Roger Mortimer, to declare Gloucester king, and when Mortimer refused, he planned to depose Richard and partition the kingdom between himself, his two brothers, and the Earl of Arundel. It was in response to news of this plot that Richard had him arrested and imprisoned, with the full concurrence of Gloucester's brothers, Gaunt and York. Richard had little choice in the matter. As Hume notes, he "saw that either his own ruin or that of Gloucester was inevitable."[12]

Richard's treatment of Bolingbroke, first in banishing him and next in destroying his power base in England,[13] is motivated by the same fear. Richard suspects that Bolingbroke is after his job from the moment he accuses Mowbray. His suspicions are confirmed when he observes Bolingbroke's behavior as he departs for exile in France:

> Ourself and Bushy
> Observ'd his courtship to the common people,
> How he did seem to dive into their hearts
> With humble and familiar courtesy;

What reverence he did throw away on slaves,
Wooing poor craftsmen with the craft of smiles
And patient underbearing of his fortune,
As 'twere to banish their affects with him.
Off goes his bonnet to an oyster-wench;
A brace of draymen bid God speed him well,
And had the tribute of his supple knee,
With "Thanks, my countrymen, my loving friends"—
As were our England in reversion his,
And he our subjects' next degree in hope. (I.iv.23–36)

On Richard's view, Bolingbroke is brazenly campaigning for his job. And while he is clearly disgusted by Bolingbroke's behavior here, I think he is also impressed by, and perhaps envious of, his talents as a campaigner.

A number of respectable critics, however, dismiss Richard's fears as paranoid and insist that Bolingbroke has no intention of dethroning the king either when he brings up Gloucester's death or when he decides to return early from banishment. According to this view, Bolingbroke is

> . . . borne upward by a power beyond his volition. He is made the first mover of trouble in the matter of the tournament and he wants to do something about Woodstock's [i.e., Gloucester's] murder. But he has no steady policy and having once set events in motion is the servant of fortune.[14]

Palmer adds a twist to this line of argument by suggesting that Bolingbroke is consciously unconscious (or some such thing) of his aims:

> Bolingbroke . . . is the most dangerous of all climbing politicians, the man who will go further than his rivals because he never allows himself to know where he is going. Every step in his progress towards the throne is dictated by circumstances and he never permits himself to have a purpose till it is more than half fulfilled. From first to last his friends and enemies alike are always more clearly aware of his intentions than the man himself.[15]

Palmer seems to equate not revealing one's purpose with lacking a purpose altogether. The poet Daniel, one of Shakespeare's possible sources for this play, gives Bolingbroke more credit: "he seems not t'affect that which he did affect."[16]

While Bolingbroke's accusation of Mowbray is presented as an attempt to avenge the murder of his uncle, "there is no particular [historical] evidence of close affection between Bolingbroke and Gloucester."[17] Of course, one doesn't need a special motive to desire to punish the murderer of one's kin, but it turns out that Bolingbroke isn't even certain that Mowbray killed his uncle. Much later in the play, when he is about to ascend the throne, Bolingbroke reopens the Gloucester case before Parliament, asking Richard's aide Bagot "what thou dost know of noble Gloucester's death, / Who wrought it with the king, and who perform'd / The bloody office of his timeless end" (IV.i.3–5). Presumably, Bolingbroke already knows the answer: he accused Mowbray and was willing to kill him in a trial by combat. But Bagot and most of those present accuse Aumerle (even Mowbray is said to have fingered Aumerle), and Bolingbroke, who may well know he's dead, repeals Mowbray's banishment so that he and Aumerle can settle the matter in a trial by combat. Bolingbroke never does make any attempt to identify and punish the real killer.[18] Once he is crowned king, the whole affair is forgotten. When Bolingbroke first accused Mowbray, he had to know that everyone would take it as a covert indictment of Richard. When he brings up Gloucester's murder a second time, he explicitly implicates Richard—"who wrought it with the king [?]" The simplest explanation is that on both occasions, Bolingbroke is seeking to undermine Richard and advance himself.

As I noted above, Richard suspects that Bolingbroke's behavior as he departs to serve his sentence of banishment is a self-serving attempt to bolster his own popularity. In a private conversation with his son in *1 Henry IV*, Bolingbroke admits as much. Recalling his departure for exile, Bolingbroke confesses that he was shamelessly campaigning for Richard's position:

> And then I stole all courtesy from heaven,
> And dress'd myself up in such humility
> That I did pluck allegiance from men's hearts,
> Loud shouts and salutations from their mouths,
> Even in the presence of the crowned King. (*1HIV* III.ii.50–54)

The departure scene appears to have been but one element in a larger effort by Bolingbroke to enhance his popular standing. Earlier in his lecture, while comparing his degenerate son Hal to Richard, King Henry shares another of his strategies for cultivating public opinion:

> Had I so lavish of my presence been,
> So common-hackney'd in the eyes of men,
> So stale and cheap to vulgar company,
> Opinion, that did help me to the crown,
> Had still kept loyal to possession [i.e., to Richard],
> And left me in reputeless banishment,
> A fellow of no mark nor likelihood. (*1HIV* III.ii.39–45)

In his attempt to carve out an appealing public image, Bolingbroke played the regal part that Richard so neglected: "[t]hus did I keep my person fresh and new, / My presence, like a robe pontifical, / Ne'er seen but wonder'd at . . . " (III.ii.55–57). But as Richard observed and Henry confirms, this actor-king is not above seducing the commonest of the people. While Richard is both common and contemptuous of the commons, a playboy as well as a snob, Bolingbroke will be both remote and solicitous of the commons. Were one casting the role of divine right king, Bolingbroke would win the part easily.

Those critics who argue that Bolingbroke had no preconcerted designs on the crown when he accused Mowbray also take him at his word when he announces, upon returning to England, that "I come but for mine own" (III.iii.196). Much of the evidence for Bolingbroke's innocence centers on his supposed swearing of an oath that he does not seek Richard's position. As Northumberland tells Richard,

> Harry Bolingbroke, doth humbly kiss thy hand;
> And by the honorable tomb he swears,
>
> . . . .
>
> His coming hither hath no further scope
> Than for his lineal royalties, and to beg
> Infranchisement immediate on his knees,
>
> . . . .
>
> This, swears he as he is a prince and just. (III.iii.104–105, 112–14, 119)

But as Herford correctly points out, "Bolingbroke has in fact given no pledge and taken no oath. Northumberland seeks merely to get possession of Richard, without committing his chief."[19] But Northumberland's claim takes on a life of its own and is repeated by his son, Hotspur, and his brother, the Earl of Worcester, in *1 Henry IV*.[20] Because Bolingbroke never swears an oath on stage in *Richard II*, we have only the word of Northumberland, and in *Henry IV*, of Worcester and Hotspur, none of whom ought to be trusted. In *Richard II*, Northumberland wants to replace Richard, and in *1 Henry IV*, Worcester and Hotspur want to replace Henry—they all have good reasons to lie. So, for that matter, does Bolingbroke. If he did swear an oath, why should one believe him? His actions seem to be a reasonably sure indication of his intentions, and soon after he returns from exile, he, not Richard, is king.

The evidence that Bolingbroke seeks only his patrimony does not, however, rely exclusively on the hearsay of untrustworthy witnesses. In *2 Henry IV*, the king himself explicitly denies ever having had designs on the crown:

> When Richard, with his eye brimful of tears,
> Then check'd and rated by Northumberland,
> Did speak these words, now prov'd a prophecy?
> "Northumberland, thou ladder by the which
> My cousin Bolingbroke ascends my throne"
> (Though then, God knows, I had no such intent
> But that necessity so bowed the state
> That I and greatness were compell'd to kiss) (*2HIV* III.i.67–74)

This is the most compelling evidence in favor of Bolingbroke's innocence. But his memory here is both self-serving and faulty, for when Richard spoke these words to Northumberland (*RII* V.i.55–56), Henry was already king and had just ordered Richard imprisoned. And Henry's explicit denial must be balanced against equally explicit admissions. In the private conversation with his son referred to above, Henry says that "[w]hen I from France set foot at Ravenspurgh, / . . . even as I was then is Percy now" (*1HIV* III.ii.95–96). In other words, like Hotspur in *1 Henry IV*, Bolingbroke in *Richard II* was engaged in a military effort to remove the sitting king. On his deathbed, Henry IV offers a general confession about his rise to power, making it clear that where Richard was concerned, he was up to no good: "God knows, my son / By what by-paths and indirect crook'd ways / I met this crown . . . It seem'd in me / But as an honour snatch'd with boist'rous hand . . . " (*2HIV* IV.v.183–85, 190–91).

But one needn't even take Henry's (unstable) word. A close reading of act 2, scene 1 shows that Bolingbroke begins to sail back to England from France before his father dies and thus before his estate has been seized, putting him in the odd position of returning to claim what hasn't yet been taken. Even if Shakespeare mistakenly botched the timing, it is difficult to reconcile Bolingbroke's innocence with the fact that Northumberland, who will serve as Bolingbroke's primary ally in unseating Richard, has "intelligence" of his imminent arrival— "[w]ith eight tall ships" and "three thousand men of war" (II.i.278, 286)—that he shares with his newly recruited fellow conspirators. Northumberland tells them that Bolingbroke may well be anchored off the coast right now, awaiting "the first departing of the king for Ireland" (II.i.290).[21] It sounds as though arrangements have been made. When Bolingbroke does arrive, the Northumberland faction treats him with a deference befitting a king[22] and he twice promises them financial reward for their loyalty.

Harold Goddard thinks that

> [t]he naive reader, encountering this play for the first time, is inclined to give Henry the benefit of the doubt and think that he came back to England from his banishment merely to recover his inheritance, not with an eye on the crown. But no one can believe that for a second when he reads the rest of the story.[23]

But a number of critics, who could hardly be called naive readers, do give Bolingbroke the benefit of the doubt, and they are provided with some textual justification in doing so. It almost seems as though Shakespeare has written two scripts about Bolingbroke's rise to power, one in which he is a well-meaning patriot who reluctantly becomes king on the encouragement of others, and only after Richard has consistently abused his power, and another in which he is an ambitious rival of the king who will seize any opportunity to advance his long-standing quest for the kingship. I hope to have made it clear that the latter script describes the real Bolingbroke; but the former script is more obviously available to the reader of the play, and provides a kind of cover for the subterranean ambition that ultimately drives Bolingbroke. But why would Shakespeare want to provide Bolingbroke with cover?

Of course, Bolingbroke provides his own cover, making sure that all of his power-plays can be plausibly interpreted as something else. But Shakespeare is an accomplice of sorts in Bolingbroke's project, for he does not give us any information that might help justify Richard's behavior or cause us to sympathize with his plight.[24] He allows us to see Bolingbroke in the best light while encouraging us to see Richard in the worst. He tells us nothing about the quarrelsome history of Richard's reign, which is the story of a legitimate boy-king constantly under assault by powerful and ambitious adults.[25] Richard comes to sight in this play not as a young king who has finally achieved some independence only to be challenged again by a man with no claim to the throne, but rather as a murderer and a thief. Shakespeare manipulates things in such a way that we are led to ask about the relative fitness of Richard and Bolingbroke to rule, and to forget about the fact that Richard is legitimate and Bolingbroke is not. The simplest explanation for Shakespeare's favoritism is that he thinks Bolingbroke deserves to be king.

If this is indeed the case, then Shakespeare must approve of the ambition, however well concealed, that carries Bolingbroke to power. But perhaps I have made Bolingbroke out to be more cynical and single-minded than he really is. His motives for seeking the crown may be more complicated than a singular desire for power for its own sake. Bolingbroke's stated aims in challenging Richard—avenging Gloucester's murder and recovering his patrimony—are, after all, unobjectionable, even praiseworthy. And they needn't be seen merely as cover for his grander ambition. Bolingbroke may, in other words, desire to be king because he thinks he would be a better, more just king than Richard is. His ambition could be seen to complement and carry into effect a concern for England's welfare that is shared by many others too timid to do anything about it. Commenting on Gaunt's passive reaction to his brother's murder, Allan Bloom notes that "if Gaunts are the subjects, the rulers will be Richards."[26]

Divine Right

Bolingbroke will depose and murder King Richard, and Shakespeare seems to want us to believe that Richard's fate is both necessary and deserved—necessary because he is unable to prevent it, deserved because he is a terrible king. Richard's fate, simply put, is a direct consequence of his belief in his divine right to rule, which causes him to abuse his power and renders him unable to maintain it.

According to Bloom, "there can be little doubt that Shakespeare teaches us that Richard is a sort of legitimate tyrant who deserves to be deposed."[27] Not everyone agrees. E. M. W. Tillyard, one of the most influential critics of the Histories in the last fifty years, argues that "in doctrine the play is entirely orthodox. Shakespeare knows that Richard's crimes never amounted to tyranny and hence that outright rebellion against him was a crime."[28] Hume says that the historical Bolingbroke concocted charges against Richard so parliament could depose him for his "*pretended* tyranny."[29] But if no tyrant, Hume's Richard, who bears a striking resemblance to Shakespeare's Richard, is certainly characterized as an irresponsible, frivolous, and corrupt king:

> Indolent, profuse, addicted to low pleasures, he spent his whole time in feasting and jollity, and dissipated, in idle show or in bounties to favourites of no reputation, that revenue which the people expected to see him employ in enterprises directed to public honor and advantage.[30]

Perhaps the term "tyrant" is technically inappropriate for a legitimate king. But if one means by the term the absolute rule of one man in the interests of himself alone, then Richard certainly fits the bill.

Richard, as noted above, refers to his subjects as "slaves" (I.iv.27). By this he means not merely that they lack political rights, an unexceptional view at the time, but that, in a loose sense, he owns them: what they produce is more or less his for the taking. Besides a high tax burden (II.i.246–48), Richard devised a number of creative ways to fill the royal coffers, most of which involved extortion and some simple theft.[31] In one of his more outrageous fund-raising schemes, Richard issued "blank charters" (I.iv.49), blank checks extorted from wealthy subjects to be filled in and cashed at the king's convenience. We first hear about all this when Richard, trying to finance a military campaign against the Irish rebels, appropriates the estate of the recently deceased Gaunt. But as Northumberland points out, Richard's behavior cannot be excused on the grounds of military necessity: "more hath he spent in peace than they [his predecessors] in war" (II.i.255). The king himself admits as much: "our coffers, with too great a court / And liberal largess, are grown somewhat light"

(I.iv.44–45). Court life under Richard is opulent and corrupt. He maintains three thousand personal servants and according to York, listens only to flattery and "lascivious meters," to reports of the latest Italian fashions and any sort of "vanity"—"so it be new, there's no respect how vile" (II.i.19, 24–25). Bolingbroke hints that the sexual escapades at court are less than respectable—Richard apparently entertains his "advisors," Bushy and Greene, who in their " . . . sinful hours, / Made a divorce betwixt his queen and him, / Broke the possession of a royal bed" (III.i.11–13). On Bolingbroke's view, at least, Richard resembles a Roman despot, ruling England for the benefit of a fashionable, party-going homosexual clique. Northumberland calls Richard a "most degenerate king!," Gaunt tags him an "unstaid youth," York a "young hot colt" (II.i.262, 2, 70). Characterizing the general tenor of Richard's reign, Gaunt says "his rash fierce blaze of riot cannot last. / For violent fires soon burn out themselves" (II.i.33–34). The most persistent charge against Richard (made by Gaunt, York, Bolingbroke, and Northumberland) is that he allows himself to be misled by self-interested court flatterers and listens to no one else. He is never characterized as anything other than frivolous, vain, depraved, and corrupt. He doesn't even pretend to be concerned with the public good.

Bolingbroke wants to replace Richard not so much because he murdered Gloucester, but because he murdered Gloucester in order to remain the kind of king he is. Bolingbroke's tireless campaign against Richard as the murderer-king is something of a pretext, for Bolingbroke surely knows that Richard had to deal decisively with Gloucester in order to save himself. But the charge of murder is sensational and generally believed to be true, which provides Bolingbroke with a perfect opening against this spoiled and despoiling king.

Strangely enough, Richard would admit to both charges while calling them different names—he is not spoiled but divinely elected, not despoiling but exercising his royal prerogative. Richard has no idea that he is doing anything wrong. He is an unselfconscious despot, utterly lacking the notion that he is getting away with something. He is simultaneously cavalier and naive, corrupt and innocent. As Jensen points out, Richard's curious political style is a direct consequence of his belief in his divine right to rule, which sometimes veers towards a belief in his divinity simply:

> Believing that he is spared the exertions of ordinary mortals, he shirks his duty to cultivate order in his own life and in his realm. His affectation of divinity essentially amounts to a wanton dereliction or neglect, an infamous evasion of responsibility toward himself and what is rightfully his own. Indolent beyond measure, as if every day were a holiday, Richard immerses himself completely in an edenic freedom from every toil and care.[32]

Like the extravagant Roman emperors or the Renaissance popes, Richard is somehow divine while remaining fanatically devoted to earthly pleasures. But unlike his dictatorial counterparts, Richard lacks political savvy. He hasn't a clue how to stay in power. As we shall see, this too is directly related to his belief in his divine right to rule.

There is a large body of critical opinion about Shakespeare's treatment of divine right in *Richard II*,[33] most of it concerned either with Shakespeare's own belief in the doctrine or with the historical justification for portraying Richard as a divine right king. While a surprising number of critics—Tillyard, for example—see Shakespeare as a believer in divine right, the logic of the play demonstrates rather clearly that he was not: Richard's faults, his very character, spring from his belief in his divine right to rule, and Shakespeare teaches in this play that Richard is unworthy of the throne. On the question of whether it is historically accurate to associate Richard with divine right, commentators and historians disagree. Hart argues that treating Richard as a divine right king is anachronistic;[34] Figgis speculates that Richard may in fact have claimed divine sanction to rule even though a full-blown doctrine had not yet been enunciated and systematically disseminated.[35] Black argues that the historical evidence supporting Shakespeare's portrait of Richard was not available to Shakespeare.[36] The most interesting and conspiratorial speculations have Shakespeare projecting Tudor ideas of kingship into the past (where they can be safely criticized), characterizing Queen Elizabeth in the guise of King Richard. There are many similarities between the reigns of the two monarchs, and Queen Elizabeth is reported to have said in a conversation about Shakespeare's play, "I am Richard II, know ye not that?"[37] The deposition scene in *Richard II* was censored during Elizabeth's lifetime and the Earl of Essex, who fancied himself a Bolingbroke to Elizabeth's Richard, had *Richard II* staged for his supporters on the eve of his (unsuccessful) rebellion against the queen. But one can find many parallels between Shakespeare's history plays and contemporary political events—e.g., Elizabeth, like Shakespeare's King John, was excommunicated by the pope—and positing a one-to-one correspondence between Shakespeare's Richard and Queen Elizabeth does not do justice to the scope of his dramas. As Palmer points out, "Shakespeare was no more responsible for the scandal caused in London by his *Richard II* in 1601 than for the scandal caused in Paris by his *Coriolanus* in 1935. He had written in each case a political play recognizably true of any period for the kind of situation and the type of public persons presented."[38] We can probably never know Shakespeare's exact intentions in treating divine right somewhat before its time in this play. But he does treat it here, and his criticisms are no less valid because they are historically precocious.

Divine right presents the curious combination of the highest political principles with the lowest practical result. A politics founded on the goodness and wisdom of God becomes the basis for the most arbitrary and pernicious tyranny, arbitrary because the ruler is accountable only to a being whose will cannot be known,[39] and pernicious because the gulf between the lofty promise of divinity and the actual king can be, and is in the case of Richard, so enormous. The divine right king is not responsible to the people or to some principle that can be clearly discerned. He is a tyrant in the precise sense, responsible to no one but himself. He is supposedly responsible to God, but it is always unclear just what God wants and, as a practical matter, what the king wants, for whatever reason or fancy, can be explained away as God's will. When the interpretation of God's will is left to one man and cannot be verified by any other man, the king is free to play God himself. And when one is allowed to play God, the results are not hard to predict: enemies are punished and passions are indulged. Nothing prevents a divine right king from using his extraordinary powers to do good, but nothing constrains him either. The Bishop of Carlisle gives the briefest statement of the perfect insularity divine right affords the king: "what subject can give sentence on his king? / And who sits here that is not Richard's subject?" (IV.i.121–22).

Well, Bolingbroke, apparently, for one. And Northumberland for another. Carlisle's defense of Richard here is academic, coming when the end is clearly in view. But the necessity of Richard's demise has been apparent for some time, and can be traced to his wide-eyed belief in his divine right to rule. The king's confidence that he is divinely ordained, perhaps even somehow divine himself, is deep-rooted and literal, blinding him to the need for the most elementary political precautions. Richard's politics is indistinguishable from his faith in the God who supports his rule, a faith that sometimes seems comically childish. In one instance, Richard addresses the earth itself, calling on God's unarmed and non-human creations to assist him in thwarting Bolingbroke's rebellion:

> Dear earth, I do salute thee with my hand,
> Though rebels wound thee with their horses' hoofs.
> As a long-parted mother with her child
> Plays fondly with her tears and smiles in meeting,
> So weeping, smiling, greet I thee, my earth,
> And do thee favours with my royal hands;
> Feed not thy sovereign's foe, my gentle earth,
> Nor with thy sweets comfort his ravenous sense,
> But let thy spiders that suck up thy venom,
> And heavy-gaited toads lie in their way,
> Doing annoyance to the treacherous feet,
> Which with usurping steps do trample thee;
> Yield stinging nettles to mine enemies;
> And when they from thy bosom pluck a flower,
> Guard it, I pray thee, with a lurking adder,
> Whose double tongue may with a mortal touch
> Throw death upon thy sovereign's enemies. (III.ii.6–22)

To counter Bolingbroke's armed revolt, Richard relies on angels ("if angels fight, / Weak men must fall"), his name ("is not the king's name worth twenty thousand names? / Arm, arm, my name!"), and finally, on York's nonexistent army (III.ii.61–62, 85–86).

While the Bishop of Carlisle is a staunch proponent of divine right, he does not believe that anointment obviates the need for political action: "The means that heaven yields," he counsels Richard, "must be imbrac'd / And not neglected" (III.ii.29–30). Aumerle is more direct:

> He means, my lord, that we are too remiss;
> Whilst Bolingbroke, through our security,
> Grows strong and great in substance and in power.
> (III.ii.33–35)

In an extraordinary rebuttal, which is meant to assure Carlisle and Aumerle rather than himself, Richard again reveals his supreme confidence that his divine authority alone will save him:

> . . . know'st thou not
> That when the searching eye of heaven is hid
> Behind the globe and lights the lower world,
> Then thieves and robbers range abroad unseen
> In murthers and outrage boldly here;
> But when from under this terrestrial ball
> He fires the proud tops of the Eastern pines,
> And darts his light through every guilty hole,
> Then murthers, treasons, and detested sins,
> The cloak of night being pluck'd from off their backs,
> Stand bare and naked, trembling at themselves?
> So when this thief, this traitor, Bolingbroke,
> Who all this while hath revell'd in the night
> Whilst we were wand'ring with the Antipodes,
> Shall see us rising in our throne the east,
> His treasons will sit blushing in his face,
> Not able to endure the sight of day,
> But self-affrighted tremble at his sin. (III.ii.36–53)

Richard believes that the mere sight of himself will shame any traitor into submission. Walter Pater comments that "the sense of 'divine right' in kings is found to act not so much as a secret power over others, as of infatuation to themselves."[40] Pater is surely right about Richard's self-infatuation, but he underestimates Richard's hold over others. Earlier in the play, as we will recall, Gaunt was convinced both that Richard murdered his brother and that nothing could possibly be done about it because Richard acted for God. Even while he is witnessing Richard's political destruction, York is mesmerized by the king's authoritative presence:

> Yet looks he like a king. Behold, his eye,
> As bright as is the eagle's, lightens forth
> Controlling majesty; alack, alack for woe
> That any harm should stain so fair a show! (III.iii.68–71)

And Carlisle, who objects to Bolingbroke's crowning in Richard's absence—

> And shall the figure of God's majesty,
> His captain, steward, deputy elect,
> Anointed, crowned, planted many years,
> Be judg'd subject and inferior breath,
> And he himself not present? (IV.i.125–129)

—thinks the very sight of Richard might still be enough to dissuade the usurper and his supporters. Richard's power over his subjects is considerable. But that power does not extend to Bolingbroke, who is armed and ambitious, and, perhaps more importantly, seems to dismiss the views of his father and Carlisle and York as "nothing more than pious myths."[41]

Arms, Machiavelli teaches, have a way of making "believers" of those inclined to disbelieve.[42] Had Richard been as concerned with English arms as he was with Italian fashions, Bolingbroke probably wouldn't have stood a chance against him. He may not even have challenged him in the first place. Richard wastes the enormous prestige conferred upon him by political tradition, instead assisting in his own deposition by relying almost exclusively on a God that seems to have no influence over Bolingbroke. Richard's passivity may seem odd considering the political skills he demonstrated earlier in the play. He was quick to discern Bolingbroke's intentions toward him and handled the Gloucester affair reasonably well. He did not rely on nettles and toads to put down the Irish rebels. But in both instances, Richard was reacting. He does not anticipate challenges and order his affairs to prevent them. He does not cultivate the people's affection or fear or reverence, content to let his title do all of the work. He makes no attempt to curb his lavish lifestyle or in any way to justify his rule. But this, I think, is Shakespeare's point: he doesn't know that he has to. His instinct for political survival is softened by his belief in the very doctrine that was designed to assure his survival. When he meets a true challenge, he is so surprised and unequipped to defend himself that he seeks refuge in a fantasy world where angels come to his rescue. In short, Richard falls to Bolingbroke because he has fallen for himself.

Richard Deposed

At least half of *Richard II* concerns itself with Richard's attempts to understand the meaning of his deposition and his suffering. Uninspired as a ruler, Richard comes alive once his kingship is lost. In the chronicling of his suffering, Shakespeare provides Richard with some of the most arresting lines in English literature. As numerous critics have pointed out, Richard is a better poet than a politician.

When it is clear that his fall is only a matter of time, Richard professes contentment with his fate:

> Say, is my kingdom lost? why, 'twas my care,
> And what loss is it to be rid of care? (III.ii.95-96)
>
> . . . .
>
> What must the king do now? Must he submit?
> The king shall do it. Must he be depos'd?
> The king shall be contented. Must he lose
> The name of king? a God's name, let it go.
> I'll give my jewels for a set of beads;
> My gorgeous palace for a hermitage;
> My gay apparel for an almsman's gown;
> My figur'd goblets for a dish of wood;
> My sceptre for a palmer's walking staff;
> My subjects for a pair of carved saints,
> And my large kingdom for a little grave,
> A little little grave, an obscure grave . . . (III.iii.143–155)

Richard's grandiose language betrays something more than simple contentment or even resignation. If he must fall, Richard will not go quietly. Lacking an army, he defends himself with poetry, singing songs about himself that he hopes others will sing long after he is dead. Richard becomes the composer of his own tragedy:

> For God's sake let us sit upon the ground
> And tell sad stories of the death of kings (III.ii.155–56)
>
> . . . .
>
> In winter's tedious nights sit by the fire
> With good old folks, and let them tell thee tales
> Of woeful ages long ago betid;
> And ere thou bid good night, to quite their griefs

Tell thou the lamentable tale of me,
And send the hearers weeping to their beds
. . . .
And some will mourn in ashes, some coal-black,
For the deposing of a rightful king. (V.i.40–45, 49–50)

Because he has wandered through life pursuing frivolous diversions and because he believes he will not be allowed to live much longer, Richard spends little time reflecting on how he could have avoided deposition and on assigning blame. Consequently, his political ruminations are not particularly coherent or revealing. He blames the people for his fall only once, when his queen, frustrated by his docility, challenges him to act like a man:

Queen: . . . and wilt thou, pupil-like,
Take thy correction mildly, kiss the rod,
And fawn on rage with base humility,
Which art a lion and the king of beasts?

Richard: A king of beasts indeed—if aught but beasts,
I had still been a happy king of men. (V.i.31–34)

Richard probably means here that if men were not beasts, if they were at all reverent, they would never have challenged his authority. Beasts do not recognize God; they have no feeling for the sacred. In the realm that beasts inhabit, brute force alone rules, and Richard is a casualty of such force.

For the most part, Richard blames himself for his fall. He says at one point that "we must [do] what force will have us do" (III.iii.207), but he usually insists that his resignation is somehow voluntary and thus never really learns the lesson of the army:

With mine own tears I wash away my balm,
With mine own hands I give away my crown,
With mine own tongue deny my sacred state,
With mine own breath release all duteous oaths . . . (IV.i.208–11)
. . . .
Nay, if I turn mine eyes upon myself,
I find myself a traitor with the rest.
For I have given here my soul's consent

T'undeck the pompous body of a king;
Made glory base, and sovereignty a slave;
Proud majesty a subject, state a peasant. (IV.i.247-52)

Richard does admit that he was a bad manager who was badly managed. He finds himself "wanting" when it comes to the "manage of unruly jades" (i.e., his nobles) and he sees, too late, what others continually warned him about, that he allowed himself to be misled by flatterers:

O villains, vipers, damn'd without redemption!
Dogs, easily won to fawn on any man! (III.ii.129–30)

. . . .

O flatt'ring glass,
Like my followers in prosperity,
Thou dost beguile me. (IV.i.279–81)

Richard also gives credit, with a hint of admiration, to Bolingbroke:

Well you deserve. They well deserve to have
That know the strong'st and surest way to get. (III.iii.200–201)

. . . .

Is this the face which fac'd so many follies,
That was at last out-faced by Bolingbroke? (IV.i.285–86)

Significantly, Richard never blames God, but only himself for failing God: "our holy lives must win a new world's crown, / Which our profane hours here have thrown down" (V.i.24-5). But his self-blame is not evidence of a new-found self-reliance. The fact that he never questions God's role in his defeat shows that Richard is truly and tragically devoted to a God who will not spare him.

Richard is more interested in who he is if he is not king than in the reasons for his fall. When he is stripped of his title, Richard feels stripped of his very being and wonders, for the first time in his life, just who he is:

I have no name, no title;
No, not that name was given me at the font
But 'tis usurp'd. Alack the heavy day,
That I have worn so many winters out,
And know not now what name to call myself! (IV.i.255–59)

At one point, Richard seems to have discovered that he is just a man, like any other man—that he is not sacred after all:

> Cover your heads, and mock not flesh and blood
> With solemn reverence; throw away respect,
> Tradition, form, and ceremonious duty;
> For you have but mistook me all this while.
> I live with bread like you, feel want,
> Taste grief, need friends—subjected thus,
> How can you say to me, I am a king? (III.ii.171–77)

But he apparently is not convinced of his ordinariness and compares himself on three separate occasions to the most famous martyr, Jesus Christ. Richard's mistaken belief that his "unkinging" was voluntary fits well with the extraordinary role he understands himself to be playing. He even engages in a little one-upmanship:

> Yet I well remember
> The favours of these men. Were they not mine?
> Did they not sometime cry "All hail!" to me?
> So Judas did to Christ. But he, in twelve,
> Found truth in all but one; I, in twelve thousand, none.
> (IV.i.167–71)

Richard's answers to the question, "who am I if I am not king?" are multiple: nothing, just a man, a martyr comparable to Christ. He never settles on a single answer, but I suspect the following lines best capture his self-understanding:

> God save the king! although I be not he;
> And yet, amen, if heaven do think him me. (IV.i.174–75)

Richard cannot really think of himself as anything other than king and while he has some doubts about his special relationship to heaven, he is usually willing to give himself the benefit of those doubts.

Richard's identity crisis is interesting in itself and, as demonstrated above, the occasion for stunning poetry. It is also politically instructive, another way of showing Richard's disastrous reliance on God, which springs from an inability to distinguish the man from the title, and results in a failure to manipulate the machinery designed to enhance his rule. In one way, Richard surely does act like a man, indulging himself in worldly pleasures. Or, if he acts like a god, he acts like a pagan god—but he neglects to employ the thunderbolts that sustain their sensual lifestyles. Richard is a political failure, finally, because he does not use the tremendous power available to him.

In his final "prison soliloquy," Richard tries once again to make some sense of what has happened to him. He seems finally willing to let go of his illusions about himself, but fails to gain any political insights. Imagining the various kinds of life available to men, Richard finds them all problematic. The Christian life, guided by hope for the afterlife, the political life of earthly ambition, and the Stoic life, which strives for contentment with one's lot, each somehow touch Richard's situation. He was a Christian king deposed by an ambitious man and he has professed, at times, to be content with his misfortune.

Consistent with the aspirations of the age in which he lives, Richard takes the Christian alternative to be the highest, "the better sort" (V.v.11). But a life lived in hopes of the afterlife is subject to doubts and uncertainties—" . . . thoughts of things divine, are intermix'd / With scruples . . . " (V.v.12–13). Our doubts are encouraged by the Bible itself, which asks us to follow Christ but then tells us that our efforts may not be rewarded:

> "Come, little ones"; and then again,
> "It is as hard to come as for a camel
> To thread the postern of a small needle's eye." (V.v.15–17)

The uncertainty of heavenly reward is neither sufficient nor particularly comforting for a man nearing death, especially one who may well have some doubts about his deservingness.

The uncertain rewards of a pious life make Richard wonder whether leading the Christian life is worth the effort. Piety and morality are apparently not their own rewards. The natural alternative to otherworldly hopes are thisworldly hopes or the life of earthly ambition. But our ambitions, Richard concludes, are resisted by a world which rarely conforms to our desires. Our hopes are greater than our chances of success:

> Thoughts tending to ambition, they do plot
> Unlikely wonders: how these vain weak nails
> May tear a passage thorough the flinty ribs

Of this hard world, my ragged prison walls;
And for they cannot, die in their own pride. (V.v.18–22)

While Richard refers here to his own impossible situation, he may derive some consolation in the thought that Bolingbroke, since "pride must have a fall," will also meet resistance in "this hard world" (V.v.88).

The first two hope-confounding alternatives lead Richard to the third and last alternative, a life lived without hope and thus without disappointment:

Thoughts tending to content flatter themselves
That they are not the first of fortune's slaves,
Nor shall not be the last—like silly beggars
Who, sitting in the stocks, refuge their shame,
That many have and others must sit there;
And in this thought they find a kind of ease,
Bearing their own misfortunes on the back
Of such as have indur'd the like. (V.v.23–30)

This is the Stoic alternative, and it points, more generally, to the life devoted to philosophy, to sober observation and the detached acceptance of what is. Shakespeare takes this alternative at least as seriously as the others. Three of his plays feature a philosopher-hero (Prospero in *The Tempest*, the Duke in *Measure for Measure*, and Ulysses in *Troilus and Cressida*), and in the history plays, the invented character of Falstaff has something of the philosopher about him, although Falstaff is hardly stoic and rarely sober. The philosophic alternative is fundamentally different than the others. The religious and political alternatives are both governed by faith or hopefulness, and are dependent on chance or fortune or the will of God. The philosophic life, however, is self-sufficient: detached observation is its own reward and is independent of the vagaries of fortune. Richard denies neither of these statements, but he implies that the philosophic life does not provide much of a reward and that it is a last resort, turned to only in misfortune.[43] It would not be chosen, or even contemplated, in the first place because human beings are above all hopeful creatures, ever confident that God will recognize and smile upon their efforts. Contentment with misfortune is nearly impossible to achieve because our thoughts tend to turn, as Richard's do now, to the time before disaster struck, which in turn reminds us of how we were robbed of our happiness. Misfortune calls forth not contentment, but a cruel cycle of nostalgia and despair:

> Then crushing penury
> Persuades me I was better when a king;
> Then am I king'd again, and by and by
> Think that I am unking'd by Bolingbroke,
> And straight am nothing. (V.v.34–38)

Richard ends, appropriately enough considering his situation, utterly hopeless and desirous of death: "but whate'er I be, / Nor I, nor any man that but man is, / With nothing shall be pleas'd till he be eas'd / With being nothing" (V.v.38–41). Richard concludes that there is no satisfaction except in annihilation, that only nothingness is without contradiction.

Thus Richard rejects the lives of piety and ambition because they are illusory or as likely as not to end in failure, and the philosophic life because it is "beggarly" and ignoble—merely making the best of a bad situation. But this is precisely what Richard is doing here: he is preparing himself for death, which is arguably the worst situation of all. Unawares, Richard opts in the end for the beggarly or philosophic alternative. He moves from false hope to no hope, a movement prompted by his earlier failure to entertain the reasonable hope—grasped by popes and cleverer politicians and taught by Machiavelli—that religion could be employed self-consciously for political ends. Richard never understands divine right. Or, he understands it as a subject might and not as a ruler should.

Moments before he is murdered, in what has been called "one of the saddest lines in Shakespeare,"[44] Richard finally takes a kind of responsibility for his demise: "I wasted time, and now doth time waste me . . . " (V.v.49). Richard may be referring here not only to the loss of his kingship but, more generally, to the frivolous way he conducted his life. It is for this, and not the fact of his deposition, that we ought to feel sorry for Richard. By the end of the play, one tends to forget that there was nothing about Richard the king that engaged our sympathies. Shakespeare may even have intended to provoke our forgetfulness. As the history plays continue, the English people themselves will forget Richard's crimes and resurrect him, as he would have hoped, as a kind of martyr, a model of simpler times when legitimacy and succession were matters only of the proper heredity and when a king spoke for God.

King Henry

With no claim whatsoever to the throne, Bolingbroke deposed, replaced, and murdered God's chosen ruler. Remarkably, his audacious feat comes off like a non-event.[45] This is due in part to the fact that while Richard was tolerated and his title respected, he was an unpopular king who inspired little loyalty or love—and a good deal of loathing—outside of his small circle of dependents. Furthermore, Bolingbroke makes every effort to lend his power-play a legal veneer, characterizing Richard's fall as a voluntary abdication, and concocting a (fanciful) hereditary claim to the throne. And because he spent years coaxing the English public to view him as king-like, Bolingbroke slides comfortably into his new role. His rise to power was gradual and engineered so deftly that his crowning seems both unanticipated and inevitable. Commenting on Bolingbroke's lack of a conventional claim to the throne, Hume says that Bolingbroke was crowned king, "nobody could tell how or wherefore."[46] It is a testimony to his political skills that few appear to care.

The divine right claim that Richard leaned on so heavily to sustain himself presents the new king with less of a problem than might have been expected. Both the language of divine right and the sentiment behind it are transferred, at least initially, to Bolingbroke. Success apparently has a religious quality. Bolingbroke himself sets the tone upon being "offered" the kingship: "[i]n God's name I'll ascend the regal throne" (IV.i.113). Later, the Duchess of York refers to King Henry as "a God on earth" (V.iii.134).[47] The Duke of York, who supported Richard until the end, sees a divine hand in the popular response to the king's defeat, and seems willing to accept Bolingbroke as God's new representative on earth:

> . . . men's eyes
> Did scowl on Richard. No man cried "God save him!"
> No joyful tongue gave him welcome home,
> But dust was thrown upon his sacred head;
> Which with such gentle sorrow he shook off,

His face still combatting tears and smiles,
The badges of his grief and patience,
That had not God for some strong purpose steel'd
The hearts of men, they must perforce have melted,
And barbarism itself have pitied him.
But heaven hath a hand in these events,
To whose high will we bound our calm contents.
To Bolingbroke are we sworn subjects now,
Whose state and honour I for aye allow. (V.ii.27–40)

These last lines are a paraphrase of Holinshed, who says in regard to the fall of Richard and the rise of Bolingbroke that "in the dejecting of the one and the advancing of the other, the prudence of God is to be respected, and his secret will to be wondered at."[48] It is perhaps unsurprising that a populace accustomed to interpreting political events as reflecting God's will should interpret this event in the same way. The people's belief in a politically active God serves Bolingbroke well. He was wise never to have attacked divine right directly, for it appears to sanctify the usurper as well as the heir.

But if Bolingbroke tries—and in the beginning succeeds—to portray himself as a continuing part of England's political tradition, Shakespeare makes it quite clear that Bolingbroke's break with the past is fundamental and, in the long run, impossible to obscure. In an elaborate conceit which compares the state of England to the Garden of Eden, and likens Richard's fall to the Fall of man from innocence, Shakespeare suggests that Bolingbroke has undermined the foundation of political legitimacy in England.

Strolling in York's garden, Richard's queen overhears a political conversation between two gardeners, who attribute Richard's fall to a simple and correctable ignorance of political science:

. . . our sea-walled garden, the whole land,
Is full of weeds, her fairest flowers chok'd up,
Her fruit-trees all unpruned, her hedges ruin'd,
Her knots disordered, and her wholesome herbs
Swarming with caterpillars . . . [49]

. . . .

Bolingbroke
Hath seiz'd the wasteful king. O, what a pity it is

> That he had not so trimm'd and dress'd his land
> As we this garden!
> . . . .
> Had he done so, himself had borne the crown,
> Which waste of idle hours hath quite thrown down.
> (III.iv.43–47, 54–57, 65–66)

Good government, the gardeners argue, is a ruler's best security; well-tended subjects do not revolt. But good government alone is not sufficient. One must also be quick to recognize and deal decisively with ambitious rivals:

> Go thou, and like an executioner
> Cut off the heads of too fast growing sprays,
> That look too lofty in our commonwealth:
> All must be even in our government. (III.iv.33–36)

The gardeners diagnose Richard as suffering from a severe case of imprudence, "ascrib[ing] to an absence of art," Bloom says, "what others understand to be a result of God's will and men's sins." In what seems to be an outright admission that politics doesn't concern him, Richard confirms their diagnosis:

> Revolt our subjects? that we cannot mend;
> They break their faith to God as well as us. (III.ii.100–101)

"One cannot help," Bloom continues, "being reminded of *Prince* XXV, where Machiavelli interprets what men call fortune or God's action in politics as a lack of prudence or foresight. Floods, he says, injure men not because they are sinners but because they did not build dams."[50]

If the gardeners' analysis seems commonsensical, even pedestrian, one must remember that in medieval England, laborers are not in the habit of subjecting legitimate kings to rational scrutiny. King's are born, not elected; they are chosen by God, not men. Richard's authority is conferred by tradition, and in order to endure, tradition must be accepted on its face. Once reverence for tradition is replaced by rational scrutiny—why *this* incompetent king?—the whole edifice upon which Richard's authority is based falls apart. In the guise of offering Richard advice, the gardeners have deprived him of his reason for political existence. Representing the traditional view, Richard's queen accuses the gardeners of political heresy, which, given the source of Richard's authority, is identical to religious heresy. Criticizing Richard is a sin:

> Thou, old Adam's likeness set to dress this garden,
> How dares thy rude tongue sound this unpleasing news?
> What Eve, what serpent, hath suggested [tempted] thee
> To make a second fall of cursed man? (III.iv.73–76)

The queen's comparison might seem like hysterical exaggeration until one considers that Bolingbroke really has tempted a nation to defy God.

But Shakespeare does not, I think, share the queen's apocalyptic interpretation of her husband's fate. Richard's "garden" was no paradise. And Bolingbroke is a better man who is almost sure to be a better king. Perhaps the fall from political innocence should be seen not as a cause for regret, but as a liberation from a harmful myth that sustained a tyrant. But as Shakespeare will show us, this is not the end of the story. The rupture in political consensus caused by Bolingbroke's victory will have long-term effects, setting in motion violent struggles for political power that will last for generations. After the Fall comes Cain.

While Shakespeare presents Bolingbroke as a radical political innovator, it's not at all clear just how innovative Bolingbroke understands himself to be. I have argued that Bolingbroke is a self-conscious usurper, but whether he sees himself as something much more than that is difficult to say. Because we are not privy in this play to Bolingbroke's most private thoughts, gauging his intentions is a tricky business. He does not present himself as a radical innovator (he doesn't, for that matter, present himself as a usurper), but rather positions himself as a continuing part of England's political tradition. He never criticizes the principle of hereditary succession, and spends a good deal of his reign grooming his troublesome eldest son to succeed him. Neither does he criticize divine right. But the fact that Bolingbroke does not present himself as a radical innovator does not mean that he isn't one and that he doesn't understand himself to be one. I think, however, that Henry's actions at the end of this play and throughout the two history plays that bear his name suggest that he is confused about what he has done and at times still under the sway of the political tradition he violated. Bolingbroke may be an unwitting revolutionary.

After murdering Richard, Bolingbroke's quiet self-assurance gives way to the question that will haunt him for the remainder of his life: what have I done? By the end of the play, the man who became king by defying God appears to have become religious:

> Lords, I protest my soul is full of woe
> That blood should sprinkle me to make me grow.
> . . . .
> I'll make a voyage to the Holy Land,
> To wash this blood off from my guilty hand. (V.vi.46–47, 49–50)

As Bloom points out, Henry is "split":

> He cannot bear to face the possibility that the sin of Cain, as Machiavelli teaches, may play a role in the establishment of earthly justice. In deposing Richard he was halfway to the realization that he was committing a crime but that such crimes are sometimes necessary for the common good. However, so strong is his faith or his fear of hell-fire, he prefers to brand himself a guilty man and cripple his political sense and dedication rather than admit what his deed has shown.[51]

In his *Henry IV* plays, to which I will shortly turn, Shakespeare will devote as much attention to the division in Henry's soul as he does to the division in Henry's kingdom.

The Question of Legitimate Rule

All of Shakespeare's history plays concern themselves with the same question: who should be king? All of them provide a provisional answer: the *legitimate* king. *Richard II* is the most important history play because it is here that the traditional principle of legitimate rule in England receives its purest expression and its most radical criticism. King Richard is undeniably legitimate; but he does not, according to Shakespeare, deserve to be king. When political tradition decrees that a murdering, thieving, self-absorbed playboy merits the kingship, something is seriously wrong with that tradition. One might argue that even though the principle of hereditary rule occasionally produces unfit rulers, they ought to be tolerated for the sake of political stability. But Richard is not tolerated precisely because he is an unfit ruler, and the result is political instability. If hereditary monarchy cannot produce either good government or stable government, then, Shakespeare seems to ask in this play, why hereditary monarchy?

While Bolingbroke never makes the case for himself in this play—the gardener does—it is clear that he represents a rational alternative to the traditions of hereditary and divine right. Reasonable men, especially those who have endured Richard, must agree that chance of birth and the mere assertion of God's favor are insufficient titles to rule; one must also consider political talent, and here Bolingbroke shows himself superior to the inept and tyrannical Richard. Bolingbroke's victory thus proves that tradition is vulnerable to reason. One might object that it proves more about the power of arms than about the power of reason. Bolingbroke, after all, forces Richard from the throne with an army, not with arguments. But that he could raise an army, that he meets so little resistance, and that he is welcomed and saluted by the same crowds in London that throw dirt upon Richard's head suggest that the English people have not been coerced. They are clearly receptive to Bolingbroke, and like Shakespeare's gardeners, they are perfectly capable of providing the arguments for his rule on their own.

I do not mean to suggest that Bolingbroke's victory over Richard is a clear-cut victory for rationalism over tradition. Obviously, it has far more to do with the character and abilities of the two individuals contending for the throne. And the people's approval of Bolingbroke is registered in the traditional way: "'God save thee, Bolingbroke!' . . . 'Jesu preserve thee!'" (V.ii.11, 17). But Bolingbroke's victory shifts the grounds of the debate about legitimacy: straightforward appeals to heredity and simple reverence for tradition will in the future be intertwined with more rational claims. The Duke of York, for example, will challenge a sitting king (Henry VI, Bolingbroke's grandson) on the basis of his superior political talent as well as on the traditional hereditary grounds:

> [I am more] like a king, more kingly in my thoughts
>
> . . . .
>
> No, thou art not king;
> Not fit to govern and rule multitudes
>
> . . . .
>
> That head of thine doth not become a crown;

> Thy hand is made to grasp a palmer's staff,
> And not to grace an awful princely sceptre. (*2HVI* V.i.29, 93–94, 97–98)

Bolingbroke's victory makes speeches like this one possible.

But if superior political ability is sufficient to carry Bolingbroke to power, it may not be enough to legitimize his rule. Henry IV will always lack that intangible quality conferred by tradition that Richard possessed and wasted. Perhaps I can best illustrate this quality by a comparison with the authority of a father over his children. It is not just that a father is bigger and stronger than his children, or that he provides for and protects them, or even that they respect his character and deeds. There is something more in his authority which is captured in the phrase, "he is my father," something often said after all reasons for obedience or reverence have been exhausted. It is somehow unreasonable or beyond reason and is difficult to put into words. Perhaps it means something like, "I am of him." In any event, it is not something a child feels for a stepfather, no matter how good a parent he may be. Fathers are legitimate in ways that stepfathers cannot be. Bolingbroke is a usurper and, as such, a kind of stepfather to England.

As Bloom notes, "Shakespeare's view of kingship and legitimacy is subtle and cannot be reduced either to reverence for tradition or bald rationalism."[52] Both Henry IV and Henry V, who are extraordinarily talented politicians and able rulers, lack the sanction conferred by tradition. And both, precisely because they are talented politicians as well as able rulers, will spend their reigns trying to devise an equally irrational substitute for the tradition-based authority that Richard enjoyed.

Chapter Four

King Henry IV, Parts 1 and 2

Parts 1 and 2 of Shakespeare's *Henry IV* dramatize the fallout from Bolingbroke's bold deposition of King Richard II. But *Henry IV* is not only or even primarily a play about how to keep what one has taken. Shakespeare is concerned here with the crisis of legitimacy caused by the ascension of an illegitimate regicide to the throne of England. All of the characters and actions in these plays, serious as well as comic, must be interpreted in light of this crisis. Whether in the war room or the barroom, in the chitchat of ostlers or the diplomacy of statesmen and generals, Shakespeare presents a picture of a country unsure of itself, a country that seems to have lost its bearings since the death of King Richard.

The crisis of political consensus is so acute that civil war appears inevitable from the first scene of the first play. Richard II was no ordinary monarch. He was a divine right king, the man God chose to rule England. Without making any divine claims for himself, Bolingbroke easily defeated Richard, apparently disabusing Englishmen of the belief that their king must be anointed by God. But while Henry is characterized in *Richard II* as a new kind of ruler, a rational alternative to the Christian king he deposed, the lingering importance of religion is everywhere evident in *Henry IV*. In the opening lines of part 1, for example, Henry calls for a Crusade to the Holy Land to cleanse the country of the guilt of King Richard's death. The rebellion against Henry in part 2 is led by the Archbishop of York, a man who "derives from heaven his quarrel and his cause," turning "insurrection to religion" (*2HIV* I.i.206, 201). Henry's skepticism about the justice of his victory over Richard is accompanied by Falstaff's skepticism about most all respectable things, including Christianity. Falstaff's relentless and delightfully entertaining iconoclasm takes center stage in these plays precisely because of Richard's defeat and the ensuing political crisis. Just what constitutes political legitimacy and the place of religion in post-Richard England are up for grabs in this uncertain new world.

But for all the high-stakes politics involved, Shakespeare's *Henry IV* strikes one as a curiously domestic drama. The question of who will win the civil war dramatized in these plays is complemented by the equally important question of whether Prince Hal will reconcile with his father. While the plot moves steadily toward the military battles that will determine who rules England, it is matters of a more personal nature that most attract and involve us. Why does the king prefer the son of his enemy to his own son? Why does the future king prefer the company of thieves and drunkards to his own family? These apparently personal concerns are, however, very much related to the confused political landscape outlined above. Henry's problems with Hal are due in large part to the influence of Falstaff, an unconventional figure who could only attract the heir-apparent in politically uncertain times. Thus Shakespeare offers us in his *Henry IV* plays the story of two wars being waged over the future of England: a civil war for the right to rule the country and a moral war for the soul of Hal, the man who will be king.

I will be treating both parts of *Henry IV* in a single chapter. This is the critical custom and parts, after all, are parts of a whole. I will, however, spend more time on part 1. It is a better play, but more importantly, the second *Henry IV* play adds very little to the first. It is only a slight exaggeration to say, as did a nineteenth-century critic, that "the second part is not a continuation of the first but rather a copy of it."[1] The two *Henry IV* plays are remarkably similar in their actions and their concerns: both dramatize rebel threats to the king that appear doomed to failure once Northumberland pulls out; both highlight Falstaff's entertaining wit in an atmosphere of drinking and carousing; both feature Hal's penchant for slumming and his "expectations strategy"; both address King Henry's concern over Hal's fitness to rule England and the question of whether father and son can reconcile. There are some notable differences which are perhaps inevitable given the passage of time. As King Henry nears the end of his life, his desire to render judgment on his career becomes more acute; and as Hal nears the throne, Falstaff's influence diminishes. But those who pay close attention to part 1 will find few surprises in part 2.

A Divided Kingdom

Part 1 of *Henry IV* begins where *Richard II* left off. Henry declares at the end of the latter play, perhaps gazing at the funeral casket encasing the murdered king, that "I'll make a voyage to the Holy Land, / To wash this blood off from my guilty hand" (*RII* V.vi.49–50) Here he repeats the desire as if no time had passed: "Therefore, friends, / As far as to the sepulchre of Christ" (*1HIV* I.i.18-19). But in fact a year has gone by—"this our purpose now is twelve month old" (*1HIV* I.i.28)—since Richard's death. Shakespeare tells us nothing of what has happened in the intervening time, but the historical King Henry was plagued by difficulties with France, a war with Scotland, and plots against his life.[2] Henry also appears to have recovered from the guilt that so consumed him following Richard's murder. One is struck immediately by the difference in tone in Henry's opening remarks. The self-doubt and urge to confess are gone, replaced by a measured, statesman-like, and, above all, politic demeanor. The armed revolt against a legitimate king and the ensuing civil war are recounted by Henry in the most abstract terms. King Richard is not mentioned, blame is neither given nor accepted, justifications are not offered. Choosing the most distant and impersonal of images to describe the civil conflict, Henry compares the warring parties to "the meteors of a troubled heaven" (*1HIV* I.i.10). It is almost as if England had suffered some natural catastrophe, a flood or a plague, for which no individuals bear responsibility. While Henry is still talking about a Crusade to the Holy Land, his motives have changed along with his inner disposition. Apparently no longer in need of personal absolution, Henry now sees a Crusade as the perfect vehicle to unite his fractious kingdom.

But a closer examination of the first scene reveals that Henry is up to his old tricks again, saying one thing while thinking another. He has no intention of going to the Holy Land. When informed by an advisor of heavy fighting in Wales that resulted in the capture of Mortimer, Richard's legal heir, by Owen Glendower, Henry responds that "the tidings of this broil / Brake off our business for the Holy Land" (*1HIV* I.i.47-48). The king is then told of another battle fought in the north between Hotspur and the Scot Archibald, but Henry knows all about it, and one wonders whether he didn't have intelligence of both battles all along. Even if he knew only of the fighting in the north, it is for "this cause," Henry later confides to Westmoreland, that "we must neglect / Our holy purpose to Jerusalem" (*1HIV* I.i.100–101). Thus while delivering his speech about a unifying trip to the Holy Land Henry knew that no Crusade would take place. He seems to want the moral credit for his piety and his high-minded call for unity without the risk of actually leaving England. Simple common sense dictates that an astute politician with a tenuous grip on power would not leave the country, and Henry knows as much from experience: he waited for Richard to leave for Ireland before launching his own military campaign for the crown. Thus a picture emerges from the first scene of a complicated man whose public rhetoric is an untrustworthy reflection of his private aims, the same man who said publicly he had no designs on Richard's kingship while furiously planning his deposition. The old Henry, recovered admirably from his guilt and self-doubt, appears to be back.

This initial impression, however, is misleading. As the plays progress, we learn that Henry has not in fact exorcised his guilt over Richard. In a private conversation with his son, Henry wonders aloud whether Hal's riotous and disrespectful behavior is not God's punishment for his political deeds:

> I know not whether God will have it so
> For some displeasing service I have done,
> That in his secret doom out of my blood
> He'll breed revengement and a scourge for me;
> But thou dost in thy passages of life
> Make me believe that thou art only mark'd
> For the hot vengeance and the rod of heaven,
> To punish my mistreadings. (*1HIV* III.ii.4–11)

Much later in part 2, in a moment of deep depression that suggests Henry knows he will soon die (*2HIV* III.i), Richard and the long deferred trip to the Holy Land are at the forefront of the king's mind. While the Holy Land is not mentioned again in part 1 after the first scene, in part 2 the subject is brought up by the king with obsessive frequency. On one of those occasions, Henry offers what appears to be decisive evidence of his true motive for wanting to go to the Holy Land. In the only private discussion of his motives, Henry confides to Hal that his desire to lead a Crusade was emphatically political, a strategy to divert his opponents from their preoccupation with deposing him (*2HIV* IV.i). This deathbed confession comes very late, and one wonders why Shakespeare didn't tell us earlier. The author must have intended for his audience to puzzle over Henry's character during the course of the two plays. In asking why Henry wants to go to the Holy Land, one is really asking what kind of a man he is: a Machiavellian or an individual plagued by a guilty conscience. There is plenty of evidence for both alternatives and this one late statement, however revealing, needn't be considered decisive: Henry's comment about the political nature of his desire has more to do with his state of mind at the time he utters it than it does with how he's felt all along. Suffice it to say for now that the Holy Land stands for different things at different times. Henry's interior career is an attempt to come to terms with his deposition and murder of a legitimate king, and his reasons for going to the Holy Land vary depending on his current judgment about whether it was worth it all. As we shall see, Henry's calculations about the justice of his political career have much to do with whether he thinks his son is worthy to succeed him.

Apart from the king's personal motives in calling for a Crusade, the whole notion seems somehow out of place, even implausible, in Henry's new England. In the highly superstitious world of King John, or in the chivalric era presided over by King Richard II, where a trial by combat is ordered as a matter of course, one can easily imagine the call for a Crusade being greeted with enthusiasm. But one would have thought that Henry's ability to depose a divine right king indicated a dampening of the religious fanaticism that led men (and some women) to drop everything for a chance at fame and glory in reclaiming the Muslim-held Holy Land. Henry's victory over Richard seemed to mark a preference by the English for practical competence over

Christian traditionalism in political affairs. But perhaps the world has not changed so dramatically after all. I think Shakespeare dwells on the Crusades primarily as a way of addressing the moral and political dilemma of Henry's deposition and murder of Richard, but also as a corrective to the impression that the medieval world has simply vanished. Henry knows the English people well enough to correctly assume he can depose a divine right king, but he also knows that the religious spirit has not disappeared and that the call for a Crusade will fall on sympathetic ears. Unlike King Richard, Henry knows his subjects. He never attacked divine right directly, and he never equates his victory over a Christian king with a rejection of Christianity.

Although I and others have argued that Henry's reign signals a break with Christian medievalism and a movement toward a more modern understanding of politics, the call for a Crusade serves as a reminder that the conservative English people may lag behind their more enlightened leadership and that appeals to religious enthusiasm continue to resonate in post-Richard England. We are a long way from Richard Coeur de Lion, the immensely popular king who spent three years fighting for Christianity in the East, but not so far that his memory is tarnished or forgotten.

While appearing to pose little or no direct threat to the king himself, the small wars fought in the north and the west were undertaken without Henry's knowledge or approval and show that the king does not control his kingdom. When independent barons command armies and allegiance, the king had better worry. With this in mind, Henry summons the victorious Percys to court and announces that

> My blood hath been too cold and temperate,
> Unapt to stir at these indignities,
> And you have found me—for accordingly
> You tread upon my patience: but be sure
> I will from henceforth rather be myself,
> Mighty, and to be fear'd, than my condition,
> Which hath been smooth as oil, soft as young down,
> And therefore lost that title of respect
> Which the proud soul ne'er pays but to the proud. (*1HIV* I.iii.1–9)

The "indignities" to which the king refers are Hotspur's refusal to hand over his prisoners of war. Hotspur will deliver the prisoners only if the king agrees to ransom Mortimer, captured by Glendower and now married to Glendower's daughter. Mortimer is Hotspur's brother-in-law, but he is also, unbeknownst to Hotspur, the deceased King Richard's declared heir.[3] The king, who must assume Hotspur knows as much and is intentionally provoking him, and who has reason to suspect, furthermore, that Worcester is behind Hotspur's demands,[4] lashes out at Hotspur:

> No, on the barren mountains let him starve;
> For I shall never hold that man my friend
> Whose tongue shall ask me for one penny cost
> To ransom home revolted Mortimer. (*1HIV* I.iii.88–91)

After calling Hotspur—among other things—a liar, the king exits, leaving the thin-skinned and impetuous Hotspur to fume. Hotspur declares to his father and his uncle that he'll "lift the down-trod Mortimer / As high in the air as this unthankful King, / As this ingrate and canker'd Bolingbroke" (*1HIV* I.iii.133–35), an ironic declaration seeing as how Hotspur doesn't know Mortimer is Richard's heir. When he is told as much, Hotspur immediately understands the reason for the king's anger: "Nay, then I cannot blame his cousin King, / That wish'd him on the barren mountains starve" (*1HIV* I.iii.156–57). But although he understands the reasons for the king's behavior, Hotspur will not excuse the insults and lets forth a flood of characteristically humorous venom:

> He said he would not ransom Mortimer,
> Forbade my tongue to speak of Mortimer,
> But I will find him when he lies asleep,
> And in his ear I'll holla "Mortimer!"
> Nay, I'll have a starling shall be taught to speak
> Nothing but "Mortimer," and give it him
> To keep his anger still in motion. (*1HIV* I.iii.218–23)

What Hotspur does not seem to notice, but what is clear enough to any observer, is that he has been set up by his father and his uncle. (Worcester admits later in the play that "all . . . [Hotspur's]...offences live upon my head/ And on his father's. We did train him on" [*1HIV*

V.ii.20-21]).[5] They do not tell him of the king's special reasons for disdaining Mortimer, or of the rebellious plot they have organized against Henry and which Hotspur has just helped to move forward. Worcester knows that Hotspur's demands will be taken by the king as close to a declaration of war, and that the king's naturally angry reaction will spur the passionate Hotspur to fiery opposition. Worcester uses Hotspur as a pretext for beginning a war and gains a motivated general in the bargain.

A pretext is all that is really needed, for civil war, as Hume points out in his *History of England*, was more or less inevitable:

> The obligations which Henry had owed to Northumberland were of a kind most likely to produce ingratitude on the one side and discontent on the other. The sovereign naturally became jealous of that power which had advanced him to the throne; and the subject was not easily satisfied in the returns which he thought so great a favor had merited. Though Henry, on his accession, had bestowed the office of constable on Northumberland for life, and conferred other gifts on that family, these favors were regarded as their due; the refusal of any other request was deemed an injury. The impatient spirit of Harry Piercy and the factious disposition of the Earl of Worcester, younger brother of Northumberland, inflamed the discontents of that nobleman; and the precarious title of Henry tempted him to seek revenge by overturning that throne which he had first established.[6]

While it true that Henry acquired the throne illegally and that he desires to keep what he has taken, the king nevertheless possesses the moral advantage in his struggle with the rebels. Henry had the courage to oppose a despot when no one else was willing to step forward. For all of Henry's stealth and deceit in acquiring the kingship, Shakespeare makes it clear in *Richard II* that his cause was just. Once Henry took the lead in challenging Richard, the Percys, it mustn't be forgotten, joined with him. Thus the rebel claim that Henry is a usurper, while true enough, is disingenuous and opportunistic. The rebels want to depose Henry in order to advance themselves, but they are motivated, at bottom, by fear. On the one hand, they fear the people, who blame them for the deposition and murder of Richard, "for whose death," Worcester says, "we in the world's wide mouth / Live scandaliz'd and foully spoken of" (*1HIV* I.iii.151–52). On the other hand, they fear the man they made king:

> And 'tis no little reason bids us speed,
> To save our heads by raising of a head;
> For, bear ourselves as even as we can,

> The King will always think him in our debt,
> And think we think ourselves unsatisfy'd,
> Till he hath found a time to pay us home. (Worcester, *1HIV* I.iii.277–82)

The rebels' lack of principle is made clear in Hotspur's pre-battle speech to the king, where instead of giving one good reason for their revolt, he offers ten bad ones. The two central complaints—we put you on the throne, so you owe us better treatment, and, you aren't the legitimate king—are contradictory and self-accusatory. The real reason is offered only in conclusion: "[you] drove us to seek out / This head of *safety*" (*1HIV* IV.iv.102–3, emphasis supplied). The only reference to Mortimer's legitimacy is made in a parenthetical aside late in the day—"(Who is, if every owner were well plac'd, / Indeed . . . [Henry's] king)" *1HIV* IV.iii.94–95—the seriousness of which is questionable since Mortimer's title to rule has not figured at all in any of the rebels' plans or declarations. Hotspur, as noted, says early on that he'll make Mortimer king, but this is in a fit of pique over Henry's refusal to ransom him and before Hotspur has any notion of his title to rule. Mortimer is treated by the rebels as a co-conspirator and, as such, due a portion of the revolutionary spoils (*1HIV* III.i). His character or fitness to rule is never discussed.

In part 2, a member of Northumberland's party who fought with Hotspur at Shrewsbury attributes their failure to a lack of principle or idealism. Ordinary soldiers were not given sufficient cause to rouse themselves in battle against a sitting king:

> My lord your son had only but the corpse,
> But shadows and the shows of men, to fight;
> For that same word 'rebellion' did divide
> The action of their bodies from their souls,
> And they did fight with queasiness, constrain'd,
> As men drink potions, that their weapons only
> Seem'd on our side; but, for their spirits and souls,
> This word 'rebellion'—it had froze them up,
> As fish are in a pond. (*2HIV* I.i.192–200)

Morton is more optimistic about the second rebel offensive because it will be led by the Archbishop of York, a man of God who can represent himself as the avenger of God's slain lieutenant:

> But now the Bishop
> Turns insurrection to religion;
> Suppos'd sincere and holy in his thoughts,
> He's follow'd both with body and with mind,
> And doth enlarge his rising with the blood
> Of fair King Richard, scrap'd from Pomfret stones;
> Derives from heaven his quarrel and his cause (*2HIV* I.i.200–206)

But this is the last we hear of the newly re-tooled and high-minded rationale for rebellion. It is significant that we hear it not from the archbishop or from one of his followers, but rather from a member of the Northumberland faction, which never had any use for Richard or for divine right. Religion is cynically appropriated, a matter of strategy rather than the foundation of a truly sacred cause. The archbishop never makes a public case for Richard in this play. Instead of exciting his ranks with inspiring rhetoric, we see him privately castigating the fickle and hypocritical populace from which he draws his troops, comparing it to a "common dog" that "didst . . . disgorge / Thy glutton bosom of the royal Richard; / And now thou wouldst eat thy dead vomit up, / And howl'st to find it. What trust is in these times?" (*2HIV* I.iii.97–100). On the eve of the battle, the archbishop is asked by the king's representative to set forth his complaints. York says that the rebels "have the summary of all our griefs, / When time shall serve, to show in articles" (*2HIV* IV.i.73–74), but he doesn't detail any of those griefs, complaining only that the king refused him audience to air them. He mentions King Richard in passing, but doesn't make the case for his legitimacy or the rebel claim to represent his cause. In short, there is nothing of substance to distinguish the two rebellions; both appear to be simple power-grabs. That the archbishop is never shown marshalling the power of religion for his cause seems to argue for its waning influence in political affairs. Henry's victory over a divine right king appears to have demystified politics and his opponents lack the energy and the belief to remystify it.

Family Affairs

If all is not well in Henry's kingdom, neither is all well in his family. We know from the end of *Richard II* that relations between father and son are strained. Hal spends no time at home and appears to be completely indifferent to his father's career (*RII* V.iii)—especially bitter medicine for a man, one of whose aims in taking the crown appears to be passing it on to his son. Although Henry professes to "see some sparks of better hope, / Which elder years may happily bring forth" (*RII* V.iii.21–22), in the first scene of *1 Henry IV* he sings a paean to Hotspur, explaining why he prefers Northumberland's son to his own:

> Yea, there thou mak'st me sad, and mak'st me sin
> In envy that my Lord Northumberland
> Should be the father to so blest a son;
> A son who is the theme of honour's tongue,
> Amongst a grove the very straightest plant,
> Who is sweet Fortune's minion and her pride;
> Whilst I by looking on the praise of him
> See riot and dishonour stain the brow
> Of my young Harry. O that it could be prov'd
> That some night-tripping fairy had exchang'd
> In cradle-clothes our children where they lay,
> And call'd mine Percy, his Plantagenet! (*1HIV* I.i.77–88)

Henry's apparent preference for Hotspur is more than a passing thought. Again at act 3, scene 2, Henry's expression of disappointment in Hal is accompanied by envious comparisons with Hotspur, whose courage and sense of honor seem to be lacking in his own son. And as Hal's earlier satire of Hotspur's famed courage seems to indicate, the comparison is a familiar one:

> I am not yet of Percy's mind, the Hotspur of the North, he that kills me some six or seven dozen of Scots at a breakfast, washes his hands, and says to his wife, "Fie upon this quiet life, I want work". "O my sweet Harry", says she, "how many hast thou killed today?" "Give my roan horse a drench", says he, and answers, "Some fourteen", an hour after; "a trifle, a trifle". (*1HIV* II.iv.99–106)

But Henry's preference for Hotspur is more complicated than it might seem. In short, he is more impressed with Hotspur's virtues as a son than he is with his virtues as a warrior and a politician.

The qualities Henry praises in Hotspur are not particularly conspicuous in himself. While no coward, Henry does not impress one primarily as a courageous man (prudence comes first to mind); and while politically daring and extraordinarily shrewd, he is not singled out, as is Hotspur, for his physical courage. Henry is never shown fighting in *Richard II*, and in the battle scenes in *1 Henry IV* the field is filled with kingly clones (this is historically accurate). Neither is Henry an especially honorable man. We know from *Richard II*, where he tells everyone, including the king, that he does not seek the throne, that Henry's word is worthless. And in a play famous for Falstaff's critique of honor, Henry offers something similar when he confides to Hal the strategy he employed to gain Richard's throne. The key to political success, Henry explains, is the clever manipulation of public opinion through the presentation of an appealing public image:

> By being seldom seen, I could not stir
> But like a comet I was wonder'd at,
> That men would tell their children, "This is he!"
> Others would say, "Where, which is Bolingbroke?"
> And then I stole all courtesy from heaven,
> And dress'd myself in such humility
> That I did pluck allegiance from men's hearts,
> Loud shouts and salutations from their mouths,
> Even in the presence of the crowned King. (*1HIV* III.ii.46–54)

There are no appeals in this discussion to God or political tradition, no talk of what is just or right or honorable, only "opinion," "popularity," and "admiring eyes." Perceptions, Henry teaches Hal, are just as important as deeds, and praise can be earned whether or not it is deserved. This is not to say that Henry's deposition of Richard was unjust, and one must take care to distinguish questionable means from the ends they serve. But Henry is clearly more comfortable talking about how to acquire and retain power than he is in outlining its ultimate purpose, and his considerable political success would not be possible if honor were a primary concern.

Unlike both Henry and Hal, who might be described as thoughtful men of action, Hotspur is all action and little thought. Sensitive to the slightest insult, loyal to a fault, ready to fight and kill at the drop of a hat, brimming over with righteous indignation, Hotspur is heroism incarnate. But like Shakespeare's Achilles, he is a simple-minded hero, the pawn of his shrewder father and uncle, who manipulate him into acting without his being aware of it. When Worcester tries to explain the rebel strategy for unseating King Henry, a riled Hotspur will not listen: "All studies here I solemnly defy, / Save how to gall and pinch this Bolingbroke" (*1HIV* I.iii.225-26). This calls to mind Ulysses' complaint about the Greek warriors in *Troilus and Cressida:*

> They tax our policy and call it cowardice,
> Count wisdom as no member of the war,
> Forestall prescience, and esteem no act
> But that of hand. (*T&C* I.iii.197–200)

As Hudson notes, "[Hotspur's] qualities unfit him, in great measure, for military leadership in regular warfare. . . . He is qualified to succeed only in the hurly-burly of border wars, where success comes more by fury of onset than by wisdom of plan. . . . "[7]

But perhaps Henry's preference for a man so unlike himself is not so unusual after all. Those qualities desired by a father in his son aren't necessarily the same as those qualities he seeks in himself. Hal is disobedient and irreverent, Hotspur the opposite. Hotspur's sense of family loyalty is impeccable. He is willing to die for the honor of an in-law, and is dutiful to a father who does not appear to be dutiful in return (Northumberland's sickness on the eve of the rebellion is suspicious; his refusal to send Hotspur reinforcements absent himself is inexcusable). Henry sees in Hotspur a loyal son, and loyal sons are ruled by their fathers. For all his impetuousness, Hotspur, like most honorable men, is rather predictable. He lives according to certain rules or traditions, for something outside himself. Hal is neither predictable nor, on his father's view, assuredly loyal. He is his own man and does no one else's bidding. Hal is far from an ideal son.

In *1 Henry IV* and in *Troilus and Cressida*, Shakespeare seems to associate traditional heroism with lack of cunning. Hotspur is without a trace of guile and this, finally, is why the king claims to prefer him to his own son. It's not only that Hal has the wrong friends and less than appropriately noble interests; more important than his moral disapproval or his fatherly disappointment, Henry *fears* Hal. In his lecture at act 3, scene 2, the king berates Hal for "thy place in council thou hast rudely lost." From what Henry's said earlier, one supposes that the loss of his position is due to Hal's neglect or incompetence or lack of interest. But according to Hume,

> The many jealousies to which Henry IV's situation naturally exposed him had so infected his temper that he had entertained unreasonable suspicions with regard to the fidelity of his eldest son; and during the latter years of his life he had excluded that prince from all share in public business, and was even displeased to see him at the head of armies, where his martial talents, though useful to the support of government, acquired a renown which, he thought, might prove dangerous to his own authority.[8]

Shakespeare's Henry confirms Hume's account later on in his lecture when he asks his son, "Why, Harry, do I tell thee of my foes, / Which art my nearest and dearest enemy?" (*1HIV* III.ii.122–23). The real purpose of the interview at act 3, scene 2 is to discover whether Henry can trust his own son. Seen in this light, his preference for Hotspur is less surprising.

The question is whether Henry's suspicions about Hal are, as Hume would have it, "unreasonable." Shakespeare's answer seems to be, probably not. Although Henry decides at the end of the interview to trust his son and although Hal's apology appears heartfelt, readers of the play will not have forgotten Hal's famous soliloquy at act 1, scene 2, where he explains his slumming as part of a calculated plan to advance his image by lowering and then exceeding expectations of himself. Hal is an admitted schemer with a plan to "falsify men's hopes." With this in mind, it is very difficult to know when he is earnest and when he is playing a role. Shakespeare is particularly interested in the ways a hereditary political system corrupts natural family feeling—one thinks immediately of *King Lear*—and Henry's fear of "premature inheritance" continues to be a concern in the second *Henry* play. In one scene Hal, thinking his father dead, lifts the crown to his head only to be discovered by a shocked and all too alive Henry, who accuses his son of wishing him dead. Henry is probably mistaken here, but his general suspicions are not without foundation. In *1 Henry IV*, after saving Henry from certain death on the battlefield, Hal tells his father

> O God, they did me too much injury
> That ever said I hearken'd for your death.
> If it were so, I might have let alone
> The insulting hand of Douglas over you,

> Which would have been as speedy in your end
> As all the poisonous potions in the world,
> And sav'd the treacherous labour of your son. (*1HIV* V.iv.50–56)

In a characteristic stroke of brutal clarification, Shakespeare has Hal remind his father that he allowed him to live. Hal, to say the least, is not prone to sentimentality. His softer father would appear to have good reason to puzzle over and even fear this strange young man.

In an uncharacteristically personal and confessional scene in *2 Henry IV*, Hal appears to set the record straight about his feelings toward his father. He confides to his friend Poins that "my heart bleeds inwardly that my father is so sick" (*2HIV* II.ii.45–46), telling him he is pained that he cannot express his true feelings without being labelled a hypocrite by the people. After long disregarding his father's wishes in associating with Falstaff and Poins and generally playing the profligate, Hal thinks he would appear unconvincing if he should show his father respect and affection only now that his father nears death and he nears the throne. Hal is so distressed by the uncaring image he presents to the world that he is compelled to tell Poins that he's not really like that. But he confides in Poins and not his father. If we readers are privy to Hal's true feelings, Henry, the object of those feelings, is not. Hal places public opinion and his own political career above his dying father's peace of mind. For Hal, *everything* is calculated for political effect; if his father must suffer because of it, so be it. Hal is not just a rebellious son but something much more difficult—a thoroughgoing politician, a man who puts politics above family and friendship.

Falstaff: Master Corrupter

Henry IV's criminal usurpation produced political faction and, eventually, civil war. It also allowed Falstaff, a corrupt and iconoclastic figure, to flourish amidst the social confusion. The times are perfectly suited to this master debunker. But Falstaff is more than a symbol of the chaotic political climate; he is the constant companion of the man who will be king. This unmarried, obese alcoholic was created by Shakespeare as Prince Hal's great friend and teacher.

And Falstaff is surely a teacher. He succeeds, for a time at least, in replacing Hal's father as the primary influence and guide in the young man's life. He presents no "doctrine" per se, but rather teaches by example, by what he cares about, what he does and does not take seriously, what he makes fun of. And so we see Falstaff drinking and carousing, listen to him talk about sack and sex, and note that his penetrating wit directs itself against the most respectable things, the law, religion, politics, and the family. But there is evidence that Falstaff once led a different kind of life. Early on he blames Hal for corrupting *him*, and says that "before I knew thee, Hal, I knew nothing, and now am I, if a man should speak truly, little better than one of the wicked" (*1HIV* I.ii.90–92).[9] Falstaff was once the owner, he claims, of "a true face, and good conscience . . . but their date is out" (*1HIV* II.iv.494–96). His numerous (and clever) biblical allusions suggest a traditional religious education and Falstaff defensively tells a drinking companion that "I have not forgotten what the inside of a church is made of" (*1HIV* III.iii.7–8). We have reason to surmise that the life we see Falstaff leading is the result of thinking through and rejecting the various prohibitions and conventions that restrain most men from acting as he does. As Masefield notes, "Falstaff is that deeply interesting thing, a man who is base because he is wise."[10]

We are introduced to Falstaff in the second scene of *1 Henry IV*. When Falstaff asks Hal what time it is, the prince, in an unexpectedly bellicose response, deftly sketches Falstaff's notorious character:

> Thou art so fat-witted with drinking of old sack, and unbuttoning thee after supper, and sleeping upon benches after noon, that thou hast forgotten to demand that truly which thou wouldst truly know. What a devil hast thou to do with the time of the day? Unless hours were cups of sack, and minutes capons, and clocks the tongues of bawds, and dials the signs of leaping-houses, and the blessed sun himself a fair hot wench in flame-coloured taffeta, I see no reason why thou shouldst be so superfluous to demand the time of the day. (*1HIV* I.ii.2–12)[11]

Falstaff is not offended. The two apparently insult each other with loving regularity, and we come to see that much of their relationship consists in witty attempts to berate one another and defend themselves from attack. Falstaff responds to Hal with a preemptive and poetic defense of yet another one of his vices, thievery:

> Marry then sweet wag, when thou art king let not us that are squires of the night's body be called thieves of the day's beauty: let us be Diana's foresters, gentlemen of the shade, minions of the moon; and let men say we be men of good government, being governed as the sea is, by our noble and chaste mistress the moon, under whose countenance we steal. (*1HIV* I.ii.23–29)

Falstaff is an admitted and unrepentant thief. The plot of the Hal/Falstaff scenes—which otherwise would consist only of trading well-aimed barbs—will revolve around a robbery. In fact, the robbery plot becomes another occasion for witty repartee. Poins suggests to Hal that the two of them hold back and then, in disguise, rob their fellow robbers. "The virtue of this jest," Poins explains, "will be the incomprehensible lies that this same fat rogue will tell us when we meet at supper, how thirty at least he fought with, what wards, what blows, what extremities he endured; and in the reproof of this lives the jest" (*1HIV* I.ii.180–85). The robbery does, however, point to the political situation in England. Under King Henry, stealing is entertained casually, without qualms, as a matter of fun and games. References among the Boar's Head crowd to hanging and Hell are so frequent and so cavalier that one suspects they arise more from habit than from any real fear. One is impressed by the general spirit of lawlessness that prevails, if not everywhere, at least in the Boar's Head circle, which, it mustn't be forgotten, includes the king's son. We are naturally led to speculate about the difficulties of reestablishing a respect for the law in light of Henry's usurpation, and more personally, how the example of a criminal father affects his son. Hal seems to have inherited from his father, along with political shrewdness and a penchant for cold calculation, a tendency to see himself as somehow above or beyond the law. But unlike his more conventional father, Hal moves comfortably in this sphere, and this has much to do with Falstaff.

But the fact that the heir to the throne spends so much time with a degenerate old man and his washed-out drinking companions at the Boar's Head Inn needs some explaining. Why does Hal bother with Falstaff? The Prince offers something of an explanation in his "expectations soliloquy" (I.ii), where he characterizes his behavior as part of a calculated political strategy:

> I know you all, and will awhile uphold
> The unyok'd humour of your idleness.
> Yet herein will I imitate the sun,
> Who doth permit the base contagious clouds
> To smother up his beauty from the world,
> That, when he please again to be himself,
> Being wanted he may be more wonder'd at
> By breaking through the foul and ugly mists
> Of vapours that did seem to strangle him.
> . . . .
> So when this loose behavior I throw off,
> And pay the debt I never promised,
> By how much better than my word I am,
> By so much shall I falsify men's hopes;
> And like bright metal on a sullen ground,
> My reformation, glittr'ing oe'r my fault,
> Shall show more goodly, and attract more eyes
> Than that which hath no foil to set it off. (*1HIV* I.ii.190–98, 203–10)

It is, however, difficult to reconcile Hal's cold plan with his evident joy in the presence of Falstaff. It all sounds a bit abstract and one wonders whether Hal hasn't invented a grand rationale for his unorthodox preference for low company. One cannot dismiss Hal's soliloquy because it fits with his career, but it doesn't seem a wholly satisfying explanation—there must be more than political utility that draws Hal to Falstaff. More convincing, perhaps because more ordinary and less conspiratorial, are Hal's drunken boasts that he can drink with the commonest of the common and be accepted by them:

> I am sworn brother to a leash of drawers, and can call them all by their christen names, as Tom, Dick, and Francis. . . . To conclude, I am so good a proficient in one quarter of an hour that I can drink with any tinker in his own language during my life. (*1HIV* II.iv.6–8, 17–19)

Hal's explanation here sounds a bit like the condescending private words of a populist politician. And yet it is clear that Hal is pleased with himself, that he likes the idea of royalty drinking toasts with commoners at questionable bars, that he likes being one of the boys: "they take it already upon their salvation, that though I be but Prince of Wales, yet I am the king of courtesy . . . and when I am King of England I shall command all the good lads in Eastcheap" (*1HIV* II.iv.8–10, 13–14). But while these two different explanations give us some insight into Hal's motives for slumming, they do not touch the heart of the matter, that is, they do not explain his desire to be with Falstaff in particular, and it is obviously with Falstaff that Hal most desires to be.

Hal and Falstaff spend most of their time together talking, so perhaps Hal's affection for Falstaff is best explained by sampling some of their conversation. As I've noted, a good deal of the pair's energy is spent exchanging inventive insults:

> *Prince*: Why, thou clay-brained guts, thou knotty-pated fool, thou whoreson obscene greasy tallow-catch,—
>
> . . . .
>
> *Falstaff*: 'Sblood, you starveling, you eel-skin, you dried neat's-tongue, you bull's-pizzle, you stock-fish—O for breath to utter what is like thee!—you tailor's-yard, you sheath, you bow-case, you vile standing tuck! (*1HIV* II.iv.221–23, 240–44).

The robbery plot was designed by Poins to catch Falstaff in "incomprehensible lies" and watch him try to wriggle out of them. Pressed about a particularly blatant contradiction, Falstaff turns the tables on his inquisitor, Hal, with a moral objection to his method of inquiry:

> What, upon compulsion? 'Zounds, and I were at the strappado, or all the racks in the world, I would not tell you on compulsion. Give you a reason on compulsion? If reasons were as plentiful as blackberries, I would give no man a reason upon compulsion, I. (*1HIV* II.iv.231–36)

Accused of cowardice in running away from the disguised Hal and Poins, Falstaff defends himself as a loyal subject: "By the Lord, I knew ye as well as he that made ye. . . . Was it for me to kill the heir-apparent? should I turn upon the true prince?" (*1HIV* II.iv.263, 264–65). None of Falstaff's ever-evolving defense is convincing, nor is it meant to be. What is on trial here is not Falstaff's valor or veracity, but his dexterity and inventiveness in defending himself with words. When Hal picks Falstaff's pocket and finds a list of debts detailing his excessive lifestyle—"O monstrous! but one halfpennyworth of bread to this intolerable deal of sack?"—Falstaff turns to the Bible for assistance: "Thou knowest in the state of innocency Adam fell, and what should poor Jack Falstaff do in the days of villainy? Thou seest I have more flesh than another man, and therefore more frailty" (*1HIV* II.iv.533–34; III.iii.164–68). The pair's teasing is not limited to one another. In an exchange with Hostess Quickly, Falstaff's sometimes bed-partner, the two enjoy their ribald selves at this silly woman's expense:

> *Falstaff*: Setting thy womanhood aside, thou art a beast to say otherwise.
>
> *Hostess*: Say, what beast, thou knave, thou?
>
> *Falstaff*: What beast? Why, an otter.
>
> *Prince*: An otter, Sir John? Why an otter?
>
> *Falstaff*: Why? She's neither fish nor flesh, a man knows not where to have her.
>
> *Hostess*: Thou art an unjust man in saying so, thou or any man knows where to have me, thou knave, thou.
>
> *Prince*: Thou says't true, hostess, and he slanders thee most grossly. (*1HIV* III.iii.121–31).

Falstaff has a way of raising others to his own level of mirth and this must be part of what attracts Hal to him. As Falstaff says, "I am not only witty in myself, but the cause that wit is in other men" (*2HIV* I.ii.8–9). As Hal demonstrates in the tasteless drawer episode with Francis, without Falstaff he is merely crude, even cruel. Perhaps it is not so extraordinary after all that a young man, burdened with enormous responsibilities, should be attracted to the illicit and profane, packaged, as they are in Falstaff, with such robust and facile gaiety. As

J. Dover Wilson remarks, "we know that that fat belly, so far from dragging him earthwards, bears him hither and thither like a balloon, at the slightest whim or desire. He is an emancipated spirit, free of all the conventions, codes, and moral ties that enwrap us. . . . What we chiefly admire him for is his abounding vitality."[12]

Falstaff's attraction to Hal needs less explaining than Hal's attraction to Falstaff. Hal will be king and Falstaff hopes to benefit from his friendship—"I'll follow, as they say, for reward" (*1HIV* V.iv.161). A man like Falstaff can flourish only in socially lax and politically confusing times, which cannot be counted on to last forever. Falstaff's only hope is to transform the politicians before they attempt to transform him. Surely part of his education of Prince Hal is directed toward making England safe for Falstaffs. Not insignificantly, Hal pays for Falstaff's drink, loosening the tongue that so entertains him; he is a patron of the art of degenerate conversation. Falstaff also likes to think of himself as a young man. He screams at the just-robbed coach riders, "they hate us youth!," justifying his crime with, "young men must live" (*1HIV* II.ii.81–82, 86). Hanging around Hal and Poins must help reinforce this pleasing illusion. In addition to his loose women and his prostitutes, Falstaff evidently delights in the company of handsome young men. Complaining to himself of the shabby treatment he's just received from Poins, Falstaff almost sounds like a frustrated lover:

> I have forsworn his company hourly any time this two and twenty years, and yet I am bewitched with the rogue's company. If the rascal have not given me medicines to make me love him, I'll be hanged. It could not be else, I have drunk medicines. (*1HIV* II.ii.15–20)

As Dr. Johnson slyly points out, "medicines" refers to "the vulgar notion of love-powders."[13] Falstaff is a master corrupter and thus naturally gravitates toward youth and innocence. If nothing else, he needs people to talk to and his particularly irreverent brand of conversation would be shocking and off-putting to most. Thus he must cultivate a receptive audience; he must corrupt others in order to enjoy himself. Falstaff is a teacher with an agenda, near the top of which is his own pleasure.

But what exactly does Falstaff teach? While Shakespeare never shows him lecturing Hal or Poins, one supposes that there must have been some kind of preparation (or seduction) that would make the freewheeling and impious banter about respectable things possible. Falstaff may or may not be an atheist, but he is the only character in the play—besides Hal, who is probably imitating him—whose conversation is peppered with biblical allusions, and his references are never respectful. We see the effects of a critique of family life in Falstaff's refusal to marry or in any way to limit his sexual appetite and, perhaps most importantly, in his utter disregard for Henry's role as father and moral educator of his son. Falstaff too is a kind of usurper: he steals sons from their fathers in a bid to make them like, and thus pleasing to, himself.

Perhaps the closest thing to a teaching Falstaff offers is his famous critique of honor. In true iconoclastic fashion, he calls his ode to self-preservation a "catechism." His argument is that living honorably, in this case on the battlefield, gets you nothing, that the costs are high and the benefits nil:

> Can honour set to a leg? No. Or an arm? No. Or take away the grief of a wound? No. Honour hath no skill in surgery then? No. What is honour? A word. What is in that word honour? What is that honour? Air. A trim reckoning! Who hath it? He that died a-Wednesday. Doth he feel it? No. Doth he hear it? No. 'Tis insensible, then? Yea, to the dead. But will it not live with the living? No. Why? Detraction will not suffer it. Therefore I'll none of it. (*1HIV* V.i.131–40)

The question, "What does honor (or any other virtue) do for me?," is obviously subversive of all morality, which must be chosen for its own sake. The moral man acts honorably because it is honorable. But according to Falstaff's very practical critique, honor is liable to bring only death and detraction. Missing from Falstaff's analysis is any mention of the afterlife and I suppose it's not accidental that such a calculation holds no sway with him. Falstaff celebrates the bodily pleasures and these require a body. But Falstaff is no simple brute. Sex is accompanied by talk of sex. Clever conversation, the exchanges of intelligent and playful souls, is also a great pleasure. What Falstaff stands for in the end is pleasure. What he stands against are all of those politically necessary constraints that tell us that we do not want or cannot have what pleases us unconditionally.

Falstaff's teaching, then, is decidedly anti-political. His broadsides against lawfulness, family, and religion, his critique of honor and ordinary ambition, and his refusal to affect even the appearance of morality or propriety serve as a devastatingly thorough rejection of all of those things that must be respected if political order is to be possible. And his radical skepticism results in an unabashed hedonism. Falstaff's life provides a thoughtful testimony to the charms of the private pleasures. This is what Falstaff offers the man who will be king.

Hal appears, in the end, to reject this teaching, choosing the political life over his friendship with Falstaff and all that he stands for. Our first intimation of Hal's preference comes in the role-playing scene, where the two take turns playing Hal's father. Falstaff plays King Henry, Hal himself, and then, reversing roles, Hal plays king to Falstaff's Hal. The issue in both cases is whether, in the father's opinion, Falstaff is a worthy companion or a corrupting influence. While Hal's negative portrait of Falstaff is truthful, Falstaff's portrait of himself is not. Falstaff tries to make himself look good to conventional eyes. He does not anticipate or answer the charges of corruption and offers no defense of his radical way of life. Like Socrates in the *Apology*, he tries to portray himself as harmless.[14] But Hal, who will be king and who is, in a sense, king at this moment, is not persuaded. He calls Falstaff "that villainous abominable misleader of youth" (*1HIV* II.iv.456), the same charge the Athenian fathers leveled against Socrates. The "play extempore" ends with a mock banishment: Falstaff is found guilty of being an undesirable and dangerous companion. Hal is prepared to act as a king must act. Lest we interpret this exchange as just another game, Hal makes clear later that he is dead serious. After his interview with Henry, Hal tells Falstaff that "I am good friends with my father and may do anything" (*1HIV* III.iii.180–81). From this point on, Hal is a warrior out to prove his political worth and Falstaff a fond reminder of his riotous past. Standing over what he mistakenly takes to be Falstaff's dead body lying on the battlefield, Hal declares that "I should have a heavy miss of thee / *If* I were much in love with vanity [foolishness]" (*1HIV* V.iv.104–5, emphasis supplied). Unfortunately for Falstaff, Hal has no use for foolishness any longer.

In *2 Henry IV*, the distance between Hal and Falstaff can be measured by the small amount of time the pair spend together on the stage. They share only two scenes, act 2, scene 4 and act 5, scene 5, the latter when the new king banishes his old friend. The banishment of Falstaff, amply foreshadowed in part 1, is preceded by Hal's new alliance with his one–time enemy and imprisoner, the Lord Chief Justice. The Lord Chief Justice has been Falstaff's most relentless and thoughtful critic. He is still pursuing Falstaff for the robbery at Gadshill, but this is really a pretext for the more serious charge of corrupting the man who will be king:

> You have misled the youthful Prince.
>
> . . . .
>
> You follow the young Prince up and down, like his ill angel.
>
> . . . .
>
> Well, God send the Prince a better companion! (*2HIV* I.ii.143, 162–3, 199)

More aware of Falstaff's peculiarly attractive subversiveness than is King Henry, who lumped the whole Boar's Head crowd together, the Lord Chief Justice accuses Falstaff of sophistry: "Sir John, Sir John, I am well acquainted with your manner of wrenching the true cause the false way" (*2HIV* II.i.107–9). The speech in which Hal pledges his support to the Lord Chief Justice and assures him he's mended his ways is as sure a sign as any that Falstaff is out and law and order are in:

> My father is gone wild into his grave,
> For in his tomb lie my affections;
> And with his spirits sadly I survive
> To mock the expectations of the world,
> To frustrate prophecies, and to raze out
> Rotten opinion, who hath writ me down
> After my seeming. (*2HIV* V.ii.123–29)

Soon after Hal's reconciliation with the Lord Chief justice, Mistress Quickly and Doll Tearsheet, tavern proprietress and prostitute, are arrested and carted off to prison.

Although it is expected, the actual banishment of Falstaff is shocking nevertheless. If Falstaff has any idea of what is in store for him, he shows no signs of it. On learning of King Henry IV's death,

Falstaff exclaims that "the laws of England are at my commandment. Blessed are they that have been my friends, and woe to my Lord Chief Justice!" (*2HIV* V.iii.132–34). Standing in the crowd to greet the new king as he and his train pass by, Falstaff, with juvenile exuberance, tells Shallow, "I will leer upon him as a comes by, and do but mark the countenance that he will give me" (*2HIV* V.v.6–8). Falstaff's calls to Hal from the street—"God save thee, my sweet boy! . . . My King! My Jove! I speak to thee, my heart!"—are met with the famous and heart-rendingly cold words of the new king: "I know thee not, old man" (*2HIV* V.v.42, 46, 47). Only after the initial shock wears off does one realize that Hal's cruel and moralistic lecture is intended for a wider audience:

> I have long dreamt of such a kind of man,
> So surfeit-swell'd, so old, and so profane;
> But being awak'd I do despise my dream.
> . . . .
> Presume not that I am the thing I was;
> For God doth know, so shall the world perceive,
> That I have turn'd away my former self;
> So will I those that kept me company. (*2HIV* V.v.49–51, 56–59)

But as Allan Bloom points out, "what is interesting and sinister about Hal is the degree to which politics consumes him even though he is the beneficiary of a powerful critique of it."[15] Why does Hal opt for a conventional political life after his unconventional experience with Falstaff? The simplest answer is that Hal was born to be king: politics is his fate. But one might have expected the companion of Falstaff to pursue a more frivolous, decadent politics than he does, to use his public authority, as Richard II does, to further his private pleasures. This, after all, is what Falstaff hopes for and what Henry IV fears. Henry's nightmare vision of England under Hal is Falstaff's utopia:

> Harry the Fifth is crown'd! Up, vanity!
> Down, royal state! All you sage counsellors, hence!
> And to the English court assemble now
> From every region, apes of idleness!
> Now, neighbour confines, purge you of your scum!

Have you a ruffian that will swear, drink, dance,
Revel the night, rob, murder, and commit
The oldest sins the newest kind of ways?
Be happy, he will trouble you no more.
England shall double gild his treble guilt,
England shall give him office, honour, might:
For the fifth Harry from curb'd license plucks
The muzzle of restraint, and the wild dog
Shall flesh his tooth on every innocent. (*2HIV* IV.v.119–32)

Henry's fears, of course, are not realized. As king, Hal seems almost a caricature of moral rectitude; he is the most vocally pious of Shakespeare's kings. And his youthful idleness gives way to a gigantic ambition, which culminates in his spectacular, against-the-odds conquest of France. Henry V's distinguishing characteristic is ambition and in this he couldn't be less like Falstaff—or more like his father.[16]

Still, the usual account of Hal's relation to Falstaff as an adolescent lark rejected in maturity fails to give either Hal or Falstaff his due. John Danby insists that "Hal's rejection of Falstaff must not be regarded as more significant than his long association with the rogue. It need not even be regarded as a final rejection."[17] Hal might well possess an inner allegiance to Falstaff's teachings at the same time he appears to reject such radical views in public. His "expectations strategy" is based upon the Machiavellian contention that the people desire the appearance of morality in their ruler:

> [A prince] should appear all mercy, all faith, all honesty, all humanity, all religion. . . . For the vulgar are taken in by the appearance and the outcome of a thing, and in the world there is no one but the vulgar.[18]

Hal knows that banishing Falstaff is the easiest and most symbolic way to acquire a good reputation. He may also know that while it is sufficient to appear virtuous to be reputed so, actual virtue can be politically counterproductive: "it is not necessary for a prince to have all the above mentioned qualities in fact . . . [only] to appear to have them. Nay, I dare say this, that by having them and always observing them, they are harmful; and by appearing to have them, they are useful. . . . "[19]

Bloom suggests that Hal's "abandonment of his old friend Falstaff, in order to improve his reputation for justice, follows from a teaching he could have learned from Falstaff."[20] Falstaff himself has no scruples about using others for his own advantage. For all of his warm humor and camaraderie, Falstaff is, at bottom, a rather cold and selfish man. What is less clear is how Falstaff could have taught Hal to be politic, to conceal unpalatable views beneath a morally upright exterior. Falstaff, after all, is not known for hiding his unorthodox views and is a careless and unconvincing liar. If the reincarnated Hal is indeed a moral imposter, how might he have learned to be so from Falstaff, a man so unconcerned with appearances?

The same unconcern Falstaff shows for conventional opinion is what allows Hal to pretend to be better than he is in order to gain an advantage: careful liars are carefree about morality. Thus beneath his new exterior, Hal may indeed remain faithful to the critique of morality that is the core of Falstaff's teaching. He surely rejects the sensual life that Falstaff chooses and opts instead for an ambitious political career. But if Hal chooses a different end, his success as king owes much to what he learns from Falstaff, for Falstaff showed Hal the possibility of freeing oneself from the moral and religious claims that govern most men, the possibility of pursuing one's selfish aims without regret. Falstaff's skepticism complements Hal's ambition. If Hal learns from his father about the mechanics of political power, he learns from Falstaff that thing Machiavelli most recommends to a prince: "to be able not to be good, and to use this and not use it according to necessity."[21] Henry IV never achieved the indifference to morality that Machiavelli thinks necessary for perfect political success. Given his experience with Falstaff, it should not be surprising that such indifference appears to characterize the reign of Henry V. At the very least, one ought to question the sincerity of Hal's "conversion" and approach his incessant professions of faith with skepticism, recalling Machiavelli's advice that "nothing is more necessary to appear to have" than religion.[22] For Henry V is just as guilty of political intrigue and treachery as his father. But unlike Henry IV, Henry V is untroubled by the pangs of conscience. Falstaff may be the ultimate source of Henry V's supreme confidence as king.

Henry IV's Death

Prince Hal's preparation for the throne is accompanied, in part 2, by King Henry's preparation for death. In the first of his two "death scenes" (act 3, scene 1), we encounter a self-pitying and insomniac king, unduly worried about and wildly exaggerating the rebel threat, feeling diminished and impotent in the face of grand forces beyond his control. As Warwick notes, Henry is very sick, but it is a spiritual, rather than a physical, weakness which is most noticeable. Falstaff earlier diagnosed the king's illness as "lethargy" caused by "much grief, from study, and perturbation of the brain" (*2HIV* I.ii.110, 114–15) and Henry's behavior here seems to confirm this diagnosis—as he says to himself, "uneasy lies the head that wears a crown" (*2HIV* III.i.31). The rebel threat does not seem significant enough to warrant Henry's deeply pessimistic and passive mood (unlike the audience, Henry is not aware of Northumberland's withdrawal; he does, however, have experience of that nobleman's extreme caution, and he knows that with Glendower dead, the western threat is nullified) and one suspects that something more is on the king's mind when he begins to ruminate out loud about how fate rules the world, oblivious to the pretensions of mere men:

> O God, that one might read the book of fate,
> And see the revolution of the times
> Make mountains level, and the continent,
> Weary of solid firmness, melt itself
> Into the sea, and other times to see
> The beachy girdle of the ocean
> Too wide for Neptune's hips; how chance's mocks
> And changes fill the cup of alteration
> With divers liquors! O, if this were seen,
> The happiest youth, viewing his progress through,
> What perils past, what crosses to ensue,
> Would shut the book and sit him down and die. (*2HIV*
> III.i.45–56)

This last phrase is telling for I think Henry has some notion that his own death is near and I suspect that his fixation with necessity and inevitability springs less from a well thought out metaphysical conviction about how the world works than from a consciousness of his own mortality. The rule of fate is evidenced, Henry continues, by King Richard's prediction—"now prov'd a prophecy?" (III.i.69)—that Northumberland would eventually turn against his one-time ally and plunge the country into civil war. Warwick tries to snap Henry out of his mystical mood by noting, quite sensibly, that Richard made a "perfect guess" (III.i.68): Northumberland betrayed his friend Richard, so why shouldn't he be expected to betray his friend Henry as well?[23] Warwick might also have argued that Northumberland's behavior proves not the rule of fate but rather the political rule that those who help one to power are most dangerous once power is acquired. Henry is aware of this Machiavellian precept,[24] but it holds no sway with him at this moment. He insists on attributing to fate what might be explained by reason. Henry also engages in a bit of revisionist history. After having admitted in part 1 that he sought all along to depose Richard, Henry denies any such intention here, insisting that "necessity so bow'd the state / That I and greatness were compell'd to kiss" (*2HIV* III.i.74). But Henry may not be convinced by his own words here for he ends the scene with another call to visit the Holy Land. He is obviously haunted by Richard, fearing that the dead king will have the last word and that he will die a failure. This is Henry's lowest moment.

When King Henry appears again at act 4, scene 4, the first words out of his mouth concern the Holy Land:

> Now, lords, if God doth give successful end
> To this debate that bleedeth at our doors,
> We will our youth lead on to higher fields,
> And draw no swords but what are sanctified. (*2HIV* IV.iv.1–4)

As death approaches, Henry is evermore preoccupied with Jerusalem. He is also concerned with Hal's ability to rule England and expresses his fears to Hal's younger brothers:

> The blood weeps from my heart when I do shape
> In forms imaginary th'unguided days
> And rotten times that you shall look upon
> When I am sleeping with my ancestors.
> For when his headstrong riot has no curb,
> When rage and hot blood are his counsellors,
> When means and lavish manners meet together,
> O, with what wings shall his affection fly
> Towards fronting peril and oppos'd decay! (*2HIV* IV.iv.58–66)

Henry's preoccupation with the Holy Land and his doubts about Hal are, I believe, related in the following way: his remorse for deposing

Richard is excited by his fear that Hal will be a failure as king. Henry's judgment about the morality of his political career appears to depend on his judgment about Hal's fitness to succeed him. When Henry is down on Hal, he's down on himself and his thoughts turn eastward, full of repentance.

This thesis is borne out in a somewhat surprising way in the next scene (IV.v), Henry's last. Asleep on his deathbed, Henry is approached by Hal, who, thinking him dead, places Henry's crown on his head—"my due from thee is this imperial crown"(*2HIV* IV.v.40)—and leaves the room. Upon his return, Hal is astonished to find his father alive:

> *Prince*: I never thought to hear you speak again.
>
> *King*: Thy wish was father, Harry, to that thought;
>
> . . . .
>
> Thy life did manifest thou lov'dst me not,
> And thou wilt have me die assur'd of it. (*2HIV* IV.v.91–92, 104–5)

After blaming his death, in advance, on Hal—"this part of his conjoins with my disease, / And helps to end me" (IV.v.63–4)—and expressing to his son the same fears he earlier expressed to Hal's brothers, the two eventually make up, Hal convincing his father of the sincerity of his grief and his long-planned "noble change." This, on my count, is the third reconciliation between father and son (*1HIV* III.ii., the interview scene; *1HIV* V.iv., the rescue on the battlefield) and, owing to Henry's health, it will have to be the last. Forgiving Hal, Henry offers "the very latest counsel / That ever I shall breathe" (*2HIV* IV.v.182–83). But before offering his advice, Henry comes clean on his deposition of Richard:

> God knows, my son,
> By what by-paths and indirect crooked ways
> I met this crown
>
> . . . .
>
> It seem'd in me
> But as an honour, snatch'd with boist'rous hand

. . . .
How I came by the crown, O God forgive. (*2HIV* IV.v.183–84, 190–91, 218)

Henry's advice to Hal is first offered by way of a commentary on his own political career:

And all my friends, which thou must make thy friends,
Have but their stings and teeth newly ta'en out;
By whose fell working I was first advanc'd,
And by whose power I might lodge a fear
To be again displac'd; which to avoid,
I cut them off, and had a purpose now
To lead out many to the Holy Land,
Lest rest and lying still might make them look
Too near unto my state. (*2HIV* IV.v.204–12)

He concludes with the direct advice to "busy giddy minds / With foreign quarrels, that action hence borne out / May waste the memory of the former days" (IV.v.213–15). In one stroke, Henry answers all of our most pressing questions. He acknowledges violently forcing Richard from the throne, expecting the betrayal of those who helped him, and devising a plan to divert them with a Crusade. Henry stands here firm and unapologetic, making no attempt, as before, to soften his deeds in order to render them more palatable to himself and others. His confidence in Hal has buoyed his confidence in himself. This is not to say that Henry was always so convinced that he'd done right or so willing to own up, in his own mind, to his deeds. And one sees some residual moral queasiness in Henry's advice to his son. The "foreign quarrels" he recommends to Hal are not specified. He does not advise a trip to the Holy Land, a project somehow intimately his own. Henry's choice of that particular political diversion was not accidental and is perfectly emblematic of this sometimes moral, sometimes Machiavellian figure. Shakespeare ends the scene with a touching reminder of Henry's dividedness. After delivering his hard-boiled political speech to Hal, Henry asks to be carried to the palace's Jerusalem room to die:

It hath been prophesied to me, many years,
I should not die but in Jerusalem,

Which vainly I suppos'd the Holy Land.
But bear me to that chamber; there I'll lie;
In that Jerusalem shall Harry die. (*2HIV* IV.v.236–40)

The Rebels

I earlier characterized both of the unsuccessful rebellions against Henry IV as simple power-grabs devoid of any genuine ideological content. But however disingenuous, the self-justifications for each rebellion are distinctive and appear to symbolize the diminishing influence of two once powerful ways of life, the one devoted to honor and heroism, the other to religion. The first rebellion, led by the Northumberlands, can be understood as an attempt to avenge an insult. Northumberland and Worcester, who helped Henry defeat Richard, feel slighted and underappreciated by the new king and Henry's curt dismissal of Hotspur's plea to ransom Mortimer is enough to set that hot-tempered nobleman on the warpath. While there is nothing heroic about Northumberland—he's a model of selfish calculation—Hotspur is cut from the traditional heroic mold. But for all of his heroic credentials, Hotspur comes off as a parody or caricature of the traditional hero. This is due in part to his decidedly unheroic sense of humor. Henry's defeat of Richard II marked the victory of shrewd calculation over the force of tradition and myth. Thus it is only appropriate that in post-Richard England, traditional heroism seems anachronistic, the subject of satire. Hotspur is, in the end, a ridiculous figure. He evokes our laughter unintentionally, and it is difficult to respect those at whom we laugh. But Hotspur is endearing, if not respected, precisely because he makes us laugh. In a brilliantly ironic scene with Glendower, Shakespeare casts this none too bright warrior as a defender of enlightened good sense (*1HIV* III.i.). When Glendower brags that he "can call spirits from the vasty deep," Hotspur snidely retorts, "Why, so can I, or so can any man, / But will they come when you do call for them?" (*1HIV* III.i.50–53). And Hotspur takes the non-intentional, scientific view of nature when confronted with Glendower's claim that nature itself responded in fear to his birth. When heroes do not challenge nature but defend its mechanical independence, one suspects that heroism is on the wane. And when a rebellious juvenile delinquent kills Hotspur, we see that a darker, more complicated hero has emerged from the new world Henry helped initiate. Henry's victory over the rebels, like King John's before him, confirms the presumption in favor of those in power. What at first appears to be a formidable rebel combination, as in *King John*, eventually dissipates. The rebels will return to fight another day, but this first defeat corrects the impression of *Richard II* that rebellion is easy.

The second rebellion, led by the Archbishop of York, justifies itself in part on the basis of religion: Henry deposed a legitimate Christian king and must therefore be removed. But as mentioned before, this religious rationale is alluded to only in terms of its strategic utility by the Northumberland faction, which helped to defeat Richard. They hope religion will supply their cause with enough energy to overcome the natural aversion of ordinary soldiers to rebel against a sitting king. There is no reason, at first glance, to question the archbishop's belief or his loyalty to Richard and divine right, but we never see him addressing his troops and never hear him discussing who will replace Henry and why. Because the two armies do not engage one another, we cannot know how effective the religious rationale may have proved in battle. Ironically enough, it is the archbishop's very Christianity which ends the war before it begins. Against the advice of the more suspicious Mowbray, the archbishop accepts Prince John's promise that if he should dismiss his troops, King Henry IV will redress his grievances. The archbishop's Christian trustingness (or gullibility) earns him only execution. (Like his father, Prince John dispenses with honor and relies on fraud.) The fact that the archbishop does not insist on Henry's removal from the throne, happily settling for (the promise of) the king's attention, combined with the rebel troops' readiness to disarm and go home without fighting, suggest that religion never played much of a part in the rebellion.

One might, then, characterize the events of the two Henry IV plays as "mopping-up exercises" after the decisive victory of a talented innovator over a traditionalist Christian order in *Richard II*. Henry's opponents are unable to resurrect those irrational forces that accounted for King Richard's authority. The rebels may, however, simply have been outmanuevered by Henry IV, who never presents himself as an innovator and who identifies his kingship with a divine purpose by calling for a redemptive Crusade to the Holy Land. Henry is an ambitious politician who recognizes the power of arms, but he never forgets the people's desire for inspired leadership. Henry is successful in part because he understood the basis of King Richard's authority better than the rebels did.

Chapter Five

King Henry V

Readers of parts 1 and 2 of *Henry IV* turn to *Henry V* with the following expectations: it will deal with Hal's problematic title to rule and his equally problematic "conversion" following his public break with Falstaff. Henry's father has already suggested—and a little bird predicted—a solution to the first problem: a diversionary foreign war.[1] Our expectations on this matter are not disappointed, for *Henry V* is a play about England's conquest of France.

The play also immediately addresses Hal's conversion, but the character of that conversion—is it genuine? is the break with Falstaff complete? is Hal really "the mirror of all Christian kings"? (II.Cho.6) —remains problematic. For those who accept Hal's conversion in 2 *Henry IV* at face value, *Henry V* offers plenty of corroborating evidence. But the play also provides evidence for those, like myself, who are skeptical about Hal's conversion.

Beneath his new moral exterior, skeptics may well see something else in Henry V, namely, a battle-hardened, sly Machiavellian prince who is only pretending to be a Christian hero-king fighting a just war—all in order to establish a patriotic basis for his illegitimate rule.[2] On this view, both the war and Hal's calculated transformation are designed to solve his legitimacy problem. In short, a crafty politician makes an unjust war seem just in the hopes of making an illegitimate king seem legitimate.

An Illegitimate King Goes to War

King Henry V is the son of a usurper: he is not supposed to be king. While it may be true, as John Alvis argues, that "for the sake of the realm even the heir of a usurper should be regarded as the rightful king and his father's breach of lineal rights ignored,"[3] the fact remains that Henry V is illegitimate. One expects, then, that the play will deal with Henry's tainted title to rule and offer some reflections on the general subject of political legitimacy. But according to Moody Prior, such expectations are not satisfied in *Henry V*:

> If *Henry V* were a consistent working out of major prefigurings in the previous plays . . . we would expect to find as a principal feature of *Henry V* a following up of Henry IV's warning about the insecurity of the succession and the consequent need for Hal to gain acceptance of his rule and thus validate his weak title by convincing the nation of his superior merits as king. However, Henry's flawed title is not the major issue in *Henry V*.[4]

Prior's conclusion is dead wrong, but it points in a useful direction. If Henry's illegitimacy does not *seem* to be a major concern of this play, it is because Henry does not want it to be. His success in "convincing the nation of his superior merits as king" renders the issue of his illegitimacy moot. In other words, Henry's skill as a politician obscures what is in fact the major issue of the play.

Henry is concerned about his illegitimacy, and this manifests itself most clearly in his preoccupation with the unquestionably legitimate Richard II. One hears unmistakable echoes of *Richard II* when the question of a ruler's relation to his subjects comes up in *Henry V*. Consider the following passages, where both Richard and Henry deny that a king is a being somehow superior to his subjects:

> Cover your heads, and mock not flesh and blood
> With solemn reverence; throw away respect,
> Tradition, form, and ceremonious duty;
> For you have mistook me all this while.
> I live with bread like you, feel want,
> Taste grief, need friends— . . . (*RII* III.ii.171–76)

> . . . I think the king is but a man, as I am: the violet smells to him as it doth to me; the element shows to him as it doth to me; all his senses have but human conditions: his ceremonies laid by, in

> his nakedness he appears but a man. . . . Therefore when he sees reason of fears, as we do, his fears, out of doubt, be of the same relish as ours are. . . . (*HV* IV.i.101–10)[5]

Both kings are playing off of the belief that they are, indeed, superior beings, a belief they are not always so eager to disavow. Richard frequently compares himself to Christ.[6] Henry V too suggests he is thought of as a kind of a god:

> And what have kings that privates have not too,
> Save ceremony, save general ceremony?
> And what art thou, thou idol ceremony?
> What kind of god art thou, that suffer'st more
> Of mortal griefs than do thy worshippers? (*HV* IV.i.244–48)

When Queen Isabel overhears a gardener predicting her husband's fall, she accuses him of making "a second fall of cursed man" (*RII* III.iv.76). Borrowing from Richard the notion that kingship is divine, Henry V accuses his rebellious subjects of the same crime: "For this revolt of thine, methinks, is like / Another fall of man" (II.ii.141–42). One need not rely on literary echoes alone to establish Henry's preoccupation with Richard II, for he admits to it outright:

> Not to-day, O Lord!
> O not to-day, think not upon the fault
> My father made in compassing the crown!
> I Richard's body have interred new,
> And on it have bestow'd more contrite tears
> Than from it issued forced drops of blood.
> Five hundred poor I have in yearly pay,
> Who twice a day their wither'd hands hold up
> Toward heaven, to pardon blood; and I have built
> Two chantries, where sad and solemn priests
> Sing still for Richard's soul. More will I do;
> Though all that I can do is nothing worth,
> Since that my penitence comes after all,
> Imploring pardon. (IV.i.298–311)

Henry V's contrition over Richard's deposition, along with his striking imitation of Richard's views on kingship, suggest that Henry is acutely conscious of his legitimacy problem. Simply put, Henry wants what Richard had and what he and his father lack: he wants to be seen as the rightful ruler of England. Richard, as we will recall, possessed a double right to rule. He was the legal heir to the throne, and, perhaps more importantly, was thought to rule by divine right. As the son of the man who stole the throne and murdered a divine right king, neither of Richard's powerful claims to rule are available to Henry V. Henry's project, which is the subject of this play, is to reestablish by other means the aura of legitimacy possessed by Richard.

What means? Henry IV, as noted above, advised war:

> Be it thy course to busy giddy minds
> With foreign quarrels, that action hence borne out
> May waste the memory of the former days. (*2HIV* IV.v.213–15)

King Henry accepts his father's advice, and the bulk of *Henry V* dramatizes the preparation for and waging of a war with France. Henry IV's proposed strategy is directed primarily toward diverting those nobles who can be expected to exploit Hal's weak credentials to further their own political ambitions. Involve them in a war, he says, and they will have neither the time nor the energy to plot against you. Once the war is under way, your suspect title will be forgotten. Hal's decision to invade France does not, as it turns out, prevent the planning of a coup against him. But when the plot is prematurely exposed, the plotters are quickly disposed of, and seem but a small nuisance to a country completely absorbed with the coming war. "[A]ll the youth of England are on fire," the chorus tells us (II.1). In such circumstances, "traitors" will have trouble winning a sympathetic audience. Once caught, the rebels seem to acknowledge as much: the fact that they planned to install Richard II's true heir as king is never even mentioned.

While Hal surely sees the logic behind his father's strategy, he has grander hopes for what a war can do for him. In addition to serving the negative end of diverting attention from his flawed title, war can serve the positive end of passionately binding the entire country to their king turned general. Henry V understands that Richard's authority had, at bottom, an irrational foundation. His legitimacy was based on custom, tradition, and religion, all of which have more to do with feeling and belief than with reasoned acceptance. A well-promoted war can tap emotions similar to those Richard relied on to sustain his authority.[7] The spectacle of war and the patriotism that accompanies it can provide Henry V with the passionate allegiance his father could not muster. Taking his cues from Richard's kingship, Henry V chooses war with France as the vehicle to remystify politics, to cover over the disenchanting impression left by his father that the right to rule belongs to whoever is strong enough to claim it. Henry plans to prove himself a legitimate king by proving himself a legitimate hero.

Viewing Henry as a savvy politician who embarks on a morally dubious war for utilitarian reasons would be easier if the play did not give the immediate impression that the war is not even Henry's idea. Rather, the idea for war appears to have been initiated and championed by the leadership of a self-interested Church that stands to lose a good deal of land if a bill currently before parliament passes. The bill in question would appropriate "the better half" (I.i.8) of Church property in order to enlarge the royal coffers and finance nearly eight thousand new positions in the nobility—it would, in effect, use Church funds to create a new aristocracy. In exchange for opposing the bill, the archbishop offers both moral and financial support for an invasion of France. A successful conquest would secure the land necessary to support a new aristocracy without endangering the Church's wealth and power. As Prior notes, "before the play is scarcely under way, we find ourselves among people who seem to have been brought up on *The Prince* and Bacon's 'Of Negotiating.'" But it is the Churchmen "who are busy being politicians, and not Henry."[8] According to a biographer of Henry V, "if Shakespeare is to be believed, the renewal of what we now call 'The Hundred Years War' was entirely due to the cynical advice of English Churchmen."[9]

Although he is a great advocate of King Henry and his war, John Dover Wilson does not see Henry as somehow above political machination: "it is not the Archbishop who sets the King awork, but the King the Archbishop. . . . "[10] A close reading of act 1, scene 2 shows that Henry is using the Church for his own ends, or, perhaps more accurately, that they are using each other for complementary ends. As noted above, the general idea for foreign war is first broached not by any Church official but by King Henry IV. At the end of *2 Henry IV*, an enemy is specified when Prince John predicts war with France:

> I will lay odds that, ere this year expire,
> We bear our civil swords and native fire

> As far as France. I heard a bird so sing,
> Whose music, to my thinking, pleased the King. (*2HIV* V.v.105–8)

Of course, the bird whose music pleases Henry could be Canterbury, but it could also be Prince John himself or anyone in agreement with Henry IV's thinking on this matter. Advice about the benefits of war, from whomever it comes, can only repeat what Hal already knows and cannot help but have thought about. When Canterbury speaks of the "offer"[11] he makes the king—financial support for the war in exchange for opposition to the bill—he notes that it is in "regard of causes now in hand" (I.i.78). Some kind of action in France has already been decided upon. Canterbury's exploratory conversation with King Henry is broken off because Henry must meet with the French ambassadors, who come to respond to Henry's *prior* claims to "some certain dukedoms, in the right / Of your great predecessor, King Edward the Third" (I.ii.247–48). Canterbury may be responsible for persuading the king to widen the scope of the war, but again, it is difficult to imagine Henry not thinking this through too. And we soon see that he has. In response to Canterbury's long argument for Henry's right to the French throne, the king first worries out loud about the danger of a Scottish invasion of England while his troops are occupied in France (I.ii.136–39). Henry has already given the French campaign a great deal of thought; he is not the Church's—or anyone else's—tool.

How is it, then, that Henry can *appear* to be a tool of the Church at the same time he's using them to his own advantage? This is exactly Henry's intention: "Henry appears to have incited the bishop to incite Henry."[12] The king may know what really moves the men who run the Church, but it is still a morally powerful institution, and Henry wants them on board. In allowing the Church to make the public case for the justice of the war, Henry allows himself to be seen as acceding to the wishes of the greatest moral authority. Lest this point be missed, Henry emphatically underlines it:

> . . . we pray you to proceed,
> And justly and religiously unfold
> Why the law Salic that they have in France
> Or should, or should not, bar us in our claim.

And God forbid, my dear and faithful lord,
That you should fashion, wrest, or bow your reading,
Or nicely charge your understanding soul
With the opening titles miscreate, whose right
Suits not your native colours with the truth

. . . .

For we will hear, note, and believe in heart
That what you speak is in your conscience wash'd
As pure as sin with baptism. (I.ii.9–17; 30–32)

Tell the truth, Henry says, and we will believe you. Since Henry already knows that Canterbury desperately wants war, he already knows the gist of what he will say. His not so subtle strategy here is to emphasize the moral credentials of the speaker who wants the same thing he wants. The notion that Henry is sincerely interested in the truth about his claim, and that he employs the archbishop and his staff as research librarians, is absurd:

> . . . it could not be seriously contended that Henry personally needs episcopal coaching regarding the historical background to his larger claim: what he does need, in addition to the public support of the great lords temporal, is the public blessing of the Church, whatever the precise goal of the invasion.[13]

But as I indicated above, Henry wants more than the Church's blessing; he wants the war to seem like their idea. Why?

I have tried to show that Henry wants war for his own reasons, independent of those of the Church. But more important than the question of who initiated the war—and of who used whom—is the question of its justice. Is the war against France just, and if not, does King Henry know as much? If the latter, then it's obvious why Henry should want the war to seem like someone else's idea. And who better to use as cover for an unjust military adventure than the Church, whose moral credentials are, at least for a great many men, unimpeachable? In fact, the war is unjust, and Henry knows it.

In calling the war unjust, I mean nothing fancier than this: it is unjust to take what doesn't belong to you, and France doesn't belong to Henry V. Theft on a grand scale is still theft. My argument that Henry knows the war is unjust rests on the fact that he always talks of the grandeur of the war, but never of its justice. The only argument for the justice of the war is made by Canterbury, in his tediously long-winded and nearly impossible to follow account of Henry's hereditary claim to the French throne. Goddard calls the argument "a colossal piece of ecclesiastical casuistry" and dispenses with it in a single sentence:

> The very thing that proves the title of a French king crooked—namely, inheritance through the female—serves by some twist of ecclesiastical logic, to prove the title of an English king good.[14]

In arguing for the justice of the war, J. H. Walter calls the archbishop's reasoning "impeccable," but still feels it necessary to bolster his case with an appeal to authority: "Gentilli, the greatest jurist of the sixteenth century, . . . quite uninvited expressed his opinion that the claim of the English kings to the French throne was legal and valid."[15] For those readers and viewers of the play who fail to see the logic of the archbishop's argument and who are uninclined to put their trust in Gentilli, the only argument for the justice of the war is, to say the least, unsatisfying. M. M. Reese, like Walter a great supporter of Henry V, acknowledges that a *modern* audience may have difficulty seeing the justice of the war: "*however it may appear to us today,* the French war was a righteous war which a virtuous king was bound in honour to undertake."[16] But why should a war that is in fact righteous, virtuous, and honourable appear any different today?

Whether it is because they lack historical sophistication or for some other reason, those readers who cannot say why this war is just have an ally in King Henry. He can't either. Disguised as a common soldier in order to surreptitiously gauge his troops' morale and bolster it where necessary, Henry declares, "I could not die any where so contented as in the king's company, his cause being just and his quarrel honourable" (IV.i.127–29). When a soldier named Williams replies, "That's more than we know" (IV.i.130), Henry is reduced to sophistical rambling. He responds not with proof of the justice of his cause, but rather with two (bad) arguments intended to absolve the king of any responsibility for those who die in battle. First, Henry says that neither the father who sends his son with merchandise to sea, nor the master who commands his servant to transport money, is responsible if the ship should sink or the servant be robbed and killed. Thus, Henry concludes,

> The king is not bound to answer the particular endings of his soldiers, the father of his son, nor the master of his servant; for they purpose not their death when they purpose their services. (IV.i.159–63)

The comparisons are inapt. The transportation of goods is a "morally innocent"[17] activity, while war is surely not. And if the sea and the highway are potentially dangerous places, the battlefield is certainly so, as Henry later admits to his troops: "a many of our bodies shall no doubt / Find native graves" (IV.iii.95–96).

Henry's second argument is even more fantastic than his first. He claims that no army is composed of "all unspotted soldiers" (IV.i.165); some are murderers, others rapists or thieves. Should any of these types die in battle, it is God's belated punishment for their crimes. Perhaps it goes without saying, but what about the innocent that die? Much earlier in the play, when he implores Canterbury to speak truthfully about his claim, Henry undermines both of the arguments he uses here, agreeing completely with Williams's assertion that "if the cause not be good, the king himself hath a heavy reckoning to make" (IV.i.135–36):

> Therefore take heed how you impawn our person,
> How you awake our sleeping sword of war:
>
> . . . .
>
> For never two such kingdoms did contend
> Without much fall of blood; whose guiltless drops
> Are everywhere a woe, a sore complaint
> 'Gainst him whose wrongs gives edge unto swords (I.ii.21-22, 24–26)

Commenting on Henry's remarks to Williams, Goddard says, "if any proof were needed that he knows in his heart of hearts that this is a bad war we have it in the squirming sophistry—almost worthy of a Pandulf—with which he vainly attempts to refute the simple and straightforward statement of Williams."[18]

If Henry is unconvincing on the question of the war's justice, he is inspiring on the question of its grandeur. His war rhetoric cannot help but arouse the passions of all but the most intransigently skeptical. The opening lines of Henry's famous Harfleur speech are stunningly memorable:

> Once more unto the breach, dear friends, once more,
> Or close up the wall with our English dead.
> In peace there's nothing so becomes a man
> As modest stillness and humility:
> But when the blast of war blows in our ears,
> Then imitate the action of the tiger . . . (I.iii.1–6)

His speech on the eve of the battle at Agincourt is even more remarkable, especially when he transports his troops into the future, allowing them to experience beforehand the everlasting glory that victory will bring. I quote here a large portion of the speech, because I think its effectiveness lies in the detail with which he imagines a scene that could take place around any veteran's table:

> This day is call'd the feast of Crispian:
> He that outlives this day, and comes safe home,
> Will stand a tip-toe when this day is nam'd,
> And rouse him at the name of Crispian.
> He that shall see this day, and live old age,
> Will yearly on the vigil feast his neighbours,
> And say, "To-morrow is Saint Crispian":
> Then will he strip his sleeve and show his scars,
> And say, "These wounds I had on Crispin's day."
> Old men forget; yet all shall be forgot,
> But he'll remember with advantages
> What feats he did that day. Then shall our names,
> Familiar in his mouth as household words,
> Harry the king, Bedford and Exeter,
> Warwick and Talbot, Salisbury and Gloucester,
> Be in their flowing cups freshly remember'd.
> This story shall the good man teach his son;
> And Crispin Crispian shall ne'er go by,
> From this day to the ending of the world,
> But we in it shall be remembered:
> We few, we happy few, we band of brothers; (IV.iii.40–60)

Underscoring the sense of pride and elitism that he has been trying to engender in his troops, Henry closes with a picture of the humiliation in store for those who did not have the privilege to fight beside him this day:

> And gentlemen in England now a-bed
> Shall think themselves accurs'd they were not here,
> And hold their manhoods cheap whiles any speaks
> That fought with us upon Saint Crispin's day. (IV.iii.64–67)

Sullivan calls Henry's Agincourt speech "magnificently stirring," but in the end judges it "strikingly vacuous" because "the King does not broach the merits of his cause. . . . "[19] Henry's speech at Harfleur could be given to any army laying siege to any city; his speech at Agincourt to any army facing overwhelming odds against a superior enemy. And none of these armies need be in the right. His rhetoric is versatile because he only addresses the greatness of victory, remaining silent about whether it is deserved. What is impressive about Henry's rhetorical talents is also alarming: he can move the souls of men while instilling forgetfulness about justice.

Shakespeare himself appears to offer a running commentary on the justice of the war by unobtrusively posing the question of whether France belongs to England. France belongs to England, he seems to answer, only if a country with a native tongue, established borders,[20] and a distinctive national character belongs to its aggressive, ambitious neighbor. I may be overstating the case here, but Shakespeare clearly goes out of his way in *Henry V* to show that whatever motivated this war, it is being fought by two separate *nations*, and that family trees and rules of monarchical succession are irrelevant in light of this larger fact. Even if Henry V's claims to the French throne could be proven genuine, "France has ruled its illegally kept possessions longer than Henry's father kept his illegally acquired throne."[21] By continually reminding us that the French and the English are different peoples, Shakespeare continually asks us to question why one country should belong to the other. Three amusing scenes in *Henry V* are devoted wholly or in part to linguistic misunderstanding (III.iv, IV.iv, V.ii). The scenes are funny, but they are funny for a reason that has direct bearing on the war: the French don't speak English, and the English don't speak French. They are two different nations with two different languages. Even more amusing are the scenes in which the national character of each side is assailed and caricatured (III.v and III.vii). The English are cold, unimaginative, and dull; the French are effeminate, frivolous, and cowardly. The French get the worst of it (they even make fun of themselves), which surely delighted Shakespeare's English audience. But the point is that you can't have patriotism without a *patrie*, and you can't caricature a people who lack a peculiar and identifiable national character. *Henry V* vividly shows that the distinctiveness of these two countries is undeniable. Supporters of the war must then show why it is just that one should govern the other. No wonder King Henry comes up short when asked to show just this. No wonder he wants the war to seem like someone else's idea.

Letting others appear to be making decisions that are in fact his own is King Henry's characteristic pose.[22] He is consistently deceitful. The duplicitous behavior he exhibits concerning the war is repeated time and again, for example when he tricks the rebels into sentencing themselves to death, making it appear that they, and not he, are responsible for their punishment (II.ii). As Sullivan notes, Henry's attempt to make the citizens of Harfleur responsible for any evil his soldiers may unleash upon them "borders on the absurd":[23]

> What is't to me, *when you yourselves are cause,*
> If your pure maidens fall into the hand
> Of hot and forcing violation? (III.iii.19–21, emphasis added)

Finally, Henry's pretense of wooing Katharine is farcical. She is Henry's war-prize—his "capital demand" (V.ii.96)—and thus can only "consent" to what has already been decided on the battlefield.

Henry is consistently deceitful for a very simple reason: he has to be. He is an illegitimate king fighting an unjust war to further his own political ambitions. He is deceitful because the war *is* unjust, the rebels *do* have a better claim to the English throne, the Harfleurians *are* innocent, and Katharine *is* a war-prize. Candor on these matters wouldn't be wise. But one might object that it is unwise as well to appear to be the pawn of others. If Henry is always seen to be doing someone else's bidding, he might appear weak and indecisive. Henry anticipates and deflects such criticism with his archetypical pose as God's servant. He does God's bidding with God's approval. By giving God the ultimate credit for all of his deeds, Henry appears not weak, but invincible. It would be a mistake, however, to understand Henry as seeking moral cover for some future calling-to-accounts of his career. Such excuses (the Church sanctioned the war; the rebels hung themselves; the Harfleurians asked to be raped and pillaged; Katharine said she wanted me . . .) would persuade no one. But this is not Henry's intention. He seeks not to blame others later, but to avoid scrutiny now. Henry's masterful strategy is to deflect attention from his true motives and let success take care of the rest. Simply put, Henry wants to be seen as careful, fair, and scrupulously moral even when he is in fact being impetuous, unjust, and unscrupulously immoral.

But if this is indeed the case, why do so many critics and viewers of the play see Henry as an "epic hero," an "ideal king," "the most straightforward, candid political man of the whole lot"?[24] Part of the reason may be that the chorus of *Henry V* tells us to view him this way. The chorus describes Henry as "the mirror of all Christian kings" (II.Cho.6) and claims that he is "free from vainness and self-glorious pride" (V.Cho.20). One ought to begin, then, by assuming that the chorus speaks the simple truth. But Henry's own words, to say nothing of his actions,[25] call the truthfulness of the chorus into question. Henry does say of himself at one point that "we are no tyrant, but a Christian king" (I.ii.241), but he is responding here to the French ambassadors, who are reluctant to deliver an insulting message. I do not kill messengers, Henry tells them. If this makes him a Christian king, then the chorus may be believed. If not, then the joke—and I take this line to be a joke by Shakespeare—is on the chorus. Later, Henry contradicts the chorus outright: "if it be a sin to covet honour, / I am the most offending soul alive" (IV.iii.28–29). Goddard thinks that "through the Choruses, the playwright gives us the popular idea of his hero."[26] I think it would be more accurate to say that the chorus expresses not public opinion *per se*, but wished-for public opinion, like a television campaign commercial. The Chorus gives us an ideal king, though "truth squads" may, upon digging, discover something different.

Shakespeare does not give us contradictory versions of the king without purpose. If one of the points of this play is to show how a king who needs to appear better than he is does so, then it must show that he isn't all that he pretends to be, as well as how he'd like to be seen:

> But how . . . could Shakespeare draw a character whose first requisite is that he shall appear to be the opposite of what he is except by drawing a character who appears to be the opposite of what he is? "If Machiavelli had had a prince for a disciple," wrote Voltaire in his *Memoirs*, "the first thing he would have recommended him to do would have been to write a book against Machiavellianism."[27]

The disjunction between the chorus and the body of the play is thus necessary for the whole message. One version may be truer than the other, but Henry's success will depend on which version is accepted as the truth by the only audience that matters: his subjects. If his subjects are mostly like the skeptical Williams, then Henry is in trouble. But if they are like Bates, who defends the king to Williams, or like Fluellen, who compares Henry to Alexander the Great, or like the Duke of York, who begs the king to be allowed to lead his troops into battle, then Henry will return to England, as the chorus would have it, as a "conqu'ring Caesar" (V.Cho.28).

Christian King or Machiavellian Prince?

I argued above that Henry knowingly wages an unjust war for domestic political reasons. Running throughout my argument is the implicit assumption that Henry's conversion, announced near the end of 2 *Henry IV* and commented on by the archbishop at the beginning of *Henry V*, is not genuine, but rather a politic pose designed to enhance his political standing. Frivolous and degenerate in his youth, once king, Henry deliberately adopts a serious and moral demeanor in order to carry out a war he trusts will legitimize his regime. But as I showed above, the chorus, as well as numerous distinguished critics, take Henry at his word. They see a changed man, a responsible statesman, a hero. Those inclined to this view of King Henry will undoubtedly find the arguments I made above unnecessarily complicated, perhaps even tortured. And if their generosity toward Henry is warranted, then my thesis is not. Thus a closer look at the character of Henry's conversion is now necessary.

Hal announces his conversion in 2 *Henry IV*, midway through a public humiliation of his close companion Falstaff. Awaiting a sign from the just-crowned king as he stands amongst a cheering crowd, Falstaff is brutally rebuked: "I know thee not, old man. Fall to thy prayers" (*2HIV* V.v.47). Of course, Hal does know Falstaff, and he proceeds to describe him in the most unflattering way as a ridiculous parody of the sensualist, as a rotund old glutton who is pitiful rather than amusing. The new king can only "despise" "such a kind of man" (V.v.51, 49). Hal has changed:

> Presume not that I am the thing I was;
> For God doth know, so shall the world perceive,

That I have turn'd away my former self;
So will I those that kept me company. (V.v.56–59)

Hal has turned away from Falstaff and all that he stands for,[28] and he has turned toward God. As Henry's tone makes plain, his is a judgmental God; this is a moral conversion.

Henry V opens with a long discussion by a bishop and an archbishop of Henry's "reformation" (I.i.33). But as Wilson observes, the conversion these religious officials are describing does not seem to be a particularly religious one:

> King Henry, as Bradley notes, "is much more obviously religious than most of Shakespeare's heroes," so that one would expect the bishops to interpret his change of life as a religious conversion. Yet they say nothing about religion except that he is "a true lover of the holy church" and can "reason in divinity"; the rest of their talk, some seventy lines, is concerned with learning and statecraft. In fact, the conversation of these worldly prelates demonstrates that the conversion is not the old repentance for sin and amendment of life, . . . but a repentance of the renaissance type, which transforms an idle and wayward prince into an excellent soldier and governor.[29]

One needn't even see it as a repentance.[30] The prince, Canterbury and Ely seem to be saying, has grown up. Or, more bluntly, he now prefers politics to prostitutes. Henry's conversion, it must be remembered, is being discussed in the context of the bill before parliament that would financially cripple the Church. Thank God we are dealing with a political grown-up—Canterbury seems to be saying between the lines—he can understand us. It is only because he knows that Henry has become a politician, and not a moralistic prude, that Canterbury dares to bribe the king, offering support for a war in exchange for squelching the bill. Canterbury knows that what is good for the Church can be good for Henry's political career. And he senses that Henry knows this too. Nothing these Church officials say is inconsistent with my earlier argument[31] that Hal's "conversion" in *2 Henry IV* was not all it appeared to be, that it was in fact a politic pose, and not a moral awakening.

But Henry's own words later in the play make us wonder whether he has not indeed changed. In two soliloquies, Henry characterizes himself not as an ambitious Machiavellian prince, but as an unhappy, reluctant politician, and a deeply repentant religious man. In his first soliloquy, Henry, like his father before him (e.g. *2HIV* III.i), complains about the great burdens of ruling. The king, he says, "must bear all." Kingship is a "hard condition." Henry even intimates that he would rather be a "peasant" or a "slave" (IV.i.279, 290, 287). Furthermore, he cannot sleep. Greenblatt's commentary on the complaints of Hal's insomniac father applies equally well to King Henry V:

> Who knows? perhaps it is even true; perhaps in a society in which the overwhelming majority of men and women had next to nothing, the few who were rich and powerful did lie awake at night. . . . We are invited to take measure of his suffering, to understand . . . the costs of power. And we are invited to understand these costs in order to ratify the power, to accept the grotesque and cruelly unequal distribution of possessions: everything to the few, nothing to the many. The rulers earn, or at least pay for, their exalted position through suffering, and this suffering ennobles, if it does not exactly cleanse, the lies and betrayals upon which this position depends.[32]

Greenblatt may be too intemperate here, but I share his view that Henry (either father or son) does not deserve our sympathy. If Henry V cannot sleep because he's worried about the war, let us not forget who started the war and why.

Henry's speech, as Alvis notes, resembles "classical anti-tyrannical writings" which "teach that the tyrant's lot suffers by comparison with the commoner's, since acceptance of such a teaching helps deter tyranny."[33] But Shakespeare could not have intended that lesson here: he makes Henry's enormous success far too attractive. Henry may lose some sleep, but in the end he gains all of France. Rather than teaching us a lesson about tyranny, Shakespeare seems to be trying to tell us something about Henry. Although, as noted above, Henry denies he is a tyrant, he does not here distinguish, as do the classical writers, between tyranny and kingship:

> . . . applied to good kings, the . . . [classical anti-tyrannical] argument meets an obvious answer: kings, as distinguished from tyrants, ought gladly to accept what Henry terms their "polished perturbation" because their end is justice. They are satisfied by knowing justice and working at it. This answer does not occur to Henry, however, nor does it occur to him that justice may be a sufficient recompense for the burdens of statecraft.[34]

That the "justice answer" does not occur to Henry ought to give pause to those who view him as a kind of political saint. But to Henry's credit, another, perhaps more troubling, answer does not occur to him either. That is, Henry does not say that the burdens of kingship are compensated for by the sheer delight of exercising power.[35] The very fact that he complains about the difficulties of ruling says something about Henry: one can imagine Richard III, for example, losing sleep because he's *not* king, but never because he is. There is something undeniably attractive about a ruler who worries about the responsibilities of office. But what about Greenblatt's argument that the political results are the same except that the people, duped by meaningless displays of suffering, swallow them more readily? I think Shakespeare would answer that the results are *not* necessarily the same, that rulers with huge ambitions who worry may be less dangerous than rulers with huge ambitions who don't. This first soliloquy, then, gives us a mixed picture of the king: Henry is neither a self-satisfied power-monger nor a squeaky-clean good government type. The first impression Henry's speech gives, that of an unhappy, reluctant politician, is misleading. One would have to balance it against the (unwritten) soliloquy he might have spoken after his stunning victory in France. So perhaps the picture is not so mixed after all. In any event, Henry's quite understandable insomnia and self-doubt on the eve of a battle against a superior enemy should not be taken as evidence of a moral reformation.

In his notorious second soliloquy, Henry really does seem to confound the characterization I've built of him. The "justice answer" may not have occurred to him in his first soliloquy because he knows the war is unjust and Williams's blunt reminder brings home to him the human costs of his political ambition. He may just be feeling guilty. And while the capacity to feel guilt is not synonymous with moral rectitude, neither does it gibe with Machiavellian indifference to morality. If Henry is the manipulative politician knowingly waging an unjust war for selfish reasons that I've made him out to be, why does he turn now to God, begging forgiveness for his father's usurpation of Richard II's throne?

> Not to-day, O Lord!
> O not to-day, think not upon the fault
> My father made in compassing the crown!
> . . . .
> Since that my penitence comes after all,
> Imploring pardon. (IV.i.298–300, 310–11)

Henry appears here to be both an orthodox Christian and an orthodox "Elizabethan": he believes in an active moral God, capable of intervening in human affairs, and he expresses remorse for the dethroning of a divine right king. His sentiments cannot, furthermore, be explained away as play-acting, for Henry is alone here—there is no audience to fool and impress.

How, then, can a man who prays to an active God (and is thus, in Machiavelli's view, ruled by fortune) and who apologizes for his father's success in power politics be, at the same time, a Machiavellian prince? In light of this soliloquy, Goddard's characterization of Henry V appears to need amending:

> Samuel Butler has demonstrated in convincing detail that no art or mental process is perfect until it becomes unconscious. The perfect thief is a kleptomaniac, who steals as it were automatically. In that sense, Henry V was possibly the perfect Machiavellian prince. In that sense, Richard III was a mere bungler: he was still conscious of his evil.[36]

Goddard almost seems to say here that Machiavelli prefers men who don't know what they're doing to those who do, which is surely wrong. But even if he means only that Henry has learned to do automatically, without moral qualms, what is politically necessary, then Henry's private expression of moral doubt here shows that he hasn't entirely absorbed that lesson.

There are, it is true, limits to Henry's remorse. He apologizes for his father's deeds, not his own. He does not consider relinquishing the throne. And if he believes in an active God, he does not, like Richard II, wait for Him to act, but proceeds with the plan he so carefully hatched without God's assistance.[37] In fact, Henry's fit of conscience changes nothing. If Henry shows himself to be less coolly calculating than we might have expected him to be, his moral doubt does not cause him to alter his course one iota. Henry may stray from Machiavelli's script, but he is not less effective because of it.

Thus if Henry's two soliloquies are to be taken as evidence of a moral transformation, it is a rather shallow one, for it does not impinge upon his actions. Still, these soliloquies reveal a puzzling incoherence in Henry's character. At his most private, Henry is more confusing than enlightening, not only because what he says is unexpected, but because it is unexpectedly shallow. Why doesn't Henry IV's "fault" in "compassing the crown" touch Hal as well? Henry V is curiously selective: he criticizes his father's tainted claim to rule but it never occurs to him that if his father's kingship was rotten, then so is his. But if Henry thinks himself a deserving king,[38] why then criticize the man who made that possible? Henry shows himself not only to be an ingrate, but a thoughtless ingrate. And why this sudden respect for convention? Richard II's claim to rule had no rational foundation, as Henry IV, however imperfectly, understood. Who would have expected Henry IV's more sober son to genuflect before an irrational tradition that held as pathetic a king as Richard to be God's chosen? Finally, Henry's prayer is barely worthy of a child. In effect, he asks a moral God to forget justice, *just this once,* in order to help the inheritor of an unjustly acquired throne win an unjust war.

Henry doesn't demonstrate the clarity of thought and consistency of character that one would expect given his long commerce with Falstaff. Falstaff's behavior, his drinking, carousing, stealing, and cowardice on the battlefield might strike one as an easy-going surrender to the low animal passions, a life of slothful indolence. But Falstaff is not at all easy-going. Unlike the run-of-the-mill degenerate, who knows he's doing wrong but is too weak or too lazy to mend his ways, Falstaff is degenerate by choice. He has considered and rejected the arguments against his indulgent behavior. In his famous critique of honor on the battlefield, Falstaff shows himself to be a strident skeptic of ordinary opinion. Without embarrassment, he offers up a penetrating defense of cowardice. Falstaff is rigorous. One would have thought that some of this rigor would have rubbed off on Hal, who was by no means easy-going to begin with. The two certainly engaged in enough sharp banter, which held nothing sacred, to have accustomed Hal to pushing things to extremes. That a man used to criticizing with impunity should end up so poor a reasoner, confusedly and unreflectively mixing respect for moral and political tradition with selfish ambition, is hard to swallow.

But if Henry is to be criticized for not being as rigorous as Falstaff, it should be noted that Falstaff too appears to have changed in *Henry V,* and in a remarkably similar way: like Henry, he is full of regret, and like Henry, he turns to God. Falstaff appears in *Henry V* only by report, first as dying and then as dead. But the reports from his deathbed have Falstaff crying out "'God, God, God!' three or four times" (II.iii.20–21) and railing against women and wine. Falstaff dies repentant, fearful of a God one would have thought he'd long since ceased to acknowledge. According to Michael Platt, the way Falstaff dies tells us everything about the way he lived:

> Falstaff dies a Christian, in terror of the afterlife. The most powerful passion in him is not thirst for the sweetness of life or enjoyment of the mere sentiment of existence, but terror of supernatural punishment. Though this terror is not powerful enough to make Falstaff or his kind moderate, it does make him immoderate in fear. . . . Falstaff cannot throw off Christian terrors; the result is big appetites and big fears; to hide from one's fears, one drinks and wenches and jests; but sack and women and jests fill one with dread—so one drinks and wenches and jests. Whenever the wit of Falstaff scores through Biblical allusion, it exposes Biblical fear. He seems to be a combination of bourgeois pleasures and Christian terrors.[39]

But does Falstaff's death really define his life? Should one recast Falstaff's entire life in light of his last, frightened thoughts? I think not. Were it not for these reports, few, if any, would think to describe Falstaff as filled with "dread" or terrified of "supernatural punishment." Whatever moral or religious battles he may have waged before, by the time we and Hal meet him, Falstaff seems comfortably settled in a way of life that shows little evidence of being the product of a tortured, divided soul. And if, facing death, Falstaff is frightened and seems to question the principles by which he lived, he wouldn't be the first. Perhaps Falstaff's lack of rigor on the deathbed should be taken for just that; it needn't mean that he was *always* scared, that his life was one long attempt at dodging demons.

I would like to suggest something similar in Henry's case—that in a moment of crisis he acts with uncharacteristic ordinariness, but that we shouldn't recast his entire life in light of this moment. Perhaps it is asking too much of Henry that he never be frightened, that he never suffer an uneasy conscience, that he never turn sheepishly to God in a weak moment hoping for some assistance. We are surprised by Henry's soliloquies only because he seemed so brave, so resolute in his aims, and more than any other Shakespearean king I've treated, so little in need of outside guidance and counsel, from God or anyone else. The almost inhuman autonomy Henry has always demonstrated[40] is lacking here. When he acts like an ordinary, faulty human being, Henry catches us off guard. But as I pointed out above, what Henry reveals to us about himself in these soliloquies does not resonate outward. He pursues the war with the same vigilance he did before; he continues to be friendless and self-reliant; he is a selfish calculator to the end. And if God is always on his lips, it is only to lend moral credence, or to give a retroactive seal of approval, to decisions he made alone, decisions guided by political efficacy and not justice. Thus Henry's soliloquies are puzzling not only because they seem to reveal an incoherence in his character, but because they seem so circumscribed, so isolated from the everyday world of political calculation that he inhabits.

I do not mean to suggest that Henry's private thoughts should simply be dismissed as aberrant and unimportant, a product of nerves in a weak moment. For they do reveal something interesting about Henry: he *is* incoherent, and in a peculiarly political way. I think the key to Henry's second soliloquy is the selectivity I pointed out above. He blames his father, but not himself, and asks God to make an exception in his case. Simply put, Henry believes he is exceptional. He seems to be blinded, because of his success, to the nature of his success. Henry really thinks himself a deserving king in the largest sense: not just because his father took the throne and passed it on to him, not just because he is tirelessly clever in keeping and strengthening his grip on it, but because he is somehow marked or special. Machiavelli, according to Mindle, teaches that "a prince must first divest himself of pride, lest he take for granted his right to rule and claim by right what can only be his 'by force or by fraud' (*Florentine Histories,* III.13)."[41] Henry never takes for granted the means necessary to maintain his kingship, but he does seem to take for granted his right to rule. The mixture of *realpolitik* with "cosmic" right is apparent when Henry first tries on the crown:

> My due from thee is this imperial crown,
> Which, as immediate from thy place and blood,
> Derives itself to me. Lo where it sits,
> Which God shall guard; and put the world's whole strength
> Into one giant arm, it shall not force
> This lineal honour from me. (*2HIV* IV.v.40–45)

Later, as I noted above, he equates rebellion against his rule to sin against God: "this revolt of thine, methinks, is like / Another fall of man" (*HV* II.ii.141–42). But as Henry shows both in thought and in deed, divine support is no substitute for force and fraud. Henry displays a kind of schizophrenic character: he knows what is politically necessary and does it, but he does not attribute his success to such knowledge and action alone. I call Henry's incoherence peculiarly political because like many savvy politicians who at one time knew better, Henry comes to believe that he deserves to rule. He is proud.

Perhaps Henry's combination of Machiavellian *realpolitik* with the belief that he has some right to rule is more formidable than either would be by itself. *Richard II* shows the limitations of relying on right alone: it engenders laziness and dangerous self-satisfaction. *Richard III* is often read as pointing out the limitations of *realpolitik*. The lack of clear-sightedness that Henry sometimes displays about the true grounds of his authority may then be a political advantage: his proud belief that he deserves to rule makes it easier to convince others of this fact because it is easier to act as though one deserves to be king if one truly believes one deserves to be king. But is this really the case? Are self-conscious liars less convincing than unconscious liars?[42] Shakespeare's plays are filled with spectacularly successful cases of deliberate fraud. Richard III, for example, in order to establish a claim to the crown he covets but has no right to, convinces the widow of a man he murdered that he loves her and that she should marry him—during her father-in-law's funeral, and after admitting he'd killed both her husband and her husband's father (*RIII* I.ii.). One can criticize Henry for his lack of clear-sightedness, but the alternative, politically speaking, is the single-minded clarity and almost casual brutality of a Richard III. Of course, Henry is brutal too,[43] but he often seems to want to justify it in a way that Richard III would not. Before executing the nobles who had plotted against him, Henry makes them listen to an unbearably moralistic lecture (II.ii). He treats them not as unfortunate equals in a treacherous political game, but as genuine traitors, as sinners against divine right. At perhaps his most hypocritical, Henry orders his old drinking buddy Bardolf executed for petty wartime theft in order to show his fairness to the French (III.vi). Henry, who is no stranger to petty theft himself, and who is engaging now in the grandest theft, executes an old friend to prove he can run a decorous war.[44] Is there not something monstrous about a man who can mistake harsh deeds done in the name of political ambition with simple justice? Killing others for political gain with one's eyes wide open is no more appealing than doing so with a false sense of righteousness. But I cannot help but conclude that Shakespeare thinks Henry's lack of self-knowledge somehow diminishes him.[45]

Victorious in War

With his victory in France, Henry's long journey from juvenile delinquent to legitimate statesman is complete. With just twelve thousand English troops, he defeats the sixty-thousand-strong French army (IV.iii). The French dead number ten thousand, the English but twenty-nine (IV.vii). First at Dover and then in London, Henry is welcomed home by huge crowds as a hero; the chorus, as is its habit, must reach back to ancient Rome to find suitable images of his greatness:

> Behold, the English beach
> Pales in the flood with men, with wives, and boys,
> Whose shouts and claps out-voice the deep-mouthed sea . . .
> (V.Cho.9–11)

> How London doth pour out her citizens.
> The mayor and all his brethren in best sort,
> Like to senators of th' antique Rome,
> With the plebeians swarming at their heels,
> Go forth and fetch their conqu'ring Caesar in . . . (V.Cho.24–28)

Questions about Henry's title to rule have long since been forgotten. He is legitimate in the truest sense: no one doubts that he should rule. But is what appears in the midst of all this celebration to be a victory for England and an historically significant event really, at bottom, a personal victory for one man, a man who will soon die, and whose son and heir will lose all that he has gained? Is Henry's victory anything more than *Henry's* victory?

The war, remember, was embarked upon to secure Henry's kingship. What all of England is celebrating originated in the selfish political ambition of the son of a usurper. But the way Henry goes about securing his kingship necessarily involves others, for he attempts (for selfish reasons) to make what is most selfish seem least selfish. The war is not his idea, but the Church's; victory is not his, but God's:

> Praise be to God, and not our strength, for it! (IV.vii.89)

> And be it death proclaimed through our host
> To boast of this or take that praise from God
> Which is his only. (IV.viii.116–18)

> . . . his lords desire him to have borne
> His bruised helmet and his bended sword
> Before him through the city: he forbids it,
> Being free from vainness and self-glorious pride;
> Giving full trophy, signal, and ostent,
> Quite from himself, to God. (V.Cho.17-22)

As Alvis notes, by attributing his victory to God, Henry gets double the honor: first for winning the war, and again for modestly foregoing the credit.[46] His troops and supporters also benefit from Henry's strategy: victory is theirs because God stood behind them. The war takes on a cosmic significance and they as participants become part of something much larger than themselves. And if God favors the English, then the English must deserve such favor. By displacing men's pride, Henry actually increases it.

In attempting to make what is selfish seem unselfish, Henry really does share his success with others. He convinces Englishmen that his good is identical to theirs, and in some sense it really is. Henry gives the English something they would not have if he weren't selfish and ambitious; he gives them the exhilaration of participating in a phenomenal military and political victory. The sense of national pride he engenders is expansive: it touches not only the participants, but, Henry promises, it will touch their children and grandchildren as well. The whole country will listen to tales of English military prowess each year on St. Crispin's Day, the Christian holiday Henry boldly appropriates on the eve of the battle at Agincourt. The chorus nicely captures the meaning of Henry's war with its strange mixture of selfish motivations and generous effects: "Small time, but in that small most greatly lived / This star of England . . . " (V.ii.Cho.5–6). King Henry is the star, but others shine in the light he gives off. Veterans of Agincourt and subjects at home can say we lived in that small time, too. We lived in a time of heroes.

There are, Shakespeare also points out, limits to patriotic fellow-feeling and memories of past glory. And there is the nagging question, greatly obscured in the flush of victory, of the justice of the war. After the intoxicating thrill of battle and pride in victory, one must still live one's life. Pistol learns in France that his wife has died of venereal disease during his absence; nothing awaits his return home but a dreary life of small-time theft (V.i.84–91). Commenting on this scene,

Rabkin notes that Shakespeare "powerfully conjures up" "the reality of the postwar world": "soldiers returned home to find their jobs gone, falling to a life of petty crime in a seamy and impoverished underworld that scarcely remembers the hopes that accompanied the beginnings of the adventure."[47] And Williams, the ordinary soldier who, the night before Agincourt, voiced skepticism about the justice of the war, appears after the victory as if to remind us of his earlier but still pertinent reservations. Upon learning that the man he boldly challenged to justify the war was the king himself, Williams politely accuses Henry of fraud. When Henry, trying to keep things light and show he meant no harm, offers Williams money, the reluctant soldier declines: "I will none of your money" (IV.viii.70). Williams, I think, represents the moral center of this play, and in this one-on-one with the king, he makes Henry look small and foolish.

In order to judge whether the war was worth it, one must then weigh the fate of all Pistols, of the French and English dead, as well as the moral reservations of a Williams, against the inspiriting and exhilarating experience of participating in a great military triumph. It is by no means an easy judgment to make. And it is not at all clear that Shakespeare himself makes that judgment here: the play is not unambiguously pro- or anti-war; it has been interpreted and produced both ways. If Shakespeare's sentiments are "pro-war," they lack the gung-ho straightforwardness of an ordinary patriot. His eyes, as we have seen, are wide open to all of the selfishness, ambition, deceit, and injustice which underlie the war. (But what war will not have similar foundations?) But if Shakespeare's sentiments are "anti-war," one would think he would have made it plainer and not made the war in many ways so appealing. If one can't discern with certainty Shakespeare's own view, the play does give us the basis to make our own judgment with all the facts in sight. If we are to celebrate the war, we will do so knowing its downsides. And if we are to oppose the war, we will do so knowing that there will be others like it because the ambition that launched this war is endemic to politics.

My own view is that Shakespeare shows us in *Henry V* the peak of politics as it is likely to be practiced: we see a nation certain of its ruler, possessing an absolute unity of purpose, animated by war-time camaraderie, the exhilaration of conquest, the pride of demonstrated superiority, and given over to the feeling that it lives in a blessed historical moment. Simply put, Henry makes men proud to be alive under his rule. If, upon scrutiny, this political peak is built on fraud and ambition and self-deception, if it is partisan and particular, if it is to be short-lived, that is because politics is all of these things. This, in other words, is politics at its best or near best—which isn't to say one must be impressed. There are other things.

There are other things, that is, besides politics. For Shakespeare seems to teach in the history plays that politics will always involve ambitious men vying for power, and that war, whether civil or foreign, will be the rule rather than the exception. He appears to reject as overhopeful and unrealistic a more moderate (and to us more familiar) view of politics, also represented in this play, according to which war is an inconvenient and unfortunate interruption of the true end of politics—peace, prosperity, and domestic tranquility. On this view, military glory and wartime heroics, however impressive, are not ends in themselves; war can be justified only by its beneficial results. The last act of *Henry V* appears to measure the war by this standard and to find it acceptable. France and England are happily and peacefully reconciled, the King of England and the daughter of the King of France in love and soon to be married: this war, at least, has a happy ending. The treachery, ambition, and violence of the first four acts are forgotten in this atmosphere of sweetness and light. The last act of *Henry V* is often criticized as unworthy of Shakespeare, a fairy-tale ending to a serious play about war. But such criticism presumes that Shakespeare believes the fairytale, and there are clear indications that he does not.

In a speech one critic calls "sincere, profound, and imaginative, a touchstone by which to try everything that is said and done in the play,"[48] the French Duke of Burgundy makes a persuasive case for the moderate politics mentioned above (V.ii.24–67). He is the spokesman for "gentle Peace." Peace, on Burgundy's account, is the fundamental political good because it is the basis of all other political goods: the "arts," the "sciences," the "plenties," the "joyful births," none of which can flourish during the "unnatural" "inconveniences" of war. But King Henry quickly punctures Burgundy's liberal sermon with a dose of political reality:

> If, Duke of Burgundy, you would the peace,
> Whose want gives growth to th' imperfections
> Which you have cited, you must buy that peace
> With full accord to all our just demands. . . . (V.ii.68–71)

Peace, Henry says, will be had only on the terms of the strong; any other view is indeed a fairytale.[49] The same lesson is conveyed in Henry's love scene with Kate. The king's boyishly awkward and painfully earnest professions of love, and Kate's delight in seeming indecision are rendered artificial by the truth of the matter: Henry won Kate on the battlefield. The play may end with images of political unity and domestic tranquility, but Shakespeare allows us no illusions about their real basis.

I tried to show above that King Henry nationalized his ambition, transforming his own cause into England's cause. But are there any long-term political consequences of Henry's extraordinary reign? One can surely say that he overcame the weight of political tradition, proving to his subjects that he deserved to rule even if he had no technical claim to do so. But he followed in his father's footsteps. Henry IV was the true innovator, the first to challenge the custom of hereditary succession. Henry IV, however, did not live long enough to give his subjects a new reason, in place of customary right, to support him. Hal does give them a new reason, but in this he is only continuing, on his father's direction, what his father began. Alvis credits Henry V with far reaching, if ominous, influence: "the ultimate effect of Henry's emancipation of the acquisitive passions is Richard III who carries ambition and avarice to their logical conclusion living for nothing but egocentric assertiveness."[50] But why make Henry V responsible for subsequent expressions of naked ambition? His father showed the way first. In fact, of the four kings I treat, only Richard II is conventionally legitimate; all the rest are usurpers. Alvis seems to imply that Richard IIIs need guides, but the history plays show time and again that ambitious men will always find their own way. Only Richard III is responsible for Richard III. The very last words in the play suggest that Henry's achievements are short-lived:

> Henry the Sixth, in infant bands crown'd King
> Of France and England, did this king succeed;
> Whose state so many had the managing,
> That they lost France and made England bleed. . . . (V.ii.Cho.9–12)

Henry VI will lose all that his father gained in war; England will again be racked by civil war; and Henry VI will be challenged in the name of tradition for being the son of the son of a usurper. There is no sense of closure at the end of *Henry V*. Always, Shakespeare seems to say, there will be more of the same. Henry V's great achievement is this: for a brief moment a great politician lifted a nation's people above the everyday and gave them a sense of greatness. It is no small achievement.

Chapter Six

Conclusion: Shakespeare and Machiavelli Revisited

Shakespeare is not a political thinker in the usual sense. He does not offer concrete policy recommendations; neither does he stake out a "position" on the best form of government. In fact, Shakespeare treats only one form of government in the history plays, hereditary monarchy.[1] He shows an awareness of its flaws—rule is arbitrary and often unjust—but this awareness is not accompanied by a claim that another form of government would be simply superior or itself without flaws.[2] If Shakespeare offers no policy recommendations or definitive statements about the justice or injustice of hereditary monarchy in the history plays, then what can one learn about politics from them?

To begin, all readers of these plays get a penetrating look at how politics is practiced. Shakespeare treats us to an inside view of the ambition and fear and desire for justice and glory that move his political actors. We see their errors and share in their successes. We second-guess, we condemn and applaud, and so in a sense become participants in the political action ourselves. And while the world Shakespeare describes has in many ways vanished, there is nevertheless something concrete and immediate about it. Shakespeare gives such a compelling and complete account of political practice that we are unlikely for long to think ourselves in a strange and foreign territory. Nothing crucial about politics seems to have escaped Shakespeare's attention; nothing seems obviously missing. It's all here, and despite the fact that it happened centuries ago, it's all familiar. More than a history lesson, then, these plays provide us with a political education.

In the course of this education, Shakespeare appears to indicate that there are limits to politics: it will always be practiced within familiar and well-traveled boundaries. More specifically, the competing desires for power and for justice will dominate politics, usually without resolution. Granted, irresolution seems like a weak branch upon which to hang a political teaching. But Shakespeare is an observer, not an advocate, and the key to his political teaching lies in his presentation of a seemingly irresolvable conflict between ambition and justice. This conflict can be seen in his maddeningly elusive account of legitimacy. It is the reason, as well, for his final disagreement with Machiavelli.

Legitimacy and Political Tradition

Shakespeare shows us that both rulers and subjects, if for different reasons, are terribly interested in legitimacy. The ambitious want to be acknowledged as true and rightful rulers in order to get and keep power. And it is easier to get and keep power if one is thought to deserve it. This means, of course, that subjects want to be ruled only by those who legitimately deserve their allegiance. But the reasons for such allegiance are not simply rational. While subjects surely judge rulers, or potential rulers, on the basis of their interest, they also expect traditions of succession to be respected. A legitimate king is first and foremost the one tradition hands down, whether or not he best serves the good of the country. As we have seen, the people will reject legitimate kings in favor of their challengers. But even the successful challengers can never quite shake the reputation that they are not supposed to be king. As a consequence, they usually have enormous difficulty sustaining their rule.

John, Henry IV, and Henry V are illegitimate kings who are superior to the alternatives, but all of them confront significant if unsuccessful challenges in the name of tradition. John's hold on the crown is tenuous from beginning to end. Even though the legitimate king, Arthur, is a young boy who has never exercised power and is allied with England's worst enemies, he plagues John throughout his reign. Henry IV is able to unseat the despotic King Richard, but his violation of political tradition spurs repeated challenges to his authority. In both of these cases, the king who is best for England must nevertheless fight a civil war to defend himself against a legitimate opponent. Henry V is the most talented and popular king of the lot, but even he must crush a conspiracy against him by those allied with King Richard's heir. So, if the people are willing to tolerate and even embrace those kings who violate custom in order to rule, they always seem to hold a place in their hearts for those who possess the sanction of tradition. Respect for tradition is often so compelling that it trumps self-interest, as the people's nearly suicidal attachment to Arthur and the pope, or their enduring nostalgia for King Richard, demonstrates.

What can account for this strangely fickle attachment to tradition, an attachment that wavers and yet endures? One is tempted to attribute it to habit, but this cannot be the end of the story. Because the English people must choose between legitimate kings and their challengers, attachment to tradition cannot be simply reflexive, the unselfconscious assent to what one is used to. Habit may be enough to sustain political tradition when it goes unchallenged, but it never goes unchallenged in these plays. Thus love of the familiar alone cannot explain the depth of attachment Shakespeare's characters feel toward the past. What, then, can?

Shakespeare shows us that there is a moral element involved in the attachment to tradition. Human beings love the old because they think, or would like to think, that it is good. And it is good because in the beginning everything was good. Put otherwise, if the oldest is the God-given, then "the past . . . ," to quote Pocock again, "was perfect indeed."[3] Attachment to political tradition may then arise out of the desire to be connected in the present to what was simply good in the past. And how better to achieve this connection to a perfect past than to be governed by a perfect being or one associated with a perfect being? This is the deepest case for divine right, but it tells us more about the hopes and desires of subjects than about the actual status of rulers. Shakespeare teaches that men want to believe in and even worship their rulers, that they want to serve, rather than be served by, a being somehow superior to themselves. Perhaps, then, popular attachment to political tradition is best explained by the desire to believe in and subordinate oneself to something simply good.

Unlike King John, who relies exclusively on arms to maintain himself, both Henry IV and Henry V seem to understand the people's deeply moral desire for a connection to the past. Henry IV tries to characterize his rule as consistent with tradition, concocting a hereditary claim to the throne. When this fails to convince anyone, he plans a Crusade to the Holy Land, hoping to associate his kingship, like Richard's, with a divine purpose. Lacking the authority of tradition, Henry appeals to the passions and desires that justify and sustain tradition. In a sense, his son wages the Holy War that he died too soon to carry out. Henry V deliberately characterizes his conquest of France as an expression of God's will, and he as its leader the executor of God's purpose. Like his father, he rightly understands that legitimacy is founded on a passionate desire to be ruled by a morally superior being.

Since attachment to political tradition is ultimately driven by powerful moral longings, this may well explain the willingness of subjects to reject those rulers who enjoy the sanction of tradition but who do not live up to the perfection it promises. Tradition often delivers up ordinary and corrupt rulers, and those excluded from power can hardly be expected to leave well enough alone. Ambitious men will point out and exploit the gap between the promise of tradition and the reality; they will try to manipulate the very passions that sustain tradition, redirecting men's longings for perfection toward themselves. So while customs of succession are designed to clarify who should rule and to enhance their authority, they raise expectations so high that legitimate kings are sure to be challenged by the ambitious. Political traditions are thus both powerful and unstable—powerful because they appeal to high moral longings, unstable because they cannot possibly satisfy them. Put oversimply, if men want gods for rulers, there will be plenty of contenders. Most will eventually disappoint, because we want more than we can have.

Shakespeare and Machiavelli

While no direct evidence exists that Shakespeare read Machiavelli, or, if he did, that he was responding to him, critics have frequently tried to locate Shakespeare's politics in relation to Machiavelli's, a project that is defensible if only because Shakespeare's political actors often resemble the kinds of men Machiavelli celebrates. Like Machiavelli, Shakespeare is preoccupied with the acquisition and maintenance of political power. And as we have seen, the ambition for power often entails violence and deceit, machination, calculation, and ruthless villainy. So the question, "What does Shakespeare think about Machiavelli?," is both understandable and useful. Wyndham Lewis's contention that "the answer would have to be complex"[4] seems to me correct. Shakespeare is not, as the critical consensus holds, a simple opponent of Machiavelli; but he doesn't wholly agree with him either.

If Shakespeare is neither simply pro- or anti-Machiavelli, he does seem to share Machiavelli's view of the likely character of the political world. The history plays confirm Machiavelli's contention that "it is a very natural and ordinary thing to desire to acquire."[5] As a consequence, politics will almost always involve force and fraud, the struggle for power between ambitious and unscrupulous men; polities will almost always be at or near war, whether foreign or civil. Shakespeare shares Machiavelli's political realism: he too begins from the premise that the struggle for power is more central and more reliable than the struggle for justice.

Those who are willing to concede Shakespeare's realism but unwilling to believe him a true "Machiavellian" often argue that Shakespeare is what I will call a "moral realist." He thinks that for good guys to succeed, they must be willing and able to compete with the bad guys, to use Machiavellian methods for laudable ends. On this view, Shakespeare provides in the history plays a road map to help the well-meaning negotiate a terrain populated by unscrupulous men. At first glance, this is an attractive position, and it makes sense of plays like *The Tempest*, the *Henry VI* series, and *As You Like It*, where well-intentioned but politically naive rulers lose out to ambitious and savvy rivals concerned only with securing power. The moral realist position is probably best illustrated by *Macbeth*, where Duncan (too good) loses out to Macbeth (too bad), who loses out to Malcolm (just right).[6] But the history plays I have written about cast doubt upon the moral realist thesis. For one thing, unambiguously moral actors are in short supply. The obvious problem of finding the requisite qualities—hard-headed realism and moral scruples—in the same individual is exacerbated by the fact that genuinely moral men are as rare in politics as ambitious men are common. The usual case in the history plays is not good men losing out to bad men (Duncans falling to Macbeths), but equally selfish and ambitious men contending for power. John, Richard, Henry IV, and Henry V may have their good moments, but no one could confuse them with Prospero or Duke Senior or Henry VI. Even if one could teach men who love justice more than power to care equally for both, one must first find them in the political arena. Furthermore, moral intentions are not always beneficial. As I have tried to show throughout this book, Shakespeare agrees with Machiavelli that moral scruples can be a hindrance to prudent and necessary acts. He agrees, as well, that the self-interest of the ambitious can be politically beneficial, that one needn't intend good to effect good. So however attractive, the moral realist thesis does not adequately address three objections: (1) the moral often lack realism, (2) the realistic often lack morality, and (3) selfish men can, however inadvertently, serve the common good. I doubt Shakespeare would object to moral realism; he just wouldn't find it very realistic.

If Shakespeare is skeptical about the possibilities of moral realism, then what is his purpose in exposing the often brutal and unseemly world of English politics? If he is not simply interested in warning good men what they are up against, then what is he doing? Perhaps we should take a step back and ask about Machiavelli's purpose: why does *he* write openly and admiringly about men whose daily bread is force and fraud? Paradoxically, Machiavelli's purpose in exposing the unsavory realities of political life is somehow moral. He brings to light the seamy underbelly of political practice in the hope that such honesty will contribute to a more stable political order. Liberating ambition might sound like a prescription for disaster, but Machiavelli makes a good case—and by now a familiar one—that elevating self-interest over moral concerns can benefit both ruler and ruled. If we could all just acknowledge self-interest, rulers wouldn't need to pretend to be better than they are, and subjects wouldn't insist on more than is humanly possible. Machiavelli thus anticipates Adam Smith's "invisible hand" and Hamilton and Madison's argument that the prudent management of self-interest is our best political hope.

Those who read *The Prince* as a handbook for the ambitious rather than a blueprint for the common good are half right.

Machiavelli forthrightly addresses his teaching to the ambitious, to those who care more for power than the public good. But since it is the ambitious who cause the problem of civil disorder, and since one cannot just wish them away, it is to the ambitious that Machiavelli looks in providing a solution. His strategy has always alarmed decent men, for Machiavelli advises the ambitious to be more selfish, to think ceaselessly and imaginatively of their own interests. Perhaps most famously, he advises princes "to learn to be able not to be good,"[7] to cultivate moral indifference in the service of their ambition to rule. He underlines this point with numerous examples of princes who lose power when they place the welfare of the people, or moral scruples, above their own security. A prince should only concern himself with others to benefit himself, should only be "moral" when a prudent regard for his own safety requires it.

Once one recovers from Machiavelli's bold alliance with the ambitious and his audacious assault on morality, it becomes clearer how his policy might benefit the people as well as the prince. If a weak prince invites society-wracking challenges to his power, a strong and prudently self-regarding prince discourages and eliminates rivals, providing a peaceful and stable environment for everyone. A prince's security is the people's security too. Machiavelli goes one step further: a prudent prince will treat the people well. Machiavelli's well-deserved reputation as an unscrupulous advisor to the ambitious gets more attention than his often benign advice: in order to stay in power, a prince must "satisfy the people." This, it turns out, requires very little. Unlike the nobility, who themselves want to rule, the people want simply "not to be oppressed." Since "one of the most powerful remedies that a prince has against conspiracies is not to be hated by the people," and since "[w]hat makes him hated above all . . . is to be rapacious and a usurper of the property and the women of his subjects," a successful ruler need only let the people pursue their lives in peace: "he should inspire his citizens to follow their pursuits quietly, in trade and in agriculture and in every other pursuit of men, so that one person does not fear to adorn his possessions lest they be taken away from him, and another to open up a trade for fear of taxes."[8] When Machiavelli counsels reliance on one's own arms, he really means that one ought to arm the people: "[f]or when they are armed, those arms become yours; those whom you suspected become faithful, and those who were faithful remain so; and from subjects they are made into your partisans."[9] In short, a ruler's security is best preserved by not abusing the very subjects upon whom he must rely to defend himself. The key to political stability is a de facto contract, or prudent accommodation, between ruler and ruled. While the liberal elements I have emphasized do not constitute the whole of Machiavelli's thought,[10] they are consistent with the overarching argument of *The Prince* that we ignore self-interest in politics at our peril.

Does Shakespeare have something similar in mind? Does he, like Machiavelli, think that there is too much concern with morality in politics, that we need a more realistic appreciation of ambition in order to arrive at a political solution? It seems at first glance absurd to think that Shakespeare, who in the course of five plays shows us three political murders, numerous executions, four civil wars, and an unjust conquest, might agree with Machiavelli that politics suffers from too much morality. But as I have argued, a ruler's tender conscience often causes more political harm than does a prudent regard for his own security. King John, for example, serves England's welfare while pursuing his own ambition to rule because his (legitimate) opponent is allied with England's enemies. But John's fit of conscience after ordering the assassination of his opponent Arthur leads him into an unwise alliance with the pope, and to neglect preparations for the defense of England against the French invasion. John's guilt over his treatment of Arthur only imperils England. Similarly, Shakespeare shows us how Bolingbroke's selfish ambition for power benefits England by ridding her of a corrupt despot. But Bolingbroke's subsequent doubt about the justice of his usurpation prevents him from acting as decisively as he should have against his opponents. As a consequence, his reign is dominated by civil war. Finally, if Richard II had shown a more prudent regard for his own security by paying attention to the needs of his subjects, he too might have spared England a civil war. So the history plays certainly offer support for the Machiavellian thesis that self-interest, rather than a concern with morality, can benefit both ruler and ruled, and so provide a more reliable formula for stability and peace.

But Shakespeare has doubts about the benefits of self-interest because he has doubts about the possibility of reconfiguring politics on a more "realistic" basis. He does not seem to think that politics can be understood in terms of power alone, as a system of contending interests that can be arranged in a way that will satisfy all. Politics is always a moral arena too. The history plays lead us to wonder whether actual rulers can act consistently with the moral indifference that Machiavelli recommends. Perhaps more importantly, Shakespeare appears to teach that subjects will not tolerate such behavior. Even if princes could "learn to be able not to be good" when necessity requires it, they might not be able to sustain the support of subjects who expect far more of them.

To be sure, Machiavelli is aware of this problem. Because the people are more moral than the ambitious men competing to rule them, he repeatedly advises princes to *appear* virtuous, which, while hardly the same thing as being virtuous, nevertheless calls into question the possibility of stripping the political world of moral concerns. When he notes that the people "are taken in by the *appearance* and the outcome"[11] of a prince's actions, he suggests that praise will be given not to success simply, but to the right kind of success. Appearing moral, Machiavelli assures us, is sufficient, for "men are so simple and so obedient to present necessities that he who deceives will *always* find someone who will let himself be deceived."[12] The fact that moral deceivers will *always* find a sympathetic audience suggests that most men always need a moral message. Thus the brutally effective Agathocles, who won and kept power by practicing "savage cruelty and inhumanity," will not "be celebrated among the most excellent men."[13] There are limits to the kinds of behavior human beings will praise, or even, in the long run, tolerate. Attention to the moral expectations of the people is apparently necessary.

But on other occasions, Machiavelli downplays the need for a prince to appear moral: "one should not care about incurring the reputation of those vices without which it is difficult to save one's state."[14] He even offers assurance to those who cannot, or do not, pay attention to the moral expectations of the people: "[a]nd truly it is a very natural and ordinary thing to desire to acquire, and *always*, when men do it who can, they will be praised or not blamed."[15] Nothing succeeds like success. On this view, the *way* one succeeds is apparently unimportant. Perhaps that is too strong, for Machiavelli does acknowledge a line that no prudent prince should cross: he should not, as I noted above, violate the women or the property of his subjects. The question is whether this bottom-line concession to the interests and sensibilities of the people can provide an enduring substitute for higher moral needs. When he describes the success of Ferdinand, who appealed to the moral fanaticism of his Catholic subjects and followed a policy of "pious cruelty" toward Muslims and Jews, Machiavelli suggests at the very least that one can use extreme moral rhetoric and policy to one's advantage. But Machiavelli may well have looked forward to a time when such appeals would ring hollow, when most men would consult their interest as a matter of habit, and ignore or condemn in the name of peace and stability such dangerous appeals to fanatical moral longings.[16]

If Machiavelli is ambiguous about the need to address the moral concerns of the body politic, and hopeful about the possibility of reconfiguring politics on a more realistic (i.e., less moral) basis, Shakespeare is neither. He does not think it possible to strip politics of moral concerns, or to reduce morality to Machiavelli's bottom-line prohibition against despoiling one's subjects. But, to repeat, his objection to the Machiavellian project is not the usual one, that moral scruples provide a useful check on the excesses of ambition. Moral concerns are not, as I pointed out above, reliably present in the ambitious; and when they are present, they either come too late (the deed is done), or do not alter subsequent behavior.[17] Furthermore, moral concerns sometimes get in the way of beneficial actions. John's and Henry's fits of conscience inhibit their ability to think clearly about their own interest, which happens in both cases to coincide with England's interest. And the Bastard's sympathy for John's murdered opponent Arthur, while understandable and in some ways commendable, indicates a blindness on his part to the threat Arthur posed to the autonomy of England.

The hope that only moral men rule is unrealistic, and in some cases contrary to what is most needed. But the notion that the people could come to accept these facts, as Machiavelli sometimes seems to hope, is also unrealistic. It is here that Shakespeare's substantial agreement with Machiavelli comes to an end. Shakespeare is far more sensitive to the moral expectations of the ruled than Machiavelli is. In *King John*, for example, the people turn against their own king—and their own interest—at the behest of the pope. When the choice is between an ambitious and self-serving usurper and the spokesman for

God, the people choose the latter, even though the pope's meddling will result in civil war and foreign invasion. Perhaps John should have eliminated the pope, as Machiavelli might have advised.[18] But when he moves against the Church in England, John finds himself more unpopular than ever. The longing on the part of the people for moral authority, even when it contradicts their true interest, calls into question Machiavelli's hope that politics can be reconstituted on the basis of self-interest.

What is at issue is the extent to which politics can be made more rational, more realistic, more consistent with the actual behavior of ambitious men. Can we simply abandon our longing for "imagined republics and principalities that have never been seen or known to exist in truth"?[19] Or is our longing for perfect justice so powerful that it cannot in any significant way be suppressed? In his treatment of legitimacy and its relation to custom, issues to which Machiavelli pays comparatively little attention,[20] Shakespeare concludes that it is unrealistic to underestimate the power of idealism in politics. As I pointed out above, attachment to political tradition, as well as the willingness to ignore it, is motivated by a deep desire to be ruled by a morally superior being. The people do not so much consent as they submit to authority; they do not choose the ruler who best serves their interest, but the one who seems to come to them from on high. Their moral expectations are so great that they are willing to believe their rulers descend upon them from a glorious past, or are recommended by God.

If Shakespeare's analysis is correct, then Machiavelli's assertion that the people want only "not to be oppressed" is questionable at best. This is not because they themselves want to rule, as the nobles surely do; the people want not to be left alone, but to obey a morally worthy ruler. So Machiavelli's contention that a ruler can, when necessary, safely disregard the moral expectations of his subjects is also doubtful. Shakespeare gives a number of examples of prudent and necessary acts that provoke popular dissent of varying degrees. King Richard was forced to eliminate his rival Gloucester in order to remain in power, but popular disapproval of that act was so powerful that Bolingbroke made it the centerpiece of his successful effort to unseat Richard. Bolingbroke's subsequent elimination of Richard, an unpopular despot, spawned years of civil war. King John's assassination of Arthur, while arguably justified and in the best interest of England, was considered so abhorrent that a portion of the English joined the French in trying to unseat John and replace him with the dauphin. On Shakespeare's view, Machiavelli's hope to diminish the influence of morality in politics is overly optimistic.

So where does this leave us? I have argued, first, that Shakespeare agrees with Machiavelli that political practice can be accurately described in terms of force and fraud, and second, that he questions Machiavelli's hope that most men can be persuaded to abandon their demands for perfect justice. If our expectations are unrealistic, so too is the hope that we can moderate them. The gulf between the way politics is actually practiced and the way we would like it to be practiced is significant and probably unresolvable. Because the ambitious and the moral want such different things, the quest for power and the quest for justice are ultimately irreconcilable. I think it might be fair to say that Shakespeare's view of politics is tragic. At the very least, he points to a fundamental split between what we want and what we can have without proposing a solution.

Shakespeare's deep pessimism about the prospects for ever overcoming the limits of politics may account for the difference in the way he and Machiavelli present the political world. Machiavelli is famous for his bold and almost gleeful exposure of all that is ugly about politics: the hypocrisy, the ruthless ambition, the violence and deceit. He does so, as I have argued, in the hopes of refounding politics on a more realistic basis. Shakespeare exposes the same ugly things, but he does so with reticence and evident disappointment, and without any sense that something good may come of such honesty. Perhaps as an act of kindness, Shakespeare, unlike Machiavelli, delicately covers over again the ugliness he has exposed. He allows us to believe that his political actors are better than they really are, camouflaging the low motives which frequently underlie apparently public-spirited acts. He encourages us to attribute political failure to moral defects when simple miscalculation would suffice to explain it. And his toughest characters are never as tough as they first seem; all eventually experience moral misgivings. Shakespeare is perhaps most delicate in his treatment of conscience: he exaggerates its hold over the ambitious. It is difficult to believe that those capable of doing the kinds of things Shakespeare's political actors do must suffer from them. When the astonishingly brutal Richard III says "I rather hate myself / For hateful deeds committed by myself!" (V.iii.190–91), we naturally wonder whether this is truly so. He certainly doesn't hate himself enough to abandon the quest for power. Henry V's expressions of regret are equally suspicious. Shakespeare must know that power can be and is pursued without regret. But instead of showing us that, he shows us self-doubt and repentance; in the end, the ambitious are somehow humane. Even if these expressions of regret are in every case genuine, they always come after the fact, or fail to transform subsequent behavior: conscience is shown to be an insufficient restraint on ambition. So we are left with ambition on the one hand, and the desire for justice on the other. While neither of these impulses can get the upper hand, Shakespeare allows us to hope that justice will prevail because he knows that we cannot do otherwise. Shakespeare is gentler than Machiavelli because he is more pessimistic than Machiavelli.

Appendix

The Omission of the Magna Carta in *King John*

One of the questions most frequently asked about *King John* is prompted not by the play itself but by a general knowledge of history: why doesn't Shakespeare deal with, or even mention, the Magna Carta in *King John*? This is a legitimate question, for a play about King John could have provided Shakespeare with a perfect opportunity to make clear his views about constitutionalism. As the heirs and beneficiaries of that liberal document, we are taught in high school history classes that John was its villainous opponent and are thus surprised that Shakespeare does not dramatize perhaps the only thing we know about that time.

John was pressured by force of arms to sign the Magna Carta toward the end of his reign (1215) and spent the rest of his life resisting it. The document limited the king's hitherto (more or less) unlimited powers, giving his subjects greater control over their property and putting some regularity and uniformity into the judicial system. A council of twenty-five barons, chosen by the nobility, became the rightful legislators and executors of the law. Hume's characterization of the Magna Carta in his *History of England* strikes an immediate and sympathetic chord in all of those for whom liberal doctrine is but boilerplate politics:

> . . . the former articles of the great charter contain such migrations and explanations of the feudal law as are reasonable and equitable and . . . the later involve all the chief outlines of a legal government, and provide for the

> equal distribution of justice and the free enjoyment of property—the great objects for which political society was at first founded by men, which peoples have a perpetual and unalienable right to recall, and which no time, nor precedent, nor statute, nor positive institution, ought to deter them from keeping ever uppermost in their thoughts and attention.[1]

Speculation on why Shakespeare did not include the Magna Carta in *King John* reveals more about the critics' political narrow-mindedness than it does about Shakespeare's own motives. It is thought by many that if Shakespeare knew about the Magna Carta he would have included it in his play; he didn't include it, therefore, he must not have known about it. This argument rests on the questionable premise that what is important to us must have been important to Shakespeare. A variation on this argument is that Shakespeare had some knowledge of the document, but "a very inadequate sense of its importance."[2] Lest this be seen as condescending to Shakespeare's intelligence, the critics point out that constitutionalism was neither popular nor much talked about during the well-liked Queen Elizabeth's reign, so Shakespeare, like the rest of the Elizabethans, couldn't have been expected to give it much thought. He was, to use contemporary parlance, "culturally bound." Supposedly textual arguments point out that Shakespeare's main source for this play, *The Troublesome Raign of King John*, does not mention the Magna Carta, and thus neither does Shakespeare. But the earlier play was based on Holinshed's *Chronicles*, and Holinshed records all of the events surrounding the signing of the charter. Why Shakespeare, who was a great reader of Holinshed and who based many of his other plays on Holinshed's accounts, should have neglected to read him while preparing this play is unclear. And besides Holinshed, there were plenty of other accounts of John and the Magna Carta available to Shakespeare. Because we cannot know for certain just what Shakespeare did or did not read, these textual arguments are really just the same old politically influenced speculations that Shakespeare couldn't have read these accounts because if he did he would have included them in his play.

Unless there is overwhelming evidence to the contrary, I think it only fair to suppose that Shakespeare knew what he was doing here. The evidence that he had no knowledge of the charter or that he failed to understand its significance is flimsy enough that one can assume with equal confidence that he did know about it and that its absence from *King John* was intentional. The question, then, is why? I offer below some suggestions.

One reason may be that Shakespeare thought constitutionalism was posterior to, and less fundamental than, those political problems it was meant to address. Shakespeare's history plays always deal with the most extreme political situations, with intrigue and political murder, with civil and foreign wars, with religious and political fanaticisms. He seems to teach that these extreme situations and the extreme actions they elicit reveal politics at its most elemental. Our contemporary understanding of the political elevates the peaceful and stable times and the constitutional processes they allow to the norm, while relegating crises to the realm of the exceptional. But by equating politics with the more or less smooth operation of institutional structures, we forget the reasons for their original existence. These legal arrangements were proposed as antidotes to the very problems Shakespeare dramatizes in *King John*: doubtful legitimacy, civil war, and religious fanaticism. What was once understood as an antidote is now taken to be the whole political ballgame. Shakespeare's history plays provide us with a panoramic picture of pre-liberal politics, restoring to our imagination a much fuller (and more dangerous) vision of the political than we are accustomed to.

Shakespeare, in other words, may have thought it more important to expose the fundamental political problems than to examine a possible legal solution. But the fact that he doesn't even mention the charter, that he doesn't point toward a constitutional way of deciding how power should be allocated and employed, is surely significant. Shakespeare may very well have thought that the political ambition of men could not be tamed by constitutional means and that the same old struggles for power would continue under any political arrangement. On this understanding, political legitimacy will always be tenuous, the threat of civil war always real. Shakespeare understands these problems to be permanent ones, co-existent with politics as such.

We must remember that the Magna Carta was proposed by self-interested politicians. The barons were less interested in the "rights of man" than they were in avoiding taxation, protecting their property, and generally taking for themselves as much of the king's powers as they could. The nobles, according to Hume, "were necessitated to insert in [the charter] other clauses of a more extensive and more beneficent nature" only because "they could not expect the concurrence of the people without comprehending, together with their own, the interests of inferior ranks of men."[3] On Hume's account, the liberalism of the Magna Carta was almost accidental, a matter of political expedience. "Had the charter contained nothing further," Hume says, "national happiness and liberty had been very little promoted by it, as it would only have tended to increase the power and independence of an order of men who were already too powerful, and whose yoke might have become more heavy on the people than even that of an absolute monarch."[4] King John was forced to sign the document and as soon as he was safe declared it null and void. The struggle for power between the nobles and the king continued for hundreds of years. If Shakespeare thought constitutionalism would not work, he was right for a very long time concerning England and is still right for a good deal of the world. Even in the United States, where succession is smooth and public and where legitimacy is unquestioned, the Civil War testifies to the fact that the constitutional arrangements we adopted are not foolproof. When the institutional mechanisms broke down, we were forced back upon a more rudimentary politics, relying on the force of arms and the prudence of statesmen. In the crunch, at least, men matter more than constitutions.

Notes

Chapter 1. Shakespeare's Politics

1. The popular opinion about Shakespeare's "universalism" is challenged and criticized by a number of influential contemporary academics. Howard and O'Connor argue that

> claims about Shakespeare as the bearer of universal truths serve an oppressive function when they render illegitimate readings produced outside the dominant ideologies which secure a society's understanding of what the true is. As feminists and Third World critics, among others, have suggested, when texts are said to speak for humankind, humankind often shrinks radically to include only those within a traditional pale of privilege. This volume aims to question claims of Shakespeare's universality and to reveal ways in which historically specific factors determine the "Shakespeare" produced in criticism, in the classroom, and on the stage. (Jean E. Howard and Marion F. O'Connor, *Shakespeare Reproduced: The Text in History and Ideology* [New York: Methuen, 1987], 4)

According to Ivo Kamps, it is the political Right that perpetuates the notion of Shakespeare's universalism, and some on the Left take it as their critical duty to expose and question that view:

> the prevailing sentiment on the Right is that Shakespeare transcends his historical moment—he is not for an age but for all time—because his genius allowed him to capture what is most true, universal, and enduring about human nature. A recent wave of counter-criticism, however, has focused close attention on the various ways in which the playwright's texts participate in, are subversive of, or reflect on Renaissance institutional practice and ideologies designed to oppress and control the people. . . . In addition to a greater self-awareness, a large contingent of Marxist, cultural

> materialist, and feminist critics consider it a crucial part of their mission not only to reinterpret Shakespeare but also to expose the conservative ideologies which quietly shape the orthodox readings of his plays. (Ivo Kamps, "Introduction: Ideology and Its Discontents," in *Shakespeare Left and Right* [New York: Routledge, 1991], 1)

2. L. C. Knights, *Further Explorations* (London: Chatto and Windus, 1946), 12–13.

3. Harold Jenkins, "Shakespeare's History Plays: 1900–1951." *Shakespeare Survey VI* (Cambridge, 1953), 3.

4. A. F. Pollard, *History of England from the Ascension of Edward VI to the Death of Elizabeth* (London, 1910), 440, quoted and discussed by Howard B. White, *Antiquity Forgot: Essays on Shakespeare, Bacon, and Rembrandt* (The Hague: Martinus Nijhoff, 1978), 44. White suggests that for Pollard, "the questions with which alone political history are concerned" are constitutional questions, and that "Pollard was no doubt referring to the well-known fact that in *King John* Shakespeare makes no mention of the Magna Carta." I treat the omission of the Magna Carta in *King John* in the appendix.

5. L. C. Knights, 13.

6. Alvin B. Kernan, "Shakespeare and the Rhetoric of Politics," in *Politics, Power, and Shakespeare*, ed. Frances McNeely Leonard (Arlington: University of Texas at Arlington, 1981), 47.

7. Allan Bloom, *Shakespeare's Politics* (Chicago: University of Chicago Press, 1964), 4; Speech given at the University of Chicago, Woodward Court, May 6, 1980.

8. Letter to J. H. Hackett, August 17, 1863, from *Abraham Lincoln: His Speeches and Writings*, ed. Roy P. Basler (Cleveland: The World Publishing Co., 1946).

> 9. You may say, and Judge Douglas has intimated the same thing, that all this difficulty in regard to the institution of slavery is the mere agitation of office-seekers and ambitious northern politicians. He thinks we want to get "his place," I suppose. I agree that there are office-seekers among us. The Bible says somewhere that we are desperately selfish. I think we would have discovered that fact without the Bible. I do not claim that I am any less so than the average of men, but I do claim that I am not more selfish than Judge Douglas. (Lincoln's reply to Senator Douglas at Alton, October 15, 1858. *The Lincoln-Douglas Debates*, ed. Robert W. Johannsen [New York: Oxford University Press, 1965], 314).

10. Niccolo Machiavelli, *The Discourses,* trans. Father Leslie J. Walker. Ed. Bernard Crick (Harmondsworth, England: Penguin Classics, 1986), III.4, 395.

11. The history plays are concerned with a hereditary monarchy, but Shakespeare treats a variety of different polities, both ancient and modern, in other plays.

12. Michael Walzer, *The Revolution of the Saints: A Study in the Origins of Radical Politics* (Cambridge: Harvard University Press, 1965), 1.

13. Walzer, 8.

14. Irving Ribner, *The English History Play in the Age of Shakespeare* (Princeton: Princeton University Press, 1957), 318; see also Richard Strier, "Faithful Servants: Shakespeare's Praise of Disobedience," in *The Historical Renaissance,* ed. Heather Dubrow and Richard Strier (Chicago: University of Chicago Press, 1988), 104: "Whether there were limits to the obedience that inferiors owed to their social and political superiors was one of the great questions of Renaissance and Reformation thinking." The paragraphs that follow rely heavily on Ribner's brief summary of sixteenth-century political thought, 309–18. For more detailed accounts, see J. W. Allen, *A History of Political Thought in the Sixteenth Century* (London: Methuen and Co. Ltd., 1928); John Neville Figgis, *The Divine Right of Kings* (Cambridge: University Press, 1922); Michael Walzer, *The Revolution of the Saints*; J. G. A. Pocock, *The Machiavellian Moment* (Princeton: Princeton University Press, 1975), especially III.X, "The Problem of English Machiavellianism: Modes of Civic Consciousness before the Civil War"; and E. M. W. Tillyard, *The Elizabethan World Picture* (London: Chatto and Windus, 1943).

15. Strier calls the homily "a brilliant piece of writing . . . ," 108.

16. Ribner (*English History Play,* 313) quotes from the homily, reprinted in John Griffiths, ed., *The Two Books of Homilies Appointed to be Read in Churches* (Oxford: The University Press, 1859).

17. Walzer, 155–56.

18. Walzer, 158. The central quotation is from Hooker's *Ecclesiastic Polity,* Book VIII.

19. Ribner, *English History Play,* 314.

20. Ribner, 315–16.

21. Walzer, 158–59.

22. Edward Pechter, *What Was Shakespeare?: Renaissance Plays and Changing Critical Practice* (Ithaca: Cornell University Press, 1995), 67.

23. Pechter, 59. Pechter continues:

> We might debate the extent and flexibility of this determination and withhold or accord value as we prefer. We might also debate the purpose or the intention of new historicists in claiming not to subordinate the text to social history. Are they trying to fool their readers, or have they succeeded in fooling themselves—and in either case, why? There can be no debate, however, about the notion of dependency itself. If the new historicists abandoned the notion, they would forfeit altogether their claim to our allegiance. (59)

24. According to Richard Levin, by "historical context," feminist, neo-Marxist, and new historicist critics "almost always [mean] some conception of 'power,' defined in terms of either class or gender" (Richard Levin, "The Problem of 'Context' in Interpretation," in *Shakespeare and the Dramatic Tradition*, ed. Elton and Long [Newark: University of Delaware Press, 1989], 92).

25. Paul Cantor, "Stephen Greenblatt's New Historicist Vision," *Academic Questions* (Fall 1993): 25.

26. Cantor, "Stephen Greenblatt's New Historicist Vision," 30–31.

27. Cantor, "Shakespeare—'For All Time'?," *Public Interest* (Winter, 1993): 37–38.

28. Why Shakespeare should provoke moral outrage for expressing views that he could not have but held is puzzling. I suspect the purpose is to correct the popular opinion that Shakespeare is one of history's good guys.

29. Pechter, 70.

30. Greenblatt, *Shakespearean Negotiations* (Berkeley: University of California Press, 1988), 54.

31. Annabel Patterson, *Shakespeare and the Popular Voice* (Cambridge, MA: Basil Blackwell, 1989).

32. In her chapter on *Henry V* ("Back by Popular Demand: The Two Versions of *Henry V*," 71–92), Patterson concentrates almost exclusively on a single passage in the play, a reference to the earl of Essex, a rival of Queen Elizabeth more sympathetic than she to popular interests. Patterson establishes Shakespeare's connection with Essex, and proceeds to speculate on how the political climate (Essex launched a failed

coup against Elizabeth) could account for the difference between earlier and more patriotic, and later and more skeptical, texts of *Henry V*. Like the new historicists, Patterson is primarily interested in situating *Henry V* in historical context and thereby establishing its meaning.

33. Patterson, 9.

34. "Being an author of sorts myself, and accustomed to having my intentions elucidated in critical reviews, I have no difficulty in positing Shakespeare as a writer whose intentions, if never fully recoverable, are certainly worth debating" (Patterson, 4–5).

35. Patterson, 1.

36. Patterson, 12.

37. Patterson, 4.

38. Cantor, "Shakespeare—'For All Time'?," 37. Cantor sees a political motive in efforts to view Shakespeare as typical of his time:

> By resituating masterpieces of literature within what it calls their historical context, the New Historicism works to assimilate them to the average and everyday in their era, to diminish their aura, ultimately to strip them of their claims to genius. The New Historicism represents the egalitarianism of the contemporary world set loose to rewrite the cultural history of the past. ("Stephen Greenblatt's New Historicist Vision," 25)

I am inclined to agree with Cantor's interpretation for two reasons. First, many contemporary political critics admit forthrightly to pursuing an egalitarian agenda in their work. Second, it seems to me unlikely that so many academics could have thought through and been persuaded by one of the most difficult philosophical positions—the truth of historicism.

39. This does not mean that recovering Milton's views is easy. "Blake and Shelley had a point," according to Gerald Graff, "when they said that Milton was of the Devil's party without knowing it—that the action of *Paradise Lost* functioned as an implicit critique of the Christian theology the work was intended to justify" (Gerald Graff, "Ordinary People/Academic Critics," in *Shakespeare Left and Right*, ed. Ivo Kamps [New York: Routledge, 1991], 107). Considering his association with those contemporary critics who are deeply suspicious about our ability to say *anything* certain about an author's intention or the meaning of his work in general, Graff's comment is surprising: he speaks here as though it were possible to recover not only an author's conscious intention, but his unconscious intention as well. One frequently finds amongst contemporary critics a large chasm between stated philosophical premises and

actual critical practice. Those numerous critics committed to the position that it is impossible to arrive at a single or definitive meaning, that there can only be a plurality of "interpretations," nevertheless often find themselves attacking Shakespeare for *his* views (e.g., " . . . Shakespeare's own ideology is as patriarchal as John of Gaunt's. . . " [Graham Holderness, "'A Woman's War': A Feminist Reading of *Richard II*," in *Shakespeare Left and Right*, 179]. It should be noted that this is *not* Holderness's view). The moral outrage typically directed at Shakespeare by contemporary political critics for having the wrong opinions (about women, class, race, imperialism, etc.) seems to me an unlikely response if one truly believed Shakespeare's views were inaccessible.

40. His primary historical source is usually thought to be Holinshed, upon whom Hume also relies in his *History of England.*

41. John Locke, *Two Treatises of Government,* ed. Peter Laslett (Cambridge: Cambridge University Press, 1988), 267–68.

42. Aristotle, *Politics,* trans. Ernest Barker (London: Oxford University Press, 1981), III.xv.

43. Howard White, 55. For an interesting account of how the American political system is supposed to encourage the election of "qualified" representatives, see Martin Diamond, "The Federalist," in *History of Political Philosophy,* 3rd edition, ed. Leo Strauss and Joseph Cropsey (Chicago: The University of Chicago Press, 1987), 659–79.

44. Walzer, 5.

45. Pocock, 9.

46. Fortesque and Pocock are concerned mostly with laws, not with polities or regimes. But the same arguments here made in defense of laws could be made in defense of polities in general.

47. Sir John Fortesque, *De Laudibus Legum Anglie,* 1468, quoted by Pocock, 13–14.

48. Pocock, 23–24.

49. So powerful, according to John Stuart Mill, is "the magical influence of custom," that this second nature "is continually mistaken for the first" (J. S. Mill, *On Liberty* [London: Penguin Classics, 1974], 64).

50. Pocock, 24; cf., 17, where Pocock notes that " . . . in the concepts of 'use' and 'second nature' may be found the beginnings of the historicist doctrine that we become what we do and so make ourselves."

51. Pocock, 15.

52. Edmund Burke, from *Selected Writings and Speeches,* ed. Peter J. Stanlis (Chicago: Regnery Gateway, 1963), 223, 331, 330.

53. Pocock, 25.

54. Pocock, 15.

55. One also encounters a respect for custom in legal debates about Supreme Court jurisprudence. Arguments in favor of following legal precedent often resemble those made by Fortesque and Burke in favor of following custom: some laws are legitimate simply because we've become accustomed to them, because they have, over time, become a part of the fabric of American life.

56. Pocock, 27.

57. Machiavelli, *The Discourses,* I.25, 175–76.

58. "The first and most fundamental cause of revolution is . . . the different conceptions men have of justice" (Harry V. Jaffa, "Aristotle," in *History of Political Philosophy,* 2nd edition [Chicago: Rand McNally, 1972], 122, quoted by Grant Mindle, "Shakespeare's Demonic Prince," *Interpretation* 20, no. 3 [Spring 1993]: 260).

59. White, 49.

60. White, 49.

61. White, 49.

62. White, 49.

63. I will discuss Machiavelli at greater length in the following section.

64. Pocock, 340–41.

65. James Madison, *The Federalist,* ed. Jacob E. Cooke (Middletown: Wesleyan University Press, 1961), no. 43, 297.

66. *The Republic of Plato,* trans. Allan Bloom (New York: Basic Books Inc., 1968), 338e–339a.

67. E. M. W. Tillyard, *Shakespeare's History Plays* (London: Chatto and Windus, 1944), 21.

68. M. M. Reese, *The Cease of Majesty* (London: Edward Arnold Ltd., 1961), vii.

69. Tillyard, 21.

70. Tracy Strong, "Shakespeare: Elizabethan Statecraft and Machiavellianism," in *The Artist and Political Vision,* ed. Benjamin R. Barber and Michael J. Gargas McGrath (New Brunswick: Transaction Books, 1982), 194.

71. Reese, 92.

72. All citations to Shakespeare's plays follow the Arden edition.

73. Stephen Greenblatt, *Shakespearean Negotiations,* 20. Greenblatt is speaking here of *1,2HIV* and *HV.*

74. *Henry VI,* Part 1, V.iv.74; *Henry VI,* Part 3, III.ii.193; *The Merry Wives of Windsor,* III.i.92–93.

75. See Tillyard, 23; White, 14, note 24; and Moody Prior, *The Drama of Power* (Evanston: Northwestern University Press, 1973), 291. I tend to agree with Prior's assessment that "whether [Shakespeare] knew *The Prince* at first hand is beyond reasonable conjecture. . . . "

76. Allan Bloom, *Love and Friendship* (New York: Simon and Schuster, 1993), 330.

77. Christian Gauss, introduction to the Mentor edition of *The Prince* (New York: New American Library, 1952), 8.

78. Machiavelli, *The Prince,* trans. Harvey Mansfield (Chicago: University of Chicago Press, 1985), chapter 17, 67.

79. *The Prince,* chapter 3, 8.

80. *The Prince,* chapter 3, 16; see also chapter 20, 85–86.

81. *The Prince,* chapter 15, 61.

82. *The Prince,* chapter 15, 61.

83. Paul Cantor, "Prospero's Republic," in *Shakespeare as Political Thinker,* ed. John Alvis and Thomas G. West (Durham: Carolina Academic Press, 1981), 246.

84. *The Prince,* chapter 15, 62.

85. *The Prince,* chapter 15, 62.

86. *The Prince,* chapter 17, 66–67.

87. *The Prince,* chapter 18, 70.

88. Reese, 146.

89. John Danby, *Shakespeare's Doctrine of Nature* (London: Faber and Faber, 1949), 90.

90. Wyndham Lewis, *The Lion and the Fox* (London: G. Richards Ltd., 1927), 178.

91. Danby, 201.

92. White, 7.

93. *The Discourses,* II.2, 278.

94. John Alvis, *Shakespeare's Understanding of Honor* (Durham: Carolina Academic Press, 1990), 60.

95. *The Discourses,* II.2, 227.

96. At *Discourses* III.5, 395–97, Machiavelli seems rather favorable to monarchy and claims that there is such a thing as "liberty" under a prince.

97. *The Prince,* chapter 18, 70–71.

98. *The Prince,* chapter 18, 71.

99. *The Discourses,* I.12, 145.

100. *The Discourses,* I.12, 144.

101. Knights, 13.

102. Alvis, *Shakespeare's Understanding of Honor,* 60.

103. Tillyard, 23.

104. Reese, 102.

105. Reese, 96–97.

106. Prior, 292.

107. Reese, 102.

108. *The Discourses,* I.9, 132.

109. Reese, 93–94.

110. Prior, 299.

111. Reese, 146, emphasis supplied.

112. Ribner, 162, emphasis supplied.

113. See Nathan Tarcov, "Quentin Skinner's Method and Machiavelli's *Prince,*" in *Meaning and Context: Quentin Skinner and His Critics,* ed. James Tully (Princeton: Princeton University Press, 1988), 199, 202.

114. *The Prince,* chapter 17, 67.

115. Tillyard, 22.

116. Prior, 293.

117. Leo Strauss, *Thoughts on Machiavelli* (Chicago: University of Chicago Press, 1958), 295.

118. This is not to say that Machiavelli never distinguishes between kingship and tyranny. At *Discourses* III.5 he associates kingship with the rule of law and liberty, tyranny with their absence.

119. *The Discourses,* I.3, 112.

120. Reese, 99. Tracy Strong makes a similar point, 194:

> As befits those who do not fit well into the natural order of the world, . . . [Shakespeare's Machiavellians] . . . are almost all men of unnatural birth, men who from their very entrance into the world were somehow cut off from normal parentage and past. Their birth is an objective correlative to their role in the world: they are forces of illegitimacy, destroyers of order, men who neither have nor know a place but are forced to try to make one for themselves. Their world is a world they build, an artifact of their own creation: almost always they stand in opposition to a more regular and happy existence.

121. Reese, 119.

122. Prior, 247.

123. e.g., Hamlet.

124. Reese, 163, viii.

125. Bloom, *Love and Friendship,* 299.

Chapter 2. *King John*

1. One critic judges *King John* "more fundamentally preoccupied with violence than *Richard III*" (John Blanpied, "Stalking 'Strong

Possession' in 'King John,'" in *William Shakespeare, Histories and Poems*, ed. Harold Bloom [New York: Chelsea House, 1986], 278).

2. See E. M. W. Tillyard, *Shakespeare's History Plays* (London: Chatto and Windus, 1944), 8, 21, 23. Tillyard's Shakespeare, according to one dissenting critic, is an "all-weathers champion of the Establishment" (M. M. Reese, *Cease of Majesty* [London: Edward Arnold Ltd., 1961], vii).

3. See Stephen Greenblatt, *Shakespearean Negotiations* (Berkeley: University of California Press, 1988), 56, 60, 62–65.

4. All parenthetical references to the text of *King John* follow the fourth Arden edition, ed. E. A. J. Honigmann (Cambridge, MA: Harvard University Press, 1954).

5. Peter Saccio, *Shakespeare's English Kings: History, Chronicle and Drama* (London: Oxford University Press, 1977), 191–92, 202–3, 206. "Only if we go back to Polydore Vergil, a Catholic historian who reflects medieval monastic chroniclers hostile to John because of his defiance of the pope, do we find charges of usurpation" (203).

6. Actually Angers, the capital of Anjou, an English possession in central France.

7. The Second Folio reads "breast," which seems to me more likely.

8. The Bastard ends his speech with the following comment: "How like you this wild counsel, mighty states? / Smacks it not something of the policy?" (II.i.395–96). As the editor of the Arden edition points out, "policy" means "Machiavellian statesmanship, low cunning." Honigmann contends that "Faulconbridge delights naively in *policy* because it does not come naturally to him" (Arden *King John*, 43). This is borne out later in the Bastard's stunned reaction to King John's policy—murder—toward Arthur.

9. While the historical King John gave Lewis some French lordships as dowry for his wedding, "[t]hese were neither as numerous or as extensive as they appear to be in the play, where John foolishly gives away most of France" (Saccio, 192).

10. John's compromise is a disaster for those interested in preserving the Angevin Empire. Whether England should be large or small, an empire or an island, is a theme running throughout many of the English history plays. Earlier in the play, Austria called England "[t]hat water-walled bulwark, still secure / And confident from foreign purposes . . . "

(II.i.27). In one of the most famous encomiums to England in the history plays, John of Gaunt also identifies England with the island ("this scept'red isle," "this little world," "[t]his precious stone set in the silver sea"), emphasizing its strategic value: "[t]his fortress built by Nature for herself / Against infection and the hand of war . . . " (*Richard II,* II.i.40, 45, 46, 44–45).

11. John knows firsthand about Pandulf's ruthlessness, persuasiveness, and persistence: he was present when Pandulf excommunicated him and promised sainthood to his killer, and he remained present when Pandulf convinced a reluctant King Philip to renege on the peace agreement. John's actions after his victory at Angiers all seem designed to secure his kingship, which he must think remains threatened. Finally, when France does invade England, John is only surprised by the lack of warning from his mother, whom he left behind in France to provide him with such intelligence (see III.ii.11 and IV.ii.116–19).

12. As John makes emphatically clear here, he intends Arthur's murder (see also IV.ii.208–10). But in the scene where Hubert confronts Arthur, he apparently intends (only) to blind Arthur with "hot irons" (IV.i.56–59). Shakespeare seems to combine in a rather confusing way elements of different historical accounts of Arthur's fate. In one account, John orders Arthur blinded and castrated in order to bar him from the throne; in another, Arthur drowns while attempting to escape from prison. In a third account, " . . . considered probable by several recent biographers of John . . . ," a drunken King John kills Arthur with his own hands, then weights him with stones and throws him into the Seine (Saccio, 193–94).

13. Pandulf's magic must already be affecting Lewis, for both King John and his son Henry have superior claims to the throne after Arthur. Lewis, who must know this, either isn't thinking or doesn't think it matters.

14. Speed, *History of Great Britain,* 499, quoted in the New Variorum edition of Shakespeare, *The Life and Death of King John,* ed. Horace Howard Furness (Philadelphia: J. B. Lippincott Company, 1919), 317. Future references to scholarship cited in the New Variorum edition will give author, title, and whatever other information is available, as well as the page number in the New Variorum edition.

15. Quoted by Saccio, who adds that Innocent was "...possibly the greatest ruler of the Middle Ages, and a man indefatigable in his efforts

to assert the authority of the papacy over all the affairs of mankind" (196).

16. " . . . in that beautiful passage where he speaks of the mischiefs following the King's loss of his subjects' hearts . . . [Pandulf's] conduct is remarkable, and was intended, I suppose, to show how much better politicians the Roman courtiers are than divines" (W. Warburton, from his 1747 edition of Shakespeare's works [New Variorum edition, 222]).

17. John's mother Eleanor is a possible exception. Had she lived, she might have given Pandulf more of a run for his money than John does.

18. Furness concurs (New Variorum edition, 319). Porter speculates that John has decided to grant power-sharing concessions to the nobility (New Variorum edition, 319), but I, like most others, can find no reference whatsoever to the Magna Carta in this play (see appendix, below). Calderwood suggests that John has already decided to submit to Pandulf in order to stop the war, but I find this unlikely (see James L. Calderwood, "Commodity and Honour in *King John*," in *Shakespeare: The Histories,* ed. Eugene M. Waith [Englewood Cliffs, NJ: Prentice-Hall, Inc., 1965], 96). Just fifteen lines earlier, John ordered Peter of Pomphret imprisoned, to be hanged "on that day at noon, whereon he says / I shall yield up my crown" (IV.ii.156–57). John sounds defiant, unlike a man planning to yield up his crown to the pope. Later in the play, after he has submitted to the pope, John recalls his earlier words about Peter, making it clear that he had no intention *then* of making a deal with Pandulf: "Is this Ascension-day? Did not the prophet / Say that before Ascension-day at noon / My crown I should give off? Even so I have: / I did suppose it should be on constraint; / But, heaven be thank'd, it is but voluntary" (V.i.25–29). When Hubert tells John at the end of act 4, scene 2 that Arthur is alive, John immediately orders him to inform the nobles and thus "make them tame" (IV.ii.262). He no longer has any need to blame Hubert, and actually apologizes for accusing him of murder.

19. Calderwood argues that John's "self-deposition" is "merely a tactic by which to insure his crown" (96, note 5). But as I have just shown, John is no longer interested in the crown. Colmo argues that John is "consumed by guilt when he thinks Hubert has carried out his order to kill Arthur" and that in his interview with Hubert, John's "concern seems to be with his own damnation" (Christopher Colmo, "Coming Home: The Political Settlement in Shakespeare's *King John,*" in *Shakespeare's Political Pageant: Essays in Politics and Literature,* ed. Joseph Alulis and

Vickie Sullivan [Lanham, MD: Rowman and Littlefield, 1996], 94, 95). I think this concern with "damnation"—for having *intended* Arthur's murder—best explains John's submission.

20. "The state which . . . [Pandulf] invoked to subject State to Church very naturally refuses to be subjected itself" (D. J. Snider, *System of Shakespeare's Dramas,* 1877, ii, 314 [New Variorum edition, 396]). This, of course, is one of Machiavelli's most famous teachings. See *The Prince,* chapters 11–13.

21. "It is our safety, and we must embrace / This gentle offer of the perilous time," says Lord Salisbury to the other disaffected nobles (IV.iii.12–13).

22. Calderwood (100) sees the Bastard as more complicated, and points to the following lines as evidence of his "simultaneously acknowledging an impulse to kingship and admitting the dishonourableness of that impulse": "[w]ithold thine indignation, mighty heaven, / And tempt us not to bear above our power!" (V.vi.37–38). While Calderwood's interpretation is possible, I think the context suggests a more likely reading of these lines. The Bastard has just received the good news that the nobles have returned to John's side and, upon Henry's recommendation, have been pardoned. He seems to be counseling against overconfidence or pride, for immediately after his warning against "temptation," he informs Hubert that he has lost half of his army in a flood (V.vi.38–42).

23. John may have suspected as much, and so recruited Hubert instead of the Bastard to kill Arthur.

24. "Holinshed, Foxe, M. Paris etc. say that the French navy was defeated by an English force. Only Coggeshall also mentions the storm . . . " (Arden *King John*, appendix A, 166).

25. Honigmann calls "the loss of John's army in the Wash, an act of criminal stupidity accredited to the Bastard by Shakespeare and dwelt upon twice to belittle him . . . " (from his introduction to the 4th Arden edition of *King John,* lxxi–lxxii). I think Shakespeare means rather to show that political misfortune afflicts both good and bad men. The converse is also true.

26. Toward the end of his early soliloquy criticizing John and Philip for their selfish, hypocritical politics, the Bastard asks himself "why rail I on this commodity?," and answers, "because he hath not woo'd me yet. . . . " In the closing lines, he declares himself perfectly willing to accommodate

himself to the ways of the world: "Since kings break faith upon commodity, / Gain, be my lord, for I will worship thee!" (II.i.587–88, 597–98).

27. Colmo, 98.

28. Commenting on the "execution" scene between Hubert and Arthur, Gentleman thinks it "conveys so much horror that it rather strains humanity too far" and Duport asks, "are there not certain spectacles too violent for the human soul which are quite unfit for its entertainment, and which art should spare it?" (F. Gentleman, from his 1774 [Bell] edition of Shakespeare's works [New Variorum edition, 280]; Paul Duport, *Essais Litteraires sur Shakspeare,* 1828, I.189 [New Variorum edition, 281]).

Chapter 3. *King Richard II*

1. In his study of the historical King Richard, A. B. Steel notes that Richard was "the last king ruling by hereditary right, direct and undisputed, from the Conqueror. The kings of the next hundred and ten years . . . were essentially kings *de facto* not *de jure*, successful usurpers recognized after the event, upon conditions, by their fellow magnates or parliament" (Steel, *Richard II* [Cambridge, 1941], quoted by Tillyard, *Shakespeare's History Plays,* 253).

2. Figgis, 45.

3. Figgis, 51.

4. "Of the historic dramas, *King John* is perhaps the worst constructed, and *King Richard II,* which wants little to be a tragedy, is certainly the best" (H. Coleridge, *Essays and Marginalia* [London, 1941], ii, 152 [New Variorum edition of *King John*, 606]). In the earliest texts of the play—the first five Quartos, published between 1597 and 1615—the title appeared as *The Tragedie of King Richard the Second.* In the First Folio (1623), the title appeared as *The life and death of King Richard the Second.*

5. As Matthew Black points out, "that Mowbray murdered [Gloucester] by Richard's order is regarded by historians as not proved, though extremely likely. It seems to have been generally believed at the time." There is "little doubt," he continues, "that Shakespeare's audience believed that Gloucester was murdered at Richard's instigation" (Matthew Black, ed., the New Variorum edition of *The Life and Death of King Richard the Second,* [Philadelphia: J. B. Lippincott Co., 1955], 4).

Future references to scholarship cited in the New Variorum edition will give the author, title, and whatever other information is available, as well as the page number in the New Variorum edition.

6. Bolingbroke's inheritance was substantial: "Gaunt was the greatest magnate in England, the possessor of castles, forests, manors, and other estates scattered throughout the realm. As Lancaster was a county palatine, a semiautonomous political entity, Gaunt had nearly regal powers within it . . . " (Saccio, 20).

7. Jensen thinks Bolingbroke's decision to return is itself a regal act: "[l]ike a godlike king, he repeals his own sentence . . . " (Pamela K. Jensen, "Beggars and Kings: Cowardice and Courage in Shakespeare's *Richard II*," *Interpretation* 18, no. 1 [Fall 1990]: 123).

8. The only testimony about Gloucester's character in the play is favorable—and misleading. As Dover Wilson notes, "Holinshed, Froissart and Daniel unite in depicting [Gloucester] most unfavorably" (from his 1939 Cambridge edition of *Richard II*, xlviii).

9. Quoted by Saccio, 24. See also New Variorum edition, 409.

10. Hume, *The History of England*, vol. 2 (Philadelphia: Porter and Coates, n.d.), 156.

11. Hume, vol. 2, 163.

12. Hume, vol. 2, 168.

13. Perhaps I am giving Richard more credit than he deserves here. He may have simply needed money and found Gaunt's property conveniently available. If, on the other hand, he was more thoughtful, he would have been waiting for Gaunt to die, for Richard can only move decisively against Bolingbroke after Bolingbroke's father Gaunt, a powerful nobleman and a fairly reliable supporter, is dead.

14. E. M. W. Tillyard, seconding John Dover Wilson, *Shakespeare's History Plays*, 260.

15. J. L. Palmer, *Political Characters of Shakespeare* (1945), 134 (New Variorum edition, 228).

16. Quoted by Jensen, 125.

17. Saccio, 25.

18. The purpose of the trial is to deflect attention from his criminal usurpation toward Richard's past crimes.

19. Charles Harold Herford, from his 1893 (Warwick) edition of *King Richard II* (New Variorum edition, 219).

20. Hotspur's information is secondhand: "My father . . . heard him swear and vow to God / He came but to be Duke of Lancaster" (IV.iii.59–61). Northumberland's brother Worcester claims to have heard Bolingbroke swear an oath upon arriving in England, but he is not a character in *Richard II*, and the scene is not dramatized in that play: "You swore to us, / And you did swear that oath at Doncaster, / That you did nothing purpose 'gainst the state, / Nor claim no further than . . . The seat of Gaunt" (V.i.41–45). Holinshed reports that (the historical) Bolingbroke did in fact swear an oath at Doncaster. See the Arden edition of *King Richard II*, IV.iii. note 54.

21. Perhaps Bolingbroke was told of the troubles in Ireland and assumed Richard would leave the country to attend to them.

22. Herford (New Variorum edition, 160).

23. Harold C. Goddard, *The Meaning of Shakespeare* (Chicago: University of Chicago Press, 1951), 148.

24. Once he has fallen, Shakespeare will give us plenty of reasons to sympathize with Richard—but not before.

25. Some in Shakespeare's audience would have been aware of the details of Richard's turbulent reign, but one has to remember that the events took place two hundred years prior to Shakespeare's play.

26. Allan Bloom, "Richard II," in *Shakespeare as Political Thinker*, ed. Alvis and West (Durham: Carolina Academic Press, 1981), 54.

27. Bloom, "Richard II," 51.

28. Tillyard, 261.

29. Hume, vol. 2, 177, emphasis supplied.

30. Hume, vol. 2, 166. See also 156–57.

31. "Farming the realm" involved the payment of a sum of money to the king in exchange for a portion of future tax profits; forced loans were euphemistically called "benevolences" (I.iv.46 and II.i.250).

32. Jensen, 112, 113.

33. For a good summary of various views, see the appendix of the New Variorum edition of *Richard II*, 529–33.

34. See New Variorum edition, 530.

35. Figgis, 66–67.

36. New Variorum edition, 186–87.

37. See Peter Ure's introduction to the Arden edition of *King Richard II*, lix.

38. Palmer, 119–20 (New Variorum edition, 585).

39. Even if his will could be known, no other human being is authorized to do anything about it.

40. Walter H. Pater, *Appreciations: With an Essay on Style*, 1889 (New Variorum edition, 528).

41. Dain Trafton, "Shakespeare's Henry IV: A New Prince in a New Principality," in *Shakespeare as Political Thinker*, 86. According to Trafton, Bolingbroke is "more thoroughly a rebel in thought than in action. He does not blink at his own impiety; on the contrary, he guides his career consistently by a view of the world that is totally opposed to the one on which the traditional politics of the realm are grounded" (85). I think this is an accurate description of Henry's consciousness prior to murdering Richard. Afterwards, his Machiavellianism is often interrupted by periods of religious dread. I will treat this subject at length in the following chapter.

42. See *The Prince*, chapter 6, 24.

43. According to Bloom, "Richard II," (59), "[t]his is the popular view of philosophy, as expressed when one says, 'he's taking it philosophically,' a phrase never used when good things happen."

44. T. M. Parrott, *Shakespearean Comedy* (NY, 1949), 229 (New Variorum edition, 332).

45. "Later generations looking back upon Richard's deposition saw the event as more catastrophic than did most of those who actually lived through it" (Saccio, 33). In his *Henry IV* plays, Shakespeare dramatizes the reappraisal of Bolingbroke's usurpation.

46. Hume, vol. 2, 182.

47. The duchess is probably only thanking Henry for answering her prayers by sparing her loyalist son. But I think the language she employs is significant, if only to show that addressing the new king in the old way is acceptable.

48. Holinshed, quoted by Palmer (New Variorum edition, 557).

49. A reference to Richard's "advisors."

50. Bloom, "Richard II," 57.

51. Bloom, "Richard II," 60.

52. Bloom, "Richard II," 52, note 1.

Chapter 4. *King Henry IV*, Parts 1 and 2

1. Roderich Benedix, *Die Shakespearomanie. Zur Abwehr* (Stuttgart, 1873), 122, quoted in the New Variorum edition of *The Second Part of Henry the Fourth*, ed. Matthias A. Shaaber (Philadelphia: J. B. Lippincott Co., 1940), 559.

2. H. Ax, *The Relation of Shakespeare's Henry IV to Holinshed*, 1912, 13, quoted in the New Variorum edition of *Henry the Fourth, Part I*, ed. Samuel Burdett Hemingway (Philadelphia: J. B. Lippincott Co., 1936), 6.

3. "Edmund Mortimer, Earl of March" is listed in the dramatis personae, but Shakespeare sometimes confuses him with his father Roger, Richard's declared heir who died before him in 1398 and whose funeral Richard was traveling to Ireland to attend when Bolingbroke landed in England, and his uncle, Sir Edmund, who married Glendower's daughter. The young earl would have been thirteen at the time the play dramatizes. After his father's death, parliament declared the young earl Richard's heir. According to Hume, both Edmund and his uncle of the same name were captured and held by Glendower (vol. 2, 197–98). Holinshed also confuses the three Mortimer's in his *Chronicles*, one of Shakespeare's sources for this play (see the discussion in the New Variorum edition, note 80, 61–62).

4. *1HIV* I.i.95–98.

5. "Hotspur is a figurehead, allowed the role in order to bring honor, glamour, and the tone of moral integrity to the enterprise" (Prior, 66).

6. Hume, vol. 2, 199.

7. Henry N. Hudson, *Shakespeare: His Life, Art, and Characters*, 4th edition, revised, 1882 (New Variorum edition, 467).

8. Hume, vol. 2, 211.

9. Falstaff is, admittedly, joking here.

10. John Masefield, *William Shakespeare*, 1932 (New Variorum edition, 439).

11. If comments like these seem to call into question my characterization of the Hal/Falstaff relationship as one between student and teacher, one must remember that Hal is heir to the throne.

12. John Dover Wilson, *The Essential Shakespeare* (Cambridge: Cambridge University Press, 1932), 88–89. Dr. Johnson's discussion of Falstaff's allure culminates in a warning about its danger:

> Yet the man thus corrupt, thus despicable, makes himself necessary to the prince that despises him, by the most pleasing of all qualities, perpetual gaiety, by an unfailing power of exciting laughter, which is the more freely indulged, as his wit is not of the splendid or ambitious kind, but consists in easy escapes and sallies of levity, which make sport but raise no envy. It must be observed that he is stained with no sanguinary crimes, so that his licentiousness is not so offensive but that it may be borne for his mirth. The moral to be drawn from this representation is, that no man is more dangerous than he that with a will to corrupt, hath the power to please; and that neither wit nor honesty ought to think themselves safe with such a companion, when they see Henry seduced by Falstaff. (From his 1765 edition of *1 Henry IV*, [New Variorum edition, 405]).

13. Dr. Johnson, 1765 edition of *1 Henry IV* (New Variorum edition, 104).

14. On Falstaff's relation to Socrates, see Bloom, *Love and Friendship*, 406–8.

15. Bloom, *Love and Friendship*, 409.

16. Toward the end of his reign, Henry IV took an active role in French affairs. He attempted, according to Hume, "to foment the animosities between the families of Burgundy and Orleans, by which the government of France was, during that period, so distracted." Hal finished what his father began. (Hume, vol. 2, 204-5.)

17. Danby, 97.

18. *The Prince*, chapter 18, 70–71.

19. *The Prince*, chapter 18, 70.

20. Bloom, *Love and Friendship*, 408.

21. *The Prince*, chapter 15, 61.

22. *The Prince*, chapter 18, 70–71.

23. Warwick's common sense explanation of supposed "prophecy" answers as well those numerous critics who see in the history plays a providential theory of history, a cycle of sin and retribution. I think, following Warwick, that in explaining the rise and fall of particular kings, one ought to look to their virtues and failings, which are amply recorded by Shakespeare. One needn't attribute to God or to fate what can more simply and convincingly be explained by the actions of men.

24. *2HIV* IV.v. 192–95, 204–12. See *The Prince*, chapter 3.

Chapter 5. *King Henry V*

1. *2 Henry IV*, IV.v.213–15; V.v.105–8.

2. "The clues to such an ironic reading of *Henry V* are not," according to Prior, "to be found within that play" (Prior, 314). Reese calls this (ironic) reading "purely subjective," and accuses critics who subscribe to it of "rationalising their prejudice" against King Henry ("In all the canon only Isabella, in *Measure for Measure,* has stirred so much personal distaste") (Reese, 317). Critical reaction to *Henry V* seems to be divided into two opposed camps, whose views are aptly summarized by Karl Wentersdorf:

> For some, the play presents the story of an ideal monarch and glorifies his achievements; for them the tone approaches that of an epic lauding the military virtues. For others the protagonist is a Machiavellian militarist who professes Christianity but whose deeds reveal both hypocrisy and ruthlessness; for them the tone is predominately one of mordant satire." "The Conspiracy of Silence in *Henry V*," *Shakespeare Quarterly* 27, (Summer 1976): 264.

Norman Rabkin argues that both views are plausible, and neither is truer than the other (Rabkin, *Shakespeare and the Problem of Meaning* [Chicago: University of Chicago Press, 1981], chapter 2, 33–62).

3. Alvis, 223.

4. Prior, 264.

5. Henry is in disguise when he makes this speech to his troops.

6. Richard refers to his enemies as "Judases" and "Pilates" and compares his deposition to Christ's crucifixion (*RII* III.ii.132; IV.i.167–71; IV.i.239–42).

7. There is, of course, a difference between strong passion and habit, but the first may, over time, become the second. Furthermore, Richard, as I show in chapter 3, relies too much on tradition and too little on arms. But no one ever publicly questions his right to rule, and most accept his claim to rule with God's favor.

8. Prior, 270, 271.

9. Harold Hutchinson, *Henry V: A Biography* (London, 1967), 36, quoted by Prior, 270.

10. John Dover Wilson, introduction to the Cambridge edition of *Henry V* (Cambridge: Cambridge University Press, 1947), xxi.

11. "There is another word, also of five letters, that would define the nature of the proposed transaction more precisely . . . " (Goddard, 219).

12. Alvis, 224.

13. Wentersdorf, 267.

14. Goddard, 220, 221. Wentersdorf calls the archbishop's speech "a masterpiece of ambiguous prolixity" (266).

15. J. H. Walter, introduction to the Arden edition of *Henry V* (1990), xxiii. According to Wentersdorf, "Walter does not point out . . . that Gentilli was writing while a refugee in England and is not necessarily an impartial witness" (265, note 2).

16. Reese, 323, emphasis supplied.

17. Alvis, 243.

18. Goddard, 242.

19. Vickie Sullivan, "Princes to Act: Henry V as the Machiavellian Prince of Appearance," in *Shakespeare's Political Pageant: Essays in Politics and Literature* (Lanham, MD: Rowman and Littlefield, 1996), 231.

20. Portions of France are, admittedly, the object of frequent contention. But Henry wants all of France.

21. Alvis, 223.

22. Sullivan makes an excellent case for this thesis.

23. Sullivan, 223.

24. Walter, xvi; Reese, 319; Prior, 271.

25. Goddard (217) states:

> can anyone believe that Shakespeare in his own person would have called Henry 'the mirror of all Christian kings' and then let him threaten to allow his soldiers to impale French babies on their pikes and dash the heads of old men against the walls; or called him 'this grace of kings' and then let him declare of the prisoners,
>
> we'll cut the throats of those we have,
> And not a man of them that we shall take
> Shall taste our mercy . . .

26. Goddard, 218.

27. Goddard, 267.

28. For what Falstaff stands for, see chapter 4, Falstaff: Master Corrupter.

29. John Dover Wilson, *The Fortunes of Falstaff* (Cambridge: Cambridge University Press, 1943), 140.

30. When chastising the dauphin for underestimating him, Henry seems far from repentant about his youth: "he comes over us with our wilder days, / Not measuring what use we made of them" (I.ii.267–68).

31. See chapter 4, Falstaff: Master Corrupter.

32. Greenblatt, *Shakespearean Negotiations*, 54.

33. Alvis, 200–201. "What infinite heart's ease / Must kings neglect that private men enjoy!" (*HV* IV.i.242–43).

34. Alvis, 200–201.

35. A motive with which Shakespeare is thoroughly familiar, but by no means thoroughly contemptuous of. See chapter 6, Conclusion.

36. Goddard, 267.

37. He is not, then, ruled by fortune.

38. As he appears to think in 2 *Henry IV*: "My due from thee is this imperial crown . . . " (IV.v.40).

39. Michael Platt, "Falstaff in the Valley of the Shadow of Death," in *Falstaff,* ed. Harold Bloom (New York: Chelsea House Publishers, 1992), 185.

40. For example, in pursuing his "expectations" strategy, where concern about his political image takes precedence over his relationship with his father, or in his ability to cut off Falstaff, the man he seemed closest to.

41. Mindle, 266.

42. Henry, of course, is both, but I am concerned here with his tendency toward self-deception.

43. See note 25.

44. In both cases, it is true, Henry is playing to an audience; but one has the distinct impression that some part of him believes what he's saying, that Henry gets caught up in his own performance.

45. " . . . Henry V turns off more people than does his father, the political man who knew himself for what he was" (Prior, 331).

46. Alvis, 241.

47. Rabkin, 57.

48. Goddard, 262.

49. The placement of Burgundy's speech in the play almost makes Henry's response unnecessary. It is given after the colossal and embarrassing French military defeat, and might be read less as a serious political theory than as an attempt to make the best of a bad situation, to cover over the humiliating French loss with high-sounding rhetoric. The historical Burgundy was in fact an opponent of the dauphin, the French king's son and heir, and had formed an alliance with King Henry a year before the peace treaty was signed. Shakespeare mentions none of this, but Burgundy's speech could be understood, consistent with the historical facts, as an attempt to convince the French king to accept Henry's terms (thus advancing his own self-interested agenda) by arguing that peace is the greatest good.

50. Alvis, 229.

Chapter 6. Shakespeare and Machiavelli Revisited

1. Of course, the elements of any government—the monarch (kingship), the nobility (aristocracy), and the people (democracy)—are present in the feudal monarchy Shakespeare dramatizes. In his Roman plays, Shakespeare shows an awareness of the fluidity of governmental forms, tracing the transformation of an aristocratic republic into a monarchy or popular despotism. While the situation is clearly less fluid in the English history plays, Henry V does abandon the nobility for the people, earning praise as a "conquering Caesar."

2. In *King John*, Shakespeare characterizes the people as rash and superstitious. In *Henry VI*, Part 2, he treats Jack Cade's rebellion as farce ("The first thing we do, let's kill all the lawyers" [IV.ii.73]). There is no indication that Shakespeare ever seriously entertained the desirability—and probably the possibility—of popular rule.

3. Pocock, 25. Shakespeare has no illusions about "perfect beginnings." As I argue in my treatments of *King John* and *Richard II*, the doctrine of the divine right of kings is ultimately the cynical invention of ambitious popes. In the beginning, one is most likely to find force or fraud.

4. Wyndham Lewis, *The Lion and the Fox* (London: G. Richards Ltd., 1927), 178.

5. *The Prince*, chapter 3, 14.

6. One should note that the Macbeth of Shakespeare's sources ruled for nearly two decades.

7. *The Prince*, chapter 15, 61.

8. *The Prince*, chapter 9, 39; chapter 9, 39; chapter 19, 73. "[T]he best fortress there is, is not to be hated by the people" (chapter 20, 87); chapter 19, 72; chapter 21, 91.

9. *The Prince*, chapter 20, 83.

10. At times, Machiavelli seems unconcerned with the welfare of the people, or with a successful prince's need for their support (sometimes, the support of the army will do). Furthermore, in *The Discourses*, republican principles (popular participation) receive far more attention than liberal ones (freedom from oppression). As Mansfield and Tarcov note, "the relation between [*The Prince* and *The Discourses*] is notoriously obscure" (from the introduction to Niccolo Machiavelli's

Discourses on Livy, trans. Mansfield and Tarcov, [Chicago: University of Chicago Press, 1996], xx).

11. *The Prince*, chapter 18, 71. Emphasis supplied.

12. *The Prince*, chapter 18, 70. Emphasis supplied.

13. *The Prince*, chapter 8, 35.

14. *The Prince*, chapter 15, 62.

15. *The Prince*, chapter 3, 14. Emphasis supplied.

16. Certainly Machiavelli makes every effort in *The Prince* to attack and undermine Christian moral teaching.

17. John and Henry IV only feel remorse *after* assassinating their rivals. And instead of reforming, both seem to lose interest in politics. Henry V and Richard III express some regret for their deeds, but this has no effect on the way they practice politics afterwards.

18. At *Discourses* I.27, Machiavelli criticizes G. Baglioni, tyrant of Perugia, for failing to kill the pope when he had the opportunity.

19. *The Prince*, chapter 15, 61.

20. For Machiavelli, legitimacy is based on the mutual interest of ruler and ruled. On one occasion, however, Machiavelli does acknowledge a desire on the part of the people to sacrifice for their ruler, counseling princes under siege to remember that "the nature of men is to be obligated as much by benefits they give as by benefits they receive" (*The Prince*, chapter 10, 44).

Appendix. The Omission of the Magna Carta in *King John*

1. Hume, vol. 1, 446.

2. F. S. Boas, *Shakespeare and His Predecessors*, 1896, 243 (New Variorum edition of *King John*, 351).

3. Hume, vol. 1, 445.

4. Hume, vol. 1, 444–45.

Bibliography

All references to Shakespeare's plays in this book follow the Arden edition. The following abbreviations are used throughout: *King John (John), King Richard II (RII), King Henry IV,* Parts 1 and 2 *(1HIV, 2HIV), King Henry V (HV), King Henry VI,* Parts 1, 2 and 3 *(1HVI, 2HVI, 3HVI), King Richard III (RIII), Troilus and Cressida (T&C).*

Primary Sources

Shakespeare, William. *Henry the Fourth, Part I.* New Variorum edition, ed. Samuel Burdett Hemingway. Philadelphia: J. B. Lippincott Co., 1936.

———. *King Henry IV,* Part 1. Arden edition, ed. A. R. Humphreys. London: Routledge, 1992.

———. *King Henry IV* Part 2. Arden edition, ed. A. R. Humphreys. London: Routledge, 1989.

———. *King Henry V.* Arden edition, ed. J. H. Walter. London: Routledge, 1990.

———. *King Henry VI,* Part 1. Arden edition, ed. Andrew Cairncross. London: Methuen, 1962.

———. *King Henry VI,* Part 2. Arden edition, ed. Andrew Cairncross. London: Methuen, 1962.

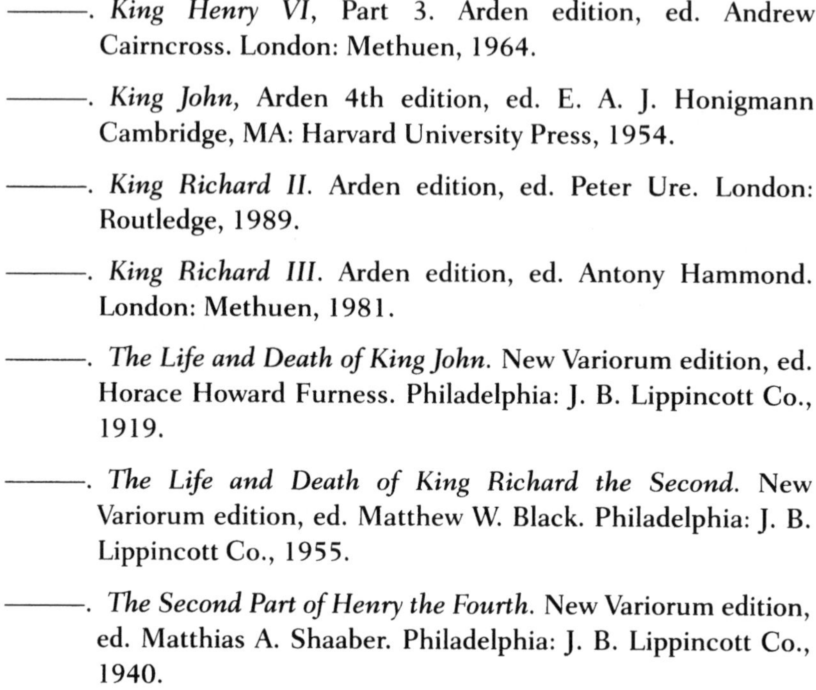

———. *King Henry VI*, Part 3. Arden edition, ed. Andrew Cairncross. London: Methuen, 1964.

———. *King John,* Arden 4th edition, ed. E. A. J. Honigmann Cambridge, MA: Harvard University Press, 1954.

———. *King Richard II*. Arden edition, ed. Peter Ure. London: Routledge, 1989.

———. *King Richard III*. Arden edition, ed. Antony Hammond. London: Methuen, 1981.

———. *The Life and Death of King John*. New Variorum edition, ed. Horace Howard Furness. Philadelphia: J. B. Lippincott Co., 1919.

———. *The Life and Death of King Richard the Second*. New Variorum edition, ed. Matthew W. Black. Philadelphia: J. B. Lippincott Co., 1955.

———. *The Second Part of Henry the Fourth*. New Variorum edition, ed. Matthias A. Shaaber. Philadelphia: J. B. Lippincott Co., 1940.

Secondary Sources

Allen, J. W. *A History of Political Thought in the Sixteenth Century*. London: Methuen and Co. Ltd., 1928.

Alvis, John. *Shakespeare's Understanding of Honor*. Durham: Carolina Academic Press, 1990.

Alvis, John, and Thomas G. West, eds. *Shakespeare as Political Thinker*. Durham: Carolina Academic Press, 1981.

Blanpied, John. "Stalking 'Strong Possession' in 'King John.'" In *William Shakespeare, Histories and Poems,* ed. Harold Bloom. New York: Chelsea House, 1986.

Bloom, Allan. *Love and Friendship*. New York: Simon and Schuster, 1993.

———. "Richard II." In *Shakespeare as Political Thinker,* ed. Alvis and West. Durham: Carolina Academic Press, 1981.

Bloom, Allan, with Harry V. Jaffa. *Shakespeare's Politics*. Chicago: University of Chicago Press, 1964.

Calderwood, James L. "Commodity and Honour in *King John*." In *Shakespeare: The Histories*, ed. Eugene M. Waith. Englewood Cliffs, NJ: Prentice-Hall, Inc., 1965.

Cantor, Paul. "Shakespeare—'For All Time'?" *Public Interest* (Winter, 1993): 34–48.

———. "Prospero's Republic." In *Shakespeare as Political Thinker*, ed. Alvis and West. Durham: Carolina Academic Press, 1981.

———. "Stephen Greenblatt's New Historicist Vision." *Academic Questions* (Fall 1993): 21–36.

Colmo, Christopher. "Coming Home: The Political Settlement in Shakespeare's *King John*." In *Shakespeare's Political Pageant: Essays in Politics and Literature*, ed. Joseph Alulis and Vickie Sullivan. Lanham, MD: Rowman and Littlefield, 1996.

Danby, John F. *Shakespeare's Doctrine of Nature*. London: Faber and Faber, 1949.

Dollimore, Jonathan, and Alan Sinfield, eds. *Political Shakespeare: New Essays in Cultural Materialism*. Ithaca: Cornell University Press, 1985.

Figgis, John Neville. *The Divine Right of Kings*. Cambridge: University Press, 1922.

Flaumenhaft, Mera. *The Civic Spectacle: Essays on Drama and Community*. Lanham, MD.: Rowman and Littlefield, 1994.

Goddard, Harold C. *The Meaning of Shakespeare*. Chicago: University of Chicago Press, 1951.

Greenblatt, Stephen. *Shakespearean Negotiations*. Berkeley: University of California Press, 1988.

———. Review of *Witches and Jesuits: Shakespeare's "Macbeth"* by Garry Wills. *The New Republic* (Nov. 14, 1994): 32–36.

Howard, Jean E., and Marion F. O'Connor, eds. *Shakespeare Reproduced: The Text in History and Ideology.* New York: Methuen, 1987.

Hume, David. *The History of England.* Volumes 1 and 2. Philadelphia: Porter and Coates, n.d.

Jenkins, Harold. "Shakespeare's History Plays: 1900–1951." In *Shakespeare Survey VI*. Cambridge, 1953, 1–6.

Jensen, Pamela K. "Beggars and Kings: Cowardice and Courage in Shakespeare's *Richard II*." *Interpretation* 18, no. 1 (Fall 1990).

Kamps, Ivo, ed. *Shakespeare Left and Right.* New York: Routledge, 1991.

Kernan, Alvin B. "Shakespeare and the Rhetoric of Politics." In *Politics, Power, and Shakespeare,* ed. Frances McNeely Leonard. Arlington: University of Texas at Arlington, 1981.

Knights, L. C. *Further Explorations.* London: Chatto and Windus, 1946.

Levin, Richard L. "The Problem of 'Context' in Interpretation." In *Shakespeare and the Dramatic Tradition*, ed. Elton and Long. Newark: University of Delaware Press, 1989, 88–106.

Lewis, Wyndham. *The Lion and the Fox.* London: G. Richards Ltd., 1927.

Lincoln, Abraham. "Letter to J. H. Hackett, August 17, 1863." In *Abraham Lincoln: His Speeches and Writings,* ed. Roy P. Basler. Cleveland: The World Publishing Co., 1946.

Locke, John. *Two Treatises of Government,* ed. Peter Laslett. Cambridge: Cambridge University Press, 1988.

Mindle, Grant. "Shakespeare's Demonic Prince." *Interpretation* 20, no. 3 (Spring 1993): 259–74.

Machiavelli, Niccolo. *The Discourses.* Trans. Father Leslie J. Walker. Ed. Bernard Crick. Harmondsworth, England: Penguin Classics, 1986.

———. *The Prince*. Trans. Harvey C. Mansfield. Chicago: University of Chicago Press, 1985.

Nuttall, A. D. *A New Mimesis*. London: Methuen, 1983.

Patterson, Annabel. *Shakespeare and the Popular Voice*. Cambridge, MA: Basil Blackwell, Inc., 1989.

Pechter, Edward. *What Was Shakespeare?: Renaissance Plays and Changing Critical Practice*. Ithaca: Cornell University Press, 1995.

Platt, Michael. "Falstaff in the Valley of the Shadow of Death." In *Falstaff*, ed. Harold Bloom. New York: Chelsea House Publishers, 1992, 171–202.

Pocock, J. G. A., *The Machiavellian Moment: Florentine Political Thought and the Atlantic Republican Tradition*. Princeton: Princeton University Press, 1975.

Prior, Moody. *The Drama of Power: Studies in Shakespeare's History Plays*. Evanston: Northwestern University Press, 1973.

Rabkin, Norman. *Shakespeare and the Problem of Meaning*. Chicago: University of Chicago Press, 1981.

Reese, M. M. *The Cease of Majesty*. London: Edward Arnold Ltd., 1961.

Ribner, Irving. *The English History Play in the Age of Shakespeare*. Princeton: Princeton University Press, 1957.

———. "Bolingbroke, a True Machiavellian." *Modern Language Quarterly* 9 (1948).

Saccio, Peter. *Shakespeare's English Kings: History, Chronicle and Drama*. London: Oxford University Press, 1977.

Strier, Richard. "Faithful Servants: Shakespeare's Praise of Disobedience." In *The Historical Renaissance*, ed. Heather Dubrow and Richard Strier. Chicago: University of Chicago Press, 1988.

Strong, Tracy. "Shakespeare: Elizabethan Statecraft and Machiavellianism." In *The Artist and Political Vision*, ed. Benjamin R.

Barber and Michael J. Gargas McGrath. New Brunswick: Transaction Books, 1982, 193–220.

Sullivan, Vickie. "Princes to Act: Henry V as the Machiavellian Prince of Appearance." In *Shakespeare's Political Pagaent: Essays in Politics and Literature,* ed. Sullivan and Alulis. Lanham, MD: Rowman and Littlefield, 1996.

Tarcov, Nathan. "Quentin Skinner's Method and Machiavelli's *Prince*." In *Meaning and Context: Quentin Skinner and His Critics,* ed. James Tully. Princeton: Princeton University Press, 1988.

Tillyard, E. M. W., *Shakespeare's History Plays.* London: Chatto and Windus, 1944.

Trafton, Dain. "Shakespeare's Henry IV: A New Prince in a New Principality." In *Shakespeare as Political Thinker*, ed. Alvis and West. Durham: Carolina Academic Press, 1981.

Walter, J. H. Introduction to the Arden edition of *King Henry V.* London: Routledge, 1990.

Walzer, Michael. *The Revolution of the Saints: A Study in the Origins of Radical Politics.* Cambridge: Harvard University Press, 1965.

Wentersdorf, Karl P. "The Conspiracy of Silence in *Henry V*," *Shakespeare Quarterly* 27, (Summer 1976): 264–87.

Wilson, John Dover. *The Essential Shakespeare.* Cambridge: Cambridge University Press, 1932.

———. *The Fortunes of Falstaff.* Cambridge: Cambridge University Press, 1943.

———. Introduction to the Cambridge edition of *King Henry V.* Cambridge: Cambridge University Press, 1947.

———. Introduction to the Cambridge edition of *Richard II.* Cambridge: Cambridge University Press, 1939.

White, Howard B. *Antiquity Forgot: Essays on Shakespeare, Bacon, and Rembrandt.* The Hague: Martinus Nijhoff, 1978.

Index